POSSIBLE DREAMS

# Possible Dreams

## A Personal History of British Christian Socialists

Chris Bryant

Hodder & Stoughton

LONDON  SYDNEY  AUCKLAND

First published in Great Britain 1996

10 9 8 7 6 5 4 3 2 1

British Library Cataloguing in Publication Data
A record for this book is available from the British Library

ISBN 0 340 64201 7

Printed and bound in Great Britain by
Mackays of Chatham PLC, Chatham, Kent

Hodder and Stoughton Ltd
A Division of Hodder Headline PLC
338 Euston Road
London NW1 3BH

# Contents

# *Foreword*

The roots of British socialism run wide and deep. Centuries before the Labour Party was founded the ideas of equality and social justice that took it forward – in 1906 to Parliament and in 1945 to power – were heard in fields and churches, meeting halls and street gatherings from speakers who were first and foremost Christians. With faith and courage and sometimes at terrible personal cost they faced not only the tyrants of the day but the suspicion and even the wrath of fellow-Christians who – under the ever extendible rubric of rendering unto Caesar – had settled for a quieter life.

This book records their stories, their struggles and their occasional shining triumphs. From it there emerges a lively gallery of activists passionate in their beliefs, and of groups sometimes awesomely complex in their own internal politics. Their legacy, here documented with masterly sweep and fascinating human detail, lives on as a powerful and complex influence in the Labour Party to this day.

As Labour revitalises itself to face the challenges of the twenty-first century we are indebted to them still. And we are indebted to Chris Bryant for bringing together this timely account of their lives and their contribution.

Gordon Brown

# Acknowledgments

Many people have helped with making this book less imperfect than it might have been: John Collins on Acland; Donald Soper, Peter Dawe and Eric Wright on CSM's own history; Frank Field and Dorothy Howell-Thomas on Temple; Ken Leech and Terry Drummond on Jubilee; Francis Davis on Catholic social teaching; Evelyn Murray on the founders of the Working Men's College; Judith Pinnington on the CSU; Graeme Smith on the twentieth century conferences; Dennis Howell on the Labour Churches; Len Murray, Jack Straw, Michael Meacher, John Battle, Chris Smith and Tony Benn on the modern Labour Party. Even more helpful have been the staff of Sion College, whose sad demise may mean the disintegration of the CSU papers. Finally, two people read most of the chapters and gave valuable and detailed advice: without David Cairns's and Nicholas Cranfield's suggestions it might well have gone hopelessly awry.

C. B.
November 1995

# *Abbreviations*

| | |
|---|---|
| CCMCO | Council of Clergy and Ministers for Common Ownership |
| CND | Campaign for Nuclear Disarmament |
| COPEC | Conference on Politics, Economics and Citizenship |
| COSPEC | Christian Organisations for Social, Political and Economic Change |
| CR | Community of the Resurrection |
| CSL | Church Socialist League |
| CSM | Christian Socialist Movement |
| CSS | Catholic Socialist Society |
| CSU | Christian Social Union |
| GSM | Guild of St Matthew |
| ICF | Industrial Christian Fellowship |
| ILP | Independent Labour Party |
| LKG | League of the Kingdom of God |
| LRC | Labour Representation Committee |
| LSE | London School of Economics |
| NEC | National Executive Committee (of the Labour Party) |
| PLP | Parliamentary Labour Party |
| PPU | Peace Pledge Union |

| | |
|---|---|
| SCL | Socialist Christian League |
| SDF | Social Democratic Foundation |
| SOGAT | Society of Graphical and Allied Trades |
| SGS | Socialist Quaker Society |
| SSC | Society of Socialist Christians |
| SSCM | Society of Socialist Clergy and Ministers |
| TUC | Trades Union Congress |
| WEA | Workers' Educational Association |

# 1

## *Posthumous Comrades*

> . . . a spirit was abroad
> Which could not be withstood, that poverty
> At least like this would in a little time
> Be found no more, that we should see the earth
> Unthwarted in her wish to recompense
> The industrious, and the lowly child of toil,
> All institutes for ever blotted out
> That legalised exclusion, empty pomp
> Abolished, sensual state and cruel power,
> Whether by edict of the one or few;
> And, finally, as sum and crown of all,
> Should see the people having a strong hand
> In making their own laws; whence better days
> To all mankind . . .
>
> William Wordsworth, *The Prelude*

'My good friends,' began the priest, 'matters will not go well in England till all things be made common; when there shall be neither serfs nor lords; when the lords shall be no more masters than ourselves.' John Ball warmed to his theme – a theme which had already landed him with a summons from the Archbishop of Canterbury on the charge of preaching sedition: 'Let us go to the King and remonstrate with him; he is young and from him we may obtain a favourable answer, and if not, we must ourselves seek to amend our constitution.'[1] The King was Richard II, and his realm was in disarray. Since Edward II's reign, waged labour had largely replaced serfdom, and when the Black Death, spreading from the ports in Dorset, killed nearly half the population during the reign of Richard's father, Edward III, the economy was plunged into crisis. There were not enough labourers to garner in the harvest. Labour was at a premium, and year after year wages rose until Parliament tried to enforce a maximum wage.

The labouring peasants rebelled. Egged on by John Ball and other itinerant peasant priests, they clamoured for equality. The Church hierarchy, however, had no sympathy for the likes of Ball and supported the nobles' attempts to scrap all tenancy agreements and to return the peasants to serfdom. So Ball was excommunicated and incarcerated by the Archbishop at Maidstone just as Wat Tyler's poll-tax revolt erupted in 1381.

Such was his popularity that he was freed by the rebels and brought with them in triumph to London, where on 13 June he preached to the mob at Blackheath on the text 'When Adam delved and Eve span, who was then the gentleman?', demanding not only equality for all, but also the solidarity of the peasants:

> in the beginning all men were created equal: servitude of man to man was introduced by the unjust dealings of the wicked ... Wherefore [Englishmen] should take courage, and behave like the wise husbandman of scripture, who gathered the wheat into his barn, but uprooted and burnt the tares that had half-choked the good grain. The tares of England [are] her oppressive rulers.[2]

By now London was in the hands of the peasants. For three days they held the city, burning down the brothels by London Bridge and throwing open the city gates. Their requirements, that bondage should cease, that all who had taken part in the uprising should be pardoned and that the price of land, not wages, should be fixed, seemed sure to be granted. But victory was short-lived. Wat Tyler was assassinated by the Lord Mayor of London, Sir William Walworth, in West Smithfield, and though Richard publicly acceded to the peasants' requests, when he persuaded them to return home they were met by the savagery of his troops on the way and thousands were slaughtered. Ball was captured in St Albans, brought before Richard and summarily hanged, drawn and quartered.

Of course, Ball's was not a sole Christian insurrectionist voice. The first time he was arrested it was because he had been identified as a follower of John Wycliffe, a philosopher-priest at Oxford who had become a ferocious critic of the Church. His distinction between the eternal, ideal Church and its temporal, material form denied the earthly Church any authority unless it embodied the principles of its founder. This struck at the very essence of the Church's power because he argued that if the clergy were manifestly not in a state of grace, then it would be quite legitimate for a civil authority to deprive them of their phenomenal endowments. Deeply critical of clerical abuses of power, he turned his guns on indulgences, pilgrimages, papal taxes, clerical celibacy and transubstantiation.

Wycliffe was no political revolutionary. His followers, nicknamed 'Lollards' because they were thought to be the tares (Latin *lolia*) hidden in the wheat, were, and his teaching spread through a group of 'poor priests' like John Ball who travelled the country barefoot, reporting to no one and preaching their own brand of egalitarian insurrection. Wycliffe was blamed for the Peasants' Revolt in 1381, and the following year his views were condemned by his colleagues at Oxford and by the Archbishop, William Courtenay, at the Blackfriars Synod, during which London was shaken by an earthquake. Wycliffe was forced to retire, and though he was allowed to continue practising as a priest, long after his death in 1383 his body was exhumed and burnt as that of an apostate, following a further condemnation at the Council of Constance in 1415. By then his two disciples, Nicholas of Hereford and John Purvey, had done considerable work on a project inspired by him and forbidden by the ecclesiastical authorities, the translation of the Bible into English.

Of course, it would be an anachronism to call either Wycliffe or Ball Christian Socialists. For the term belongs properly to the nineteenth century, when a curate, C. B. Dunn of Cumberworth, and John Sabine of Birmingham new-coined it in time for F. D. Maurice, Charles Kingsley and John Ludlow to form the first 'Christian Socialist' movement. Even to suggest that they were precursors of Christian Socialism is logically to leap ahead of ourselves. For what is Christian Socialism that we can attribute it to anyone without their claiming it for themselves? It is only in its modern history that we shall find its ideas, and to reach back into earlier centuries is to baptise innocents in a creed they could not possibly have proclaimed for themselves.

Yet a history of Christian Socialists in Britain would seem curiously incomplete without some picture of what came before the Victorians. Even a cursory glance at later writers will show how much they felt they owed to the pioneers of earlier centuries, and there are elements of later Christian Socialist thought which make little or no sense unless seen in the context of a longer tradition.

What follows, then, is a brief and non-chronological account of some of the determining influences that helped to shape later Christian Socialism.

On 1 April 1649 a merchant tailor from Wigan by the name of Gerrard Winstanley, together with a band of some twenty others, moved to Cobham in Surrey and started to 'dig up, manure and sow corn upon St George's Hill'. Proclaiming themselves 'True Levellers', they announced: 'In the beginning of Time, the great Creator, Reason, made the Earth to be a Common Treasury, to preserve Beasts, Birds, Fishes, and Man, the lord that was to govern this Creation ... but not one word was spoken in the beginning, that one branch of mankind should rule over another.'[3]

Winstanley himself was now forty. He had been made a freeman of the City of London in 1637, but had resigned at the start of the Civil War, and soon become acquainted with William Everard, a soldier in Cromwell's New Model Army who supported the *Agreement of the People, upon Grounds of Common Right, for uniting of all unprejudiced people therein*. Drawn up by the more radical delegates to the Army's democratic 'Council of Agitators', this called for near-universal male suffrage, annual parliaments, a limit of two consecutive terms for Members, an end to religious discrimination and the replacement of polls and tithing with a tax on land and personal estate. Those who supported the *Agreement* soon became known in the Army as 'Levellers', as opposed to the 'Gentlemen Independents', senior officers like Cromwell, Fairfax and Ireton, who declared it seditious. In 1648 the Levellers published *A Light shining in Buckinghamshire*, which called for 'a just portion for each man to live so that none need to beg or steal for want but that every man may live comfortably'; 'a just rule for each man to go by, which rule is to be the Scriptures'; government by 'Judges called Elders', to be elected by the people; and the confiscation of bishops' lands and Crown properties so as to provide a public fund for the maintenance of the needy. All this was to inaugurate a commonwealth 'after the pattern of the Bible in which the land would be the common property of all.'[4]

The Levellers' leader was John Lilburne, a linen draper from Greenwich who had first got into political trouble at the age of twenty-two in 1637, when he was arrested for smuggling Calvinist pamphlets from Holland. He was fined £500, was whipped from Fleet Bridge to Westminster, stood an hour and a half in the pillory and languished in the Fleet gaol for more than two years. Lilburne fought for Parliament in the Civil War but left the Army in 1644, returning to London political life, where he became an *habitué* of the Independents' meetings.

When Army support for the *Agreement* continued, Cromwell agreed to a special commission of four representatives from either side to draw up a new document. The commission eventually managed to hammer out a new version of the *Agreement*, although the differences between the Levellers and the Gentlemen Independents were dramatic. In the meantime the Presbyterian Members of the House of Commons had been expelled in December 1648, and on 27 January a Special Court sentenced the King to death. Three days later the sentence was carried out. Despite assurances that Parliament would circulate the new *Agree-*

*ment*, Cromwell ensured that in the maelstrom of events it was dropped. Lilburne and the Levellers felt that Cromwell had betrayed not only them but the whole venture of the Civil War.

Throughout March there were constant condemnations of his actions, and a new manifesto was composed, *The Second Part of England's New Chains Discovered*, calling for immediate fresh parliamentary elections. The poet John Milton, then the Foreign Secretary, was asked by the Council of State to draft a public reply to the declaration but refused out of sympathy with the Levellers' cause. April saw the Levellers' support swell, with two detachments and several whole regiments mutinying in support of the *Agreement*'s demands. The mutineers, gathered at Burford, were swiftly defeated. Lilburne managed to survive, although he was banished in 1652, and when he returned to England the following year he was tried for breach of exile. He was acquitted at the Old Bailey but was kept as a prisoner of state in Jersey and then in Dover Castle, where he died in 1657.

So when Winstanley set up on St George's Hill and proclaimed himself a Leveller in April 1649 he was allying himself with the left wing of the Army only two months and a day after Charles's execution, and the political impetus for his actions came from disillusionment with Cromwell. As Winstanley wrote, 'O thou Powers of England, though thou hast promised to make this people a Free People, yet thou hast so handled the matter, through thy self-seeking humour, that thou hast wrapped us up more in bondage, and oppression lies heavier upon us.'[5] Winstanley's reasons for gathering this 'Digger' community of about twenty were also overtly religious. He wanted to demonstrate that the earth was 'a common treasury', that Christ had ushered in a 'New Law' and that men and women were called to live in common society. The New Jerusalem was to be seen not only in the hereafter but 'within Creation'. God was not distant but to be found in the lives and experiences of ordinary men and women. The spirit of prophecy from the Old Testament was still alive, and society would be called to account, for the Second Coming of Christ would soon inaugurate a new age of community. Violence should not be met with violence, for the 'New Law' enjoined peace. As a 'true Leveller', he advocated annual local elections, for 'nature tells us that if water stands long it corrupts; whereas running water keeps sweet and is fit for the common use';[6] and demanded comprehensive, mixed-ability public education for all. Buying and selling, as the source of all warring, would also be banned within the community.

The Diggers' aim was a clean sweep, casting off the 'Norman yoke' that had been laid upon the English since the Conquest and restoring 'the pure Law of righteousness before the fall',[7] and they urged the reclaiming of the enclosures which had been 'got by that murdering sword, and given by William the Conqueror'[8] to the ancestors of the present landlords.

Winstanley's dream lasted little more than a year. The local landowners, with the support of the Army, drove the Diggers' cattle off the land, and a savage period of harassment led to the community's being disbanded at Easter in 1650. The Diggers attempted to settle elsewhere without success, but Winstanley continued to write extensively, arguing in *The Law of Freedom* for a 'True Commonwealth' with a clearly theological foundation.

His theology was certainly bold. Paraphrasing the New Testament letter of James, he argued that 'True Religion, and undefiled, is this, To make restitution of the Earth, which hath been taken and held from the Common people, by the powers of Conquests formerly, and so *set the oppressed free*.'[9] He saw exploitation in symbolic biblical terms, as the rule of Cain over Abel, 'the elder brother lives in a continual thievery, stealing the land from the younger brother.'[10] He also, in a bid as dramatic as Charles Kingsley's claim to be a Chartist and a parson in the 1840s, invoked Jesus in words that asserted a divine authority for the Levellers' cause:

This great Leveller, Christ our King of Righteousness in us, shall cause men to beat their swords into ploughshares and spears into pruning hooks, and nations shall learn war no more; and every one shall delight to let each other enjoy the pleasures of the earth, and shall hold each other no longer in bondage.[11]

As Christopher Rowland has pointed out, Winstanley's later works, after the collapse of the Cobham community, come much closer to defining the ideal society he believed in, whereas his earlier works are 'full of challenge to action and to understand the times'.[12] The irony is that his own disillusionment, in pushing him towards hope for a paradise regained, made him less and less able to relate to the world in which he lived. Rowland sees Winstanley as a Utopian who failed to keep his eye on the ball, and in part he is right, but Winstanley's fascination for later Christian Socialists remains. His use of the Bible as a tool for analysis and action lies remarkably close to much of the work of the Latin American Liberation theologians, as does his emphasis on the small community, and he advocated many elements of a modern political programme. Furthermore, where Archbishop Laud, who was executed in January 1645, simply condemned the enclosures, Winstanley was prepared to claim the whole earth as the heritage of all, a 'Common Treasury'.

When Lilburne was imprisoned in Dover Castle in 1650, he was reported to have joined the Quakers, who at the time of the Levellers and Diggers were a growing Christian movement with a radical understanding of how faith should relate to society. By 1655 there were Quakers all over England, and it seems certain that their rapid growth owes much to the ideas of the Levellers. Following in the traditions of the Anabaptists, they held a strong belief in the power of the 'inner light', as opposed to the received wisdoms of tradition or dogmatic theology, and refused to swear oaths, pay tithes or make any special acknowledgment, either by speech or manner, to social 'superiors'. Named also the Society of Friends after the Third Letter of John 1.14, 'The friends here send their greetings; greet the friends there by name', the Quakers spent much of the seventeenth century under persecution: between 1651 and 1656, 1,900 Quakers were imprisoned in England, with another 12,000 being sent down by the end of the persecution in 1697 and 450 reputedly dying in prison.

It was George Fox, born in 1624 the son of a Leicestershire silk weaver, who founded the movement in about 1650, after a period as an itinerant preacher. His message, described by Edouard Bernstein as 'a compound of rationalism and mysticism, of democracy and political abstention',[13] was simple, proclaiming that Christ's teaching was of such urgent significance that organised religion was irrelevant to the true Gospel. Instead of having ordained ministers to lead worship, Fox's followers would wait on God to inspire one of the number present with a 'word'. There would be no liturgy, no sacraments. Decision-making would be by consensus. War and forcible resistance to violence were repudiated, and all were accorded equal respect. Fox, like Winstanley, called for common ownership of the land and, in his fulminations against the rich, expected that the new era of God's reign would start only when all England recognised the 'inner light' within them.

The Quakers, like the Levellers, attracted many of Cromwell's disaffected soldiers, men like the ex-quartermaster James Naylor. Naylor was from a background very different from Fox's; he was the son of a wealthy farmer near Wakefield, and at the age of twenty-four he joined Cromwell's Army. He left after the battle of Dunbar to return to his father's farm and in 1651 heard Fox preach for the first time. That was all it took. The following year he decided to become a peripatetic missionary. Within months he was arrested for preaching blasphemy, and on his release he made for London, where there was a large Quaker group. Naylor acquired a following among the London Quakers, and when splits developed in the group he set off with some of his supporters to visit Fox, who was now in Launceston Prison. The journey rapidly became a messianic march, with new adherents starting to call Naylor the 'only son of God' and one woman claiming that he had raised her from the dead. Naylor was arrested and imprisoned again for blasphemy but, on his release, continued on his mission. Arrested yet again in Bristol, he was sent to London to be tried before the Bar of the House of Commons. He was whipped through the streets of London, his tongue was pierced through with a hot iron and the letter B for 'blasphemer' was branded on his forehead. The following year he died.

For our purposes, however, the most important of the seventeenth-century Quakers was undoubtedly John Bellers, to whom Marx referred as 'a phenomenal figure in the history of political economy'.[14] Bellers was born in 1654 of a wealthy family and in 1695 wrote an essay entitled *Proposals for raising a college of industry of all useful trades and husbandry with Profit for the Rich, a plentiful living for the Poor and a good education for Youth, which will be advantage to the government by the Increase of the People and their riches. Motto: Industry brings Plenty – The Sluggard shall be clothed with Rags. He that will not work shall not eat.* In it he advocated a communal colony where value would be measured in units of labour-time instead of money. Although Sir William Petty had already in 1662 recognised the principle that the value of commodities could be related to the amount of labour it took to make them, Bellers was the first person to argue for its being put into industrial or economic practice and thus anticipated Robert Owen by more than a century with his plans for a commune of 300. Beller's plans were very detailed, but they failed to attract sufficient interest or cash to make them viable, and it is not until Róbert Owen's early-nineteenth-century villages of Unity and Co-operation that the principles he espoused were ever tried. Even then most church people were offended by Owen's overt anti-clericalism, which he expressed forcibly in his *Denunciation of all Religions* in 1817. So Beller's ideas broke vital ground in asserting that by combining, by associating, not only could people find greater strength in numbers but they could also form an alternative economy, an idea to which the Victorian Christian Socialists would return with their co-operative associations.

If the Quakers were the radicals of the late seventeenth century, it was the Methodists who took up the torch in the early nineteenth.

The seed that John Wesley had cast among the poor in the late eighteenth century was in many respects unexceptional. There were plenty of evangelical preachers of his time who could attract significant crowds, not least his colleague George Whitefield and the likes of Samuel Walker of Truro, John Berridge of Everton and Hywel Davies in Wales. All of them capitalised on the Church of England's patent inability to meet the needs, spiritual or material, of the majority of the population. What was distinctive about Wesley, however, was the fact that his congregations were drawn almost exclusively from the poor. Wesley himself was no socialist, and much of his teaching verges on the authoritarian, but he saw his own work quite clearly as a mission to the poor. 'To speak the rough truth,' he announced, 'I do not desire any discourse with any person of quality in England.'[15]

By the start of the nineteenth century, though, Methodism was beginning to make inroads into the middle classes, and so it was not long before a split occurred between the more structured Wesleyans and the Primitive Methodists. These last were formed in 1811 largely through the work of Hugh Bourne, a Methodist based at Mow Cop in Staffordshire, and the American Lorenzo Dow, who ran Camp Meetings at Mow Cop as a way of attracting labouring men and women to Christianity without having to force them into church. Both men were expelled by the Wesleyan Conference when they continued with the Camps against the Conference's commands, as was William Clowes, a colleague who had taken the Camp idea to Tunstall. From the outset the Primitive Methodists had a distinct dissenting voice. They maintained their work among the poor, in the same mining communities that Wesley had preached to, and, as a predominantly working-class Church, were unique in appointing women ministers.

There has been a tendency in the modern Labour Party to over estimate the contribution of Methodism to British socialism, largely because few political commentators have understood the difference between the Wesleyans and Primitives, who did not combine again until 1932. The comment 'Labour owes more to

11

Methodism than to Marx', while oft-repeated, is only dubiously attributable to Morgan Phillips and may go back to Arthur Henderson, a Methodist. Either way, it would be truer to say with R. F. Wearmouth that 'Labour's ascent to political influence and authority was due more to Methodism than Marxist theories, more to the prophets and the New Testament than to the *Communist Manifesto*,'[16] and then only if one includes all of Nonconformism under 'Methodism'. In many regards Wesleyan Methodism held Labour back, still teaching a creed of self-dependence and individualism, associating Dissent with Liberalism and Free Trade, so much so that the republican Cobbett argued in *The Political Register* of 12 June 1813, 'There are, I know, persons who look upon the Methodists . . . as *friends of freedom*. It is impossible they should be.' In both 1817 and 1819, years of political turmoil in Britain, Methodists were reckoned among the more conservative of the Church leaders.

None the less there were Methodists, both Primitive and Wesleyan, who from their Methodist churchgoing had learnt to read, to write and to speak in public and from their theology had derived a radical critique of the society in which they lived.

Thus in 1834 Methodists numbered the majority among the Tolpuddle Martyrs, a group of six who were spuriously sentenced to transportation for seven years and became one of the great *causes célèbres* of the century. Their crime had been to form a trade union at a time when agricultural wages had been cut from nine shillings a week to seven in three years, with a threat of a further shilling's cut in 1834. Until 1825 the Combination Acts had made any form of trade union illegal, but with their repeal Robert Owen had inaugurated the Grand National Consolidated Trades Union, which provided advice for local groups around the country. One such was the Tolpuddle Friendly Society of Agricultural Labourers, which started in October 1833 and had taken the precautionary steps of insisting on an oath of secrecy for all members.

The leading figures in the Union formed a close-knit family and were all Methodists: George Loveless, a thirty-four-year-old lay preacher who had trained himself in theology, and his twenty-five-year-old brother James, their brother-in-law Thomas Stanfield, also thirty-four, and his son John, who was then twenty-one. On 24 February 1834 these four, together with James Brine, a member of the Church of England, and James Hammett, of no fixed religion, were arrested not for belonging to the Union but for having taken an 'unlawful oath' in supposed contravention of the 1797 Mutiny Act, which made no reference to unions. Within the month they had been tried at Dorchester Crown Court and sentenced to the extreme limit of the law: seven years' transportation. The judge, Mr Baron Williams, in passing sentence effectively admitted the excessive severity of his decision:

The object of all legal punishment is not altogether with a view of operating on the offenders themselves, it is also for the sake of offering an example and warning, and accordingly the offence of which you have been convicted ... is of that description that the security of the country and the maintenance of the laws on the upholding of which the welfare of this country depends, make it necessary for me to pass on you the sentence required by those laws.[17]

All bar George Loveless, who was ill in Dorchester Prison, set sail for New South Wales in the *Surrey* on 11 April, and Loveless followed in the *William Metcalf* on 25 May. To all intents and purposes, like any other convict, the Martyrs became slaves, working in chain-gangs on penal settlements and being exchanged between agents for money.

Meanwhile a great campaign had started back in England to ensure the remission of their punishment or at least a pardon. Owen called a Grand Meeting of the Working Classes on 24 March, which Arthur Wade, the vicar of St Nicholas, Warwick, chaired and more than 10,000 people attended. In April an even larger meeting was held on Copenhagen Fields, and Owen and Wade processed to Downing Street to present the Home Secretary,

Lord Melbourne, with a petition calling for an unconditional release. In June 1835 the new Home Secretary, Lord Russell, offered a conditional pardon, but the campaign continued until finally, on 14 March 1836, the Government caved in, and a free and full pardon was extended to all six of the Martyrs, who returned over the next eighteen months.

The story of the Martyrs is brief and contains little theology, but they came to symbolise for both the trade-union movement and the Christian Socialists the importance of solidarity, resistance to injustice and the ability of sustained campaigning to sway governments.

The same year, 1834, was also the year of the Poor Law Amendment Act, which brought in the Poor Law Commissioners and the union workhouses and abolished the 1601 paupers' right to parish support. Again one of the leading figures to stand up for the poor and to contest the Act was a Methodist, Joseph Rayner Stephens. The son of a celebrated Cornish President of Wesleyan Conference, Stephens was born in Edinburgh in 1805 and became a Wesleyan minister himself at the age of twenty, soon going to work as a missionary in Sweden. In 1832 he accepted a charge in the Aston-under-Lyme circuit, where he came out in favour of Disestablishment, thus isolating himself from the rest of Wesleyan Conference. Indeed in 1834, after charges were levelled against him at the annual conference, he resigned from the Connexion and became the pastor of the 'Ashton separationists'.

So far Stephens's notoriety centred on purely theological and ecclesiastical matters. The next two years saw him drawn inexorably into political confrontations that established him as one of the leading revolutionaries of his time.

One of Stephens's most influential friends was the prime mover in the factory-reform movement, Richard Oastler, the steward of a large country estate in Yorkshire whom he met soon after his marriage in 1835. Oastler was also a dissident Methodist of strong evangelical, radical Tory convictions. Committed to reducing the working hours of factories, he had initiated the Ten Hours campaign, of which one of the Ashton mill-owners, and since January 1835 its MP, Charles Hindley, was a keen advocate.

Not surprisingly for a minister in a town dominated by rapidly growing cotton mills, Stephens's first sallies into the political battlefield were related to factory reform, but by 1836 his opposition to the new Poor Law was just as marked. His objection to the workhouses was avowedly Christian. Christianity centred on the institutions of marriage and family, but in segregating the sexes the workhouses would destroy marriages and split fathers from their children. The Poor Law, he argued, 'treats the poor worse than the felon ... makes marriage a mockery and offers brutal violence to the holiest feelings of our nature'.[18] Furthermore, the Poor Law Commissioners' factory-migration scheme to supply rural paupers to industrial areas for money would effectively 'resuscitate slavery in the British dominions'.

So throughout 1836 and 1837 Stephens, in tandem with Oastler, proclaimed the immorality of the Poor Law and demanded factory reforms in line with Hindley's Ten Hours Bill. Inevitably Stephens was told to stick to spiritual matters, although he rebutted his critics with ease:

> I have been told by these men to stick to the Bible and leave the spindle to them. [Laughter.] I mean to stick to the Bible: and if anyone wants to know why I am a factory-reform agitator, I tell them it is because I know that the system is repugnant to the word of the living God and that as long as we have his blessed book in our hands and in our hearts we must live to see the downfall of that tyranny which is now grinding you into the dust.[19]

Stephens soon had a radical following which included the Chartist leader Feargus O'Connor, whose *Northern Star* regularly covered Stephens's attacks on the Poor Law Commission.

Although Stephens was elected to the Chartists' Convention and regularly shared platforms with Chartists, he was himself unconvinved by the demands of the five-point Charter, and despite briefly calling for universal suffrage, through 1838 he steadily distanced himself from the Chartists, arguing that it was physical force, not a tidily presented petition, that would change Britain. By the start of 1838 he had abandoned all restraint and proclaimed in Rochdale, 'If it were right to confiscate the property of the poor by abrogating the 43rd Elizabeth [the 1601 Poor Law], it is right for the poor to take a dagger in one hand and a torch in the other, and do the best for themselves.'[20] On a nationwide tour of banned torchlight meetings Stephens continued, much to the Chartist leaders' discomfort, that 'the firelock must come first and then the vote afterwards.'[21]

Eventually Stephens was arrested, tried and imprisoned for eighteen months in Chester Castle, by which time he had finally fallen out with O'Connor. Stephens's ministry after his imprisonment was a mild affair compared with his rabble-rousing itinerant evangelical mission of the 1830s. Indeed, he even became a Poor Law Guardian himself in 1848. None the less much of what he fought for did come to pass. Disraeli's Factory Acts of 1874, 1875 and 1878 improved working conditions and gave the law muscle fully to enforce reforms on factory owners. The Poor Law was also never implemented with the full rigour that had originally been intended, thanks in part to the moral force behind Stephens's forceful agitation. By the time of his death in 1879 his anti-Charter Toryism had been overtaken by political history, but his original conception of the task of ministry still stands as a model for Christian Socialists:

> let the priesthood become a real *Ministry for the Poor*, not confined to the Church and the sickroom, but operating on the daily life of the poor. To reclaim the vicious, to counsel the improvident, to raise new hopes in the desponding, to be the friend and benefactor of all, is a noble mission. To instruct and relieve the poor is more God-like than to minister to the rich.[22]

\*

The term 'Utopian' has had a prickly history, and perhaps its coinage is now so debased that it is time to melt it down and start afresh. After all, even modern Christian Socialists are scathing about Utopianism. Christopher Rowland again:

> One of the problems of Utopianism is that it can lead the reader into construction of ideal worlds which distract him or her from the demands of the present. Utopianism can lead to an escape from reality however much its attempts betoken that yearning for something better. Writers who resort to Utopianism do so as a compensation for the inability to do anything about the world as it is.[23]

All this is true, of course. With our eyes too firmly fixed on Heaven, we can fail to see the pavement under our feet, and it is fully as fraudulent to peddle impossible dreams to the poor as it is to tell them that happiness lies in the cheerful acceptance of their lot in this life so that they may attain salvation in another.

But Utopias, properly understood, are not impossible dreams, and the first Utopian was more thoroughly engaged in the *Realpolitik* of his day than the vast majority of modern Christians. Indeed, he wrote *Utopia* to explore the wisdom of getting involved in the political matters of the realm.

Every historical figure stands the risk of being adopted by causes they might never have espoused. Sir Thomas More has posthumously suffered from this almost as much as he suffered in his own lifetime from the theological and marital meandering of his King. In 1935 he was canonised by the Vatican as a stout defender of Catholic orthodoxy, yet in the same year Marxists were claiming him as an early dialectical materialist. In *Utopia* he seems to espouse religious tolerance, yet, as Anthony Kenny has pointed out, he 'put men to death for deviations from Catholic orthodoxy far less serious than those of the Utopians'.[24] It is small wonder that for the playwright Robert Bolt he was 'a man for all seasons'.

More's career is easily charted. Born in 1478, he saw England get through four kings by the time he was twenty-one. After school he followed in his father John's legal steps by going to Lincoln's Inn in 1496 and being called to the Bar. While studying law he joined the local ascetic Carthusians in their devotions, and for a time he considered a monastic life. His friend Erasmus recounts, however, that 'as he found he could not overcome his desire for a wife, he decided to be a faithful husband rather than an unfaithful priest,'[25] and he married Jane Colt, who died in 1511, shortly after giving birth to their fourth child, whereupon More remarried within a month, more, so his biographer Harpsfield maintained, 'for the ruling and governing of his children, house and family, than for any bodily pleasure'.[26]

In the year of his first marriage he entered Parliament, aged only twenty-six, and his first contribution, in which he spoke against Henry VII's request for a feudal levy, earned him the King's disfavour for the rest of his reign. In 1509 the monarch was succeeded by his son Henry VIII, and More soon began to enjoy royal patronage. He became Under-Sheriff of London in 1510 and in 1515 envoy to Flanders, where he wrote *Utopia*. Having joined the Privy Council on 1518, he was knighted in 1521 and became Speaker of the House of Commons in 1523, by which time he had helped Henry draft a robust defence of the papacy against Luther's *The Liberty of Christian Man*, for which Pope Leo X granted Henry the title *Fidei Defensor*. Luther's reply was extremely rebarbative, and More was again brought in to provide a retort. Indeed, he acquired a taste for rebutting Protestant tracts and went on, in robust Latin, to attack Lutheran 'heresies' and condemn the New Testament that William Tyndale had translated into English. When Cardinal Wolsey was summarily dismissed as Lord Chancellor in 1527, he was eventually replaced by More.

More had not sought the Chancellorship and soon felt extremely uncomfortable in the role, for Henry's divorce from Catherine of Aragon steadily became more and more contentious, and More was caught between his loyalty to the King and his own conscience. Privately he supported Catherine's claim but publicly kept his own counsel. Through 1530 and 1531 Henry's attempts to bring the clergy to heel, with an enforced vow to accept him as 'only Supreme Head of the English Church as far as the law of Christ allows', must have exasperated the ecclesiastical loyalist in More, and when, in March 1532, the bishops agreed, under pressure, to the King's demand that all clerical legislation should be subject to Royal Assent, More resigned as Chancellor. This did not take him out of harm's way, however, especially as he refused to attend Anne Boleyn's coronation in Westminster Abbey, and in 1534 More refused to swear an oath to observe the Act of Succession, whereby Catherine's marriage was declared annulled and her offspring were to be overlooked in favour of the offspring of Queen Anne. More was prepared to assent to the succession, which was a political matter for Parliament, but not to the annulment, over which he believed Parliament had no authority, so there was a delay while it was decided what to do with him, but on 17 April he was committed to the Tower of London. The new Parliament in 1534 changed the rules yet again, and More was interrogated about his views on the new Act of Supremacy and its declaration of the King as Head of the Church. Eventually, after months of interviews, solicitous requests from his daughter Margaret that he should make the oath and calm, considered asseverations from More that he was the King's loyal subject but could not make the oath, he was condemned for High Treason; though, strictly, as a Commoner he should have received the penalty of being hanged, drawn and quartered, he was beheaded on Tower Hill on 6 July 1535, passing into history as a resolute and courageous defender of truth. None of which makes More a Christian Socialist.

More's legacy, however, hinges as much on his writings as on his life, and his most fiercely debated book, *Utopia*, broke fascinating political ground. It was written in two stages. First comes the description of the 'Commonwealth of Utopia', in which he outlines an imagined island, some 500 miles long by 200 wide, incorporating fifty-four cities and about twenty miles of agricultural land. This More wrote, as we have seen, while an envoy to

Flanders, and it now forms chapter two of the book. The first chapter, written subsequently, is a dialogue between More and a Raphael Hythlodaye about the rights and wrongs of a philosopher entering into political service. When More questions Hythlodaye's beliefs that only radical change will do to convert unruly kings and that while there is still private property there can be no justice, he replies that More's doubts would disappear if only he knew the commonwealth of Utopia, which he then goes on to describe.

*Utopia* is an ironic work, and its shimmering layers of irony leave it open to misinterpretation, but what shines through is More's playfulness. At the end of Book Two he states, 'when Raphael had finished his story, it seemed to me that now a few of the customs and laws he had described . . . were quite absurd' and continues to disparage Utopia: 'my chief objection was to the basis of their whole system, that is, their communal living and their moneyless economy. This one thing alone takes away all the nobility, magnificence, splendor, and majesty which (in the popular view) are considered the true ornaments of any nation.'[27] Here More is playing with his reader, gently implying that Utopian ideals might be more valid than 'the popular view', and it is exactly this drollery that has given More so much posthumous grief.

For ostensibly *Utopia* posits an 'ideal' world: there is no private property; the inhabitants have no locks on their doors; they change houses by lot every ten years; everyone does a two-year stint on a farm; the local leaders are elected by the whole community; women are equal to men; everyone has a trade at which they work six hours a day; most meals are eaten communally; gold, silver, rubies and pearls are treated as base metals and toys for children; and the sick are cared for well. I say 'ostensibly' both because More himself seems ambivalent about his own 'ideal' and because there is much in Utopia that appals, not least the fact that the terminally ill are encouraged to practise euthanasia in rather forceful terms – 'the priests and the magistrates exhort the man, seeing he is not able to do any duty of life, and by overliving his own death, is irksome to others and grievous to himself'[28] – to commit suicide. While women are allowed to be priests in Utopia, and all women work, the marriage rituals are extremely degrading, and there is a system of serfdom which belies the equality of the rest.

So *Utopia* is a confusing book to read for those seeking a definite blueprint for how an ideal society should be. C. S. Lewis said, 'we approach it through a cloud of contradictory eulogies.'[29] More is playing with ideas, not framing a political manifesto, and it is scarcely surprising that there are marked inconsistencies between what he seems to advocate in the book and elements of his own life. More's genre in *Utopia* is not satire or polemic. It is a philosophical treatise based on the simple premise 'What if . . .?' and it is only when it is read as such that both its humour and its acute perceptiveness shines through. Certainly More held strong views, especially on matters of religious and ecclesiastical discipline, and he was prepared to go to the scaffold for them, but when he wrote *Utopia* he allowed his imagination to wander and so happened upon a whole range of political ideas that would not become possibilities until many years later.

The problem with *Utopia*, then, is not that it espouses a wild fantasy that could never be realised, or that it advocates some ludicrous policies, but that its essentially humorous nature has rarely been appreciated, and consequently the whole concept of Utopia has been misinterpreted. For let us be clear: Utopias are not intended as political manifestos, and what is most perceptive about More's vision is that he gives just enough hints to his reader to suggest that all is not quite so perfect as it might seem. Bluff and double-bluff are part of the book's technique of making us evaluate our world against a supposedly ideal society that might, after due consideration, be no more ideal, or Christian, than our own. It is, in Shakespeare's words, to 'hold a mirror up to nature', no more and no less.

We have already mentioned the poet John Milton as one of the Levellers' supporters, and an important aspect of the tradition that the Christian Socialists stood to inherit was that of the visionary wordsmiths of succeeding centuries. In Milton's own day John Bunyan described 'God's people' as 'a turbulent, seditious and factious people'[30] and was himself a preacher imprisoned as much for his political as his theological views.

In the eighteenth century the most notable figure was William Blake, who is variously described as a poet, an artist, an engraver and a visionary. Indeed, it is Blake's poem 'Milton' that has provided the modern Labour Party, thanks to Percy Dearmer and Hubert Parry, with its most enduring hymn, and successive generations of Labour activists (and Albert Hall patriots) have vowed not to let their sword sleep in their hand, 'Till we have built Jerusalem' among the 'dark satanic mills'.

Blake's life is full of shadows and half-certainties. Born the son of a hosier in Soho in 1757, he earned his living as an engraver, having studied art at the newly formed Royal Academy Schools, and spent a part of his apprenticeship drawing the royal tombs in Westminster Abbey. Much has been written of Blake's religious views, but little is definite. It seems likely he was at various times a Swedenborgian, a Muggletonian and a Ranter – certainly he held in common with them a firm belief in the life of the 'Spirit' as opposed to the 'Moral Law'. He held too powerful millenarian beliefs that were fed by intense, biblically inspired visions and matched the antinomian spirit of his age. As for his politics, he was by nature and upbringing a radical, a republican and, in his own words, 'a Son of Liberty', but, as Peter Ackroyd has pointed out, 'the fact that he never joined any particular group or society suggests that his was, from the beginning, an internal politics both self-willed and self-created.'[31] None the less he was acquainted with the radicals of his day, Thomas Paine and Mary Wollstonecraft, and in their circle was a stout defender of Christianity. He had little time for party politics, however, and never voted.

> I am really sorry, [he averred] to see my countrymen trouble themselves about Politics. If Men were Wise the most arbitrary Princes could not hurt them. If they are not Wise the

22

Freest Government is compell'd to be a Tyranny. Princes appear to me to be Fools; House of Commons and House of Lords appear to me to be Fools, they seem to me to be something else beside Human Life.[32]

Blake's poetry and paintings are permeated with images of the oppressed of London, and it is clear that his own internal struggles and those of the poor were as one in his religious imagery. In one of his 'Songs of Experience' he articulated this most clearly:

> In every cry of every Man,
> In every Infant's cry of fear,
> In every voice, in every ban,
> The mind-forg'd manacles I hear.[33]

Blake died in 1827 and was buried in the dissenters' burial ground at Bunhill. Though little of his thought translates easily into a more cynical post-Freudian era, none the less his particular concatenation of millenarian expectation, radical dissent, concern for the poor and mystical biblical imagery became a potent symbol for Christians who refused to accept the politics of their day as inevitable, and it is no accident that the early prophets of the Labour Party saw as their task to build Blake's 'New Jerusalem'.

If there is any one figure who deserves the term 'seminal' in the early nineteenth century, it is Samuel Taylor Coleridge. Today his reputation relies almost entirely on his poetic works and especially the mythic laudanum-induced words of 'Kubla Khan', but in his time he was renowned equally as a philosopher, a theologian, a biblical scholar and a political theorist, and his seemingly random views affected the thinking patterns of a whole generation. As John Stuart Mill put it, no one of his time 'contributed more to shape the opinions of those among its younger men, who can be said to have opinions at all'.[34]

His most direct disciples, however, were the likes of Julius Hare, John Sterling, and F. D. Maurice, all major protagonists in the formation of the Christian Socialist movement of 1848. Both

Hare and Maurice dedicated books to Coleridge and felt that he had rescued Christianity from a shallow debate about its veracity according to severe rationalist principles and provided it with a much more substantial philisophical grounding that was more realistically related to human experience. As Coleridge put it:

> I more than fear the prevailing taste for books of Natural Theology, Physico-Theology, Demonstrations of God from Nature, Evidences of Christianity, and the like. Evidences of Christianity! I am weary of the word. Make a man feel the want of it; rouse him, if you can, to the self-knowledge of his need of it; and you may safely trust to its own Evidence.[35]

Coleridge's approach to biblical criticism also put him at the forefront of British theologians seeking a new way of interpreting the role and significance of the Bible in modern theology. In open contradiction of the then prevailing view of the Bible as divinely dictated, he claimed it as 'the living educts of the imagination', a 'breathing organism',[36] and urged that

> the more tranquilly an inquirer takes up the Bible as he would any other body of ancient writings, the livelier and steadier will be his impressions of its superiority to all other books, till at length all other books and all other knowledge will be valuable in his eyes in proportion as they help him to a better understanding of his Bible.[37]

Similarly, Coleridge's understanding of the relation of Church and State reveals clear principles that informed, within a very different historical setting, much thinking about the Kingdom of God. Thus, in his *On the Constitution of the Church and State* he places great emphasis on 'the Christian Church' as 'the appointed opposite' to all realms collectively, '*the sustaining, correcting, befriending* opposite of the World; the compensating counter-force to the inherent and inevitable evils and defects of the State, as a State'.[38]

The implications of Coleridge's work could be deeply conservative, for all his revolutionary zeal during the years of French emancipation. After all, in matters constitutional he was arguing for the *status quo*, and, if anything, he would have supported an extension of the Church of England's established role. But his theology was new, and it liberated Hare and Maurice to rethink the purpose and method of theology, arguing more from experience than from dry philosophical principle.

Furthermore, his political thoughts were suffused with a radical concern for an ethical social order. Both Wordsworth and Coleridge had acclaimed the French Revolution in its earliest days, though they had been dismayed by its later violence, and both retained a keen sense of the moral imperative. Wordsworth wrote in his 1835 edition of his poems in defiance of the new Poor Law, 'all persons who cannot find employment or procure wages sufficient to support the body in health and strength are entitled to maintenance by law,'[39] and in the *Prelude* he attacked Adam Smith: 'How dire a thing/Is worshipped in that idol proudly named *The Wealth of Nations*.'[40] Both, then, had scant regard for the politics of their day, believing that narrow rationalism had led to the political sphere being considered off-limits to the claims of faith and morality. Coleridge, in words that in another age would sound more like snobbish bigotry than radicalism, expressed the problem as essentially religious: 'today reason governs in opposition to Christianity. The cure for his vulgarisation and anarchy is religion, more discipline, Christian ethics and faith.'[41] He attacked the concept of the right to property except in so far as it implied and demanded the performance of commensurate duties, and he was keen to extend the concept of equality:

It is a mockery of our fellow creatures' wrongs to call them equal in rights, when by bitter compulsion of their wants we make them inferior to us in all that can soften the heart or dignify the understanding. We should endeavour to diffuse these comforts and that illumination which, far beyond all political ordinances, are true equalisers of men.[42]

25

Coleridge achieved two things that made modern Christian Socialism possible. He asserted that Christianity had a legitimate claim to speak on matters political and economic, and he reasserted a faith bound into life and human experience. Both of these claims liberated theology, made possible an incarnational understanding of the significance of the material and declared the scandal of poverty.

Of course, the list of posthumous comrades could now become endless: William Penn, the Quaker founder of Pennsylvania, who outlined plans for a European Parliament in 1690; Roger Crabb, the egalitarian vegetarian hatter of the seventeenth century to whom the phrase 'mad as a hatter' refers; Bishop Shute Barrington of Durham, who opened the first Co-operative Distributive Society at Mongewell near Oxford in 1794; Dr David Davies of Barkham in Berkshire, who called for unemployment benefit and child allowances in 1795; Robert Hall, who helped sustain the Frame-knitters' Union in Leicestershire from 1819 to 1824; Dr William King of Brighton, who published the *Co-operator* in the 1830s; and George Bull, the vicar of St James's, Bradford, who published *The Oppressors of the Poor and the Poor their own Oppressors* in 1839.

What is indubitable is that by the time of the 'hungry Forties' the Christian Socialists had an eclectic tradition on which to build. Christian social thought had already explored much of the territory that they were to map out, and some key landmarks had already been identified. These took the form of four core propositions: (1) all people are of equal worth and sharp inequalities between rich and poor must be morally offensive; (2) the material welfare and personal dignity of the poor are of ultimate concern for Christians; (3) theological freedom, political dissent and the views of minorities should be accepted, honoured and respected; (4) by associating together and sharing the fruits of God's earth, men and women can create a more godly society.

At the core of all these ideas was the fundamental belief that humanity was by its very nature social. It was another poet, the former MP and Dean of St Paul's, John Donne, who expressed it best:

No man is an island, entire of it-self; every man is a piece of the Continent, a part of the main; if a clod be washed away by the Sea, Europe is the less, as well as if a Promontory were, as well as if a manor of thy friend's or of thine own were; any man's death diminishes me, because I am involved in Mankind; And therefore never send to know for whom the bell tolls; it tolls for thee.[43]

In the 'hungry Forties' thoughts such as these, mixed together by the Industrial Revolution, fermented by the Chartist clamour for reform and distilled by the growing sense of a new understanding of Christian faith and citizenship, were to prove a potent brew.

# 2

# The Band of Brothers

Is this a holy thing to see
In a rich and fruitful land,
Babes reduc'd to misery,
Fed with cold and usurous hand?

William Blake, 'Holy Thursday'

They mock at the labourer's limbs! They mock at his starved
children,
They buy his daughters that they may have power to sell his sons;
They compel the poor to live upon a crust of bread, by soft, mild
arts;
They reduce the Man to want, then give, with pomp and
ceremony;
The praise of Jehovah is chanted from lips of hunger and thirst.

William Blake, 'Jerusalem'

Frederick Denison Maurice had a cold on the morning of 10 April
1848 and was confined to his house in Queen Square, Bloomsbury, where he had lived for three years, since the death of his
wife Anna. By now forty-three, he was a well-established figure in
the Church of England, holding two jobs, as was not uncommon
at the time, as chaplain to Lincoln's Inn, one of the legal Inns
of Court, and as Professor of Theology at King's College,
London.

His sermons at Lincoln's Inn had attracted a great deal of
attention for their immediacy and topicality, and he had something of a radical young following. He had published several

works, including a lengthy semi-autobiographical novel, *Eustace Conway*, in 1834 and, far more significant, in 1838 *The Kingdom of Christ*, which set out his fundamental views and his understanding of the nature of the Christian endeavour.

His career had not been exactly normal for a Anglican priest. His father, Michael Maurice, had been sent by his own father, a Presbyterian minister, to Hoxton Academy for Dissenters in Shoreditch, which was then being run surreptitiously by Unitarian followers of Joseph Priestley. When he finished there in 1787 Michael Maurice announced that he too considered himself a Unitarian and was seeking Unitarian, not Presbyterian, ordination, and his father promptly disinherited him. In 1794 he witnessed the sacking of Priestley's house by religious bigots, and after Priestley emigrated to Pennsylvania, he married Priscilla Hurry, another Unitarian of a rich West Country family. They then moved to Yarmouth, where he taught private pupils, including the poet Southey's younger brother.

As a family the Maurices were close but not intimate, and matters of religious adherence were of constant interest. From F. D. Maurice's son Frederick's biography of his father we know that the family always wrote letters to express their keenest feelings rather than speak face to face. So when both Edmund Hurry, an orphaned cousin who lived with the family, died, and when his sister Anne decided to leave the Unitarian fold for the Society of Baptist Dissenters, rapidly followed by the three eldest Maurice sisters, all these momentous matters were relayed by letter. A respect for dissent and theological honesty, the importance of faith to the ordinary matters of life, as well as a real fear of conflict survived through into all of Maurice's work. Indeed, in a letter of 1866 to one of his sons, Maurice expressed his own indebtedness to his father:

My ends have been shaped for me, rough hew them how I would, and shape has been given to them by my father's function and this name 'Unitarian' more than by any other influences ... My father's Unitarianism was not of a fiercely dogmatic kind. But it made him intolerant of what he considered intolerance in Churchmen or Dissenters; pleased when either would work with him, sensitive to slights from them.[1]

His father's work with the anti-slave-trade movement, the new Sunday school and the Bible Society which he set up in Frenchay, as well as his mother's clothing shop and soup kitchens, all contributed as surely as any other aspect of his life to the formation of the man who is often credited as being the greatest of Anglican theologians.

The family turmoils over religion, with Priscilla's eventual decision not to worship at her husband's church in 1821, led to the young Maurice's decision not to go forward for ordination but instead to pursue a career at the Bar. So in 1823 he started a classics degree at Trinity College, Cambridge, where he immediately came under the influence of one of the most significant figures in his later life, Julius Hare, whose lectures he attended and whose friendship he instantly adopted. It was at Trinity that he also met John Sterling, who referred to his time at college as spent 'in picking up pebbles beside the ocean of Maurice's genius'.[2]

Sterling became his closest friend, and his premature death was later to cause the first half of an extended period of depression in 1844. Maurice and Sterling formed something of a dissenting political alliance, for all Cambridge seemed then to follow the utilitarian teaching of Jeremy Bentham, while they espoused the Romantic theology of the poet Coleridge, whose ideas lay behind much of Maurice's worthy novel *Eustace Conway*. Maurice's and Sterling's final year at Cambridge was spent at Trinity Hall, then the lawyer's college, although neither went on to practise law. Because of the University's restrictions on Noncomformists Maurice came down from Cambridge without a degree and started his working life as a journalist, writing scathing attacks on Bentham and lengthy magazine articles about poetry and modern literature. When his father's fortunes were badly damaged by the collapse of a bonds issue in Spain in 1828, having recently transferred his allegiance to the Church of England, he decided to restart his academic studies in order to prepare himself for ordination. Armed with a recommendation from Julius Hare, he went up to Exeter College, Oxford, in 1830, to study as an undergraduate again, since the religious requirements placed on graduands had meant that he still had no relevant degree.

In 1831, while his closest sister Emma lay desperately ill, he was baptised into the Church of England and then took a term off to stay with her. She died in July, and Maurice decided to hasten his studies, opting for immediate theological examination. A Mr Stephenson of Lympsham took him on as his parish assistant for a year before his ordination to the country parish of Bubbenhall, near Leamington, in 1834.

With the zeal of a newly received Anglican he published a major article entitled 'Subscription no Bondage', defending the Church of England. He also read some of the work of the 'Oxford Movement' leader, Dr Pusey, though he rejected most of its scathing assessment of the state of the Church. In late 1835, through Hare's intervention, he was offered the post of chaplain at Guy's Hospital in London, which he took up in January 1836. By now Sterling was Hare's curate in Hurstmonceux, in Sussex, but living in Orme Square in London, and was married to Susannah Barton. He was also seriously ill with tuberculosis and had turned substantially away from Coleridge towards the atheist Carlyle. Maurice was doubly hurt – that his close friend had so apparently become a purely professional Christian, and that he was dying. In later years he regretted the constant rows that ensued over matters sacred and secular. In 1837, however, Susannah Sterling called her sister Anna over from Germany, where she lived with their widowed mother, to help her care for him. Maurice met her and fell in love, getting engaged in the summer at Hurstmonceux and being married by the frail Sterling in October. Maurice experienced a transformation. His son wrote later, 'Any one who has realised how much of isolation, of self-restraint and of silence amid many words there was in all his relationships and in all his friendships up to this point will judge what through sympathy, eager approval of his own best thoughts, complete appreciation, she must have been to him.'[3] Maurice himself said, 'She was the most *transparently* truthful person I ever knew, the most fresh and informal.'[4] That freshness was clearly felt most strongly in her sense of humour, in many senses rather distant from her husband's intense moral earnestness: 'Mr Carlyle has been here talking for four hours in praise of silence.'

The following years were ones of extremely mixed blessings. Maurice's first major theological work, *The Kingdom of Christ*, which started life as a series of letters to a Quaker friend, was an instant success. Sterling, meanwhile, increasingly frail, moved further towards Carlyle and became part of his regular Cheyne Walk set. In 1839 Maurice's only Anglican sister, Elizabeth, died, and soon after his first child, a daughter, was stillborn. In 1840, at the recommendation of W. E. Gladstone, he was offered the additional post of Professor of English Literature and History at King's College, just as Hare was appointed Archdeacon of Lewes and the first of two sons was born.

In 1843, however, Maurice's most trying period started. First old Mrs Sterling died, and then Susannah Sterling. Anna Maurice cared for the invalid Sterling until his death in September 1844, and by the end of the year Anna herself contracted tuberculosis. In December of that same year Hare became engaged to and married Maurice's sister Esther, and Maurice met, at his house in Lavington the Archdeacon of Chichester, Henry Manning, whose support for agricultural labours he admired. At Easter in 1845 Anna Maurice died. Maurice's children, together with the Sterling children, went to live with the Hares at Hurstmonceux, where Anna was buried. Maurice was distraught, and it was not until 1847 that he really seemed to escape the ghost of his wife's death, when he openly supported Gladstone's candidature in Oxford, agreed to write a preface for Charles Kingsley's *Saint's Tragedy* and put forward a plan for the first college for governesses, Queen's College.

So by 1848 Maurice was a respected man with a significant

body of work behind him, scarred by the experience of losing nearly all those who had been close to him only a couple of years before, still unused to the easy exchange of intimacy and cautious of confrontation. Yet, as John Ruskin said later, it was as much the quality of the man as his thinking that was attractive: 'I loved Frederick Maurice, as every one did who came near him, but Maurice was by nature puzzle-headed and, though in a beautiful manner, wrong-headed.'[5]

That year, 1848, was a year of dramatic *bouleversements* throughout Europe. In France Louis Philippe abdicated in February, and the new Republic was announced. Socialist experiments, such as the *phalanstères* of Ludlow's friend Fourier, were being tried, and the old revolutionary call of '*Liberté, egalité, fraternité*' was heard again. Germany saw popular uprisings in many cities, leading to new constitutions and new rights for the people. In Vienna Metternich was deposed and fled to England. Italy was also in revolt, with new constitutions being granted to Naples, Rome, Tuscany and Piedmont. In Ireland the famine of the previous year had been brought home chillingly to Maurice and his friends by Archbishop Chenevix Trench, while in Britain too there was a whiff of cordite in the air. The Chartists had been around for some time, but the thrust of their campaign had foundered in 1839. After re-forming in 1842 they had collapsed again a year later. But now their militant demands, expressed in a six-point Charter, acquired a much stronger currency. In March 1848 there were large assemblies across the East End of London, at Stepney, Bethnal Green, Clerkenwell Green. The West End saw three days of confrontation with the police over the banning of demonstrations in Trafalgar Square. Glasgow was also in the hands of the mob for several days, and there were demonstrations up and down the land. The Chartists were sharply divided between a 'physical-force' group and a more reformist tendency, and by late March there was a distinct fear among the ruling classes that the 'physical-force' group would win the day. A hastily convened National Convention of Chartists on 4 April drafted a new petition to Parliament and resolved to march on Parliament from Kennington Common on 10 April.

What is clear from all the records of the time is that London took the threat of potential violent unrest very seriously. The Government recruited 150,000 special constables for the day, and many shopkeepers boarded up their premises. As Ludlow put it much later, 'The present generation has no idea of the terrorism which was at that time exercised by the Chartists.'⁶

The reaction of the early Christian Socialists to the general project of Chartism was mixed, but the response to the intended demonstration on 10 April was almost unanimous. Maurice himself offered to act as a special constable but was told that clergy would not be accepted. Thomas Hughes did act as a constable. Charles Kingsley, who had had his friend and publisher John Parker to stay at his rectory in Eversley the previous weekend, was deeply concerned to hear that the Parkers' shop near the Strand was to be closed for the day for fear of the demonstrations and resolved to travel back up to London with Parker, determined to go and speak to the crowds at Kennington Common. So Kingsley, having met Maurice four years before, arrived at his Queen Square house, hoping to elicit his support and help. Maurice, still thick with his cold, sent him round the corner to his young friend Ludlow. 'Meantime,' his letter of recommendation read, '(as I am confined to the house by a cough myself) will you let me introduce my friend Mr Kingsley. He is deeply earnest and seems to be possessed with the idea of doing something by handbills.'

It is difficult quite to imagine the effect Kingsley would have had on Ludlow, coming as they did from such radically different backgrounds. Ludlow's account of the meeting is probably over-generous:

[I found his] conversation fascinating by its originality, keen observation, strong sense and imaginative power; deep feeling and broad humour succeeding each other without giving the least sense of incongruity or jar to one's feelings. His stutter,

34

which he felt most painfully himself as a thorn in the flesh, in fact only added to a raciness in his talk as one waited for what quaint saying was going to pour out, as it always did, at full speed, the stutter once conquered.[7]

What Ludlow omitted was Kingsley's decidedly West Country accent, for Kingsley had been born in 1819, the same year as Queen Victoria, and brought up almost exclusively in the West of England. Kingsley's father, also named Charles, was a wealthy man who frittered away all the money his father had made in East and West Indian trade. In 1804 he had married Mary Lucas, who made him a forceful wife. He was ordained, and during his second curacy, at Holne in Devon, the young Charles was born. The family moved fairly frequently, to Burton-on-Trent, north Clifton and, in 1824, to Barnack near Peterborough. Kingsley wrote of his family in a letter to his wife in 1843, 'love and devotion were only enticed out to be played with for a moment, and when it became *de trop* in any way was rudely struck aside and made to recoil weeping upon itself.' Kingsley was not a healthy child, suffering often from croup, and it was to the regular administration of mercurous chloride that he attributed his stammer and his underdeveloped chin. None the less he was sent away to a preparatory school in Clifton, near Bristol, where he witnessed one of the scenes that most significantly affected his political understanding. For on a walk from school one day he saw the Bristol riots of 1831, when the gaol was burnt down and the docks were in uproar. He later described, somewhat improbably, seeing several casks of brandy smashed in the street and rioters bending down to lick it up, whereupon there was a 'rustling sound'. Suddenly the brandy had caught fire and all the rioters were burnt to death. More important, however, he saw the north side of Queen Square stacked with mutilated corpses, 'What I had seen made me for years the veriest aristocrat, full of hatred and contempt for those dangerous classes, whose existence I had for the first time discovered.'[8]

His next school was Helston Grammar School, in Cornwall,

which was run by the distinguished natural scientist and priest Derwent Coleridge, who was son of the poet and to whom Maurice later dedicated *The Kingdom of Christ*. Here he made friends with Cowley Powles; the friendship survived well into old age, when Powles was one of Kingsley's parishioners at Eversley.

In 1837 Kingsley's father was appointed to the parish of St Luke's, Chelsea, which had been built to provide for the population of the new Cadogan estates. In 1838, after two years at King's College, London, he went up to Magdalene College, Cambridge, where he made another of his most enduring friendships, with Charles Mansfield, another son of the rectory, who was then studying at Clare. Kingsley described him as 'so wonderfully graceful, active, and daring. He was more like an antelope than a man.'[9]

It was in the summer of 1839, when his father had exchanged duties for two months with a rector in Checkenden, in Oxfordshire, that Kingsley met Frances Eliza Grenfell and her three elder sisters, all of whom were devoted Tractarians in the Keble mould. Kingsley felt no sympathy for their high-church theology, as later events would prove, but 'Fanny' instantly became the focus of his life. Ludlow later referred to him as a 'man of rugged strength and headlong dash', but in the case of Fanny he had to wait seven years before he could overcome both his own deep sense of sexual guilt and his future-in-laws' belief in his unworthiness.

Yet in 1842, after a lengthy period of religious doubt, he was ordained to serve as curate at Eversley. Fanny sent him a copy of *The Kingdom of Christ*, which simultaneously set Kingsley off into an enthusiasm for theological debate and convinced him of his own sinfulness. He proposed a year of not corresponding with Fanny to prove their love and embarked on what became a constant pattern of self-mortification through flagellation. He wrote a biography of St Elizabeth of Hungary, which was to be a wedding present for Fanny, and adorned it with openly sadomasochistic sexual drawings. None the less by the end of their year of separation the Grenfell family had been won over, and the marriage was held in Trinity Church in Bath on 10 January 1844.

Through Fanny's family Kingsley also met one of his most important influences in the shape of the rector of Durwent, Sydney Godolphin Osborne, who wrote letters to *The Times* on every matter of social justice for more than forty years. After staying with him Kingsley knew that his politics had been transformed, so much so that he could now say, 'The refined man is he who cannot rest in peace with a coal mine, or a factory, or Dorsetshire peasant's house near him in the state they are.'[10]

In May 1844 Kingsley was appointed rector of the very parish in which he had served as curate by the patron Sir John Cope and took up residence in the splendid rectory with Fanny and Rose Georgiana, who was born in November. So began the most important aspect of Kingsley's life, his regular work as a parish priest in the tradition, as he saw it, of the country parson and poet George Herbert. His predecessor had neglected the parish, and much of the church itself was in disrepair, but Kingsley set out to visit as regularly as possible, especially among the poorer tenants. He started a reading class in the rectory, and opened a lending library, as well as initiating a variety of small savings schemes.

Between 1844 and 1848, then, Kingsley was concerned predominantly with his family, his parish and his writing. He entered into a regular correspondence with Maurice. He read a great deal, especially valuing Stanley's biography of Thomas Arnold, the headmaster of Rugby, which appeared in 1844 and through which he acquired a political taste for systems that emphasised the need for self-help and self-improvement. He was fundamentally opposed to the Charter, which he described as 'constitution-mongering', and though he had a very keen sense of the needs of the poor, he did not believe that an Act of Parliament could bring about the change that was required. His own instincts, framed partly by the rural environment in which he worked, were those of a Tory paternalist. He believed in social reform, not political reform, and his concern was as much with the morality of the poor as with their living conditions. He was also obsessed by manliness, frequently referring to the quality or its lack in others and regularly exerting himself in sport, so much so that he was the first to be referred to as a 'muscular Christian'. Yet for all the curiosity of Kingsley's temperament, which was prone to excessive exhaustion and depression, he was an eager man looking for a way of channelling his political concern into action.

The man he came to see on 10 April was of a very different kind. John Malcolm Forbes Ludlow was two years younger than Kingsley, born in Nimach, in India, in 1821 of British Indian stock. His father had been a colonel in the British Indian Army and had died within six months of his birth. His mother was the daughter of Murdoch Brown, the first Scotsman to own land in south India, whose wife had deserted him and who had taken an Indian mistress. (Her brother Frank went on to found, in 1839, the British India Society to combat the worst excesses of the virtual monopoly which was the East India Company.) Ludlow and his sister Maria were then brought up in Paris, where he studied at the Collège Bourbon. In 1830 Ludlow witnessed at close hand the Paris revolt that toppled Charles X. As with Kingsley, his first impression of public demonstrations was not favourable, as he saw a whole mob stopped in its tracks by a single student of the Ecole Polytechnique. Ludlow later interpreted his life in terms of seven spiritual crises; the first of these ensued when his elder sister Maria fell in love with Charles Liot and asked her brother's permission to marry him and leave for Martinique.

Five years later, in 1838, Mrs Ludlow decided to remove to London, and the family took up residence first with an elderly relative and then in a small house in Cadogan Square, which was still considered to be on the outskirts of London, whence Ludlow derived his nickname (and *nom-de-plume*) of Johnny Townsend. His second crisis came in 1843 with the news of an earthquake in Martinique in which he feared his sister and her husband had been killed. 'Whatsoever faith I had up till then had been intellectual only,'[11] he confessed. Yet the crisis, as on a future occasion when Liot had lost all his money and Ludlow had to help him out, merely strengthened Ludlow's religious leanings, which both in Paris and in London were at this time strictly Protestant. Heavily scriptural in his approach, he was distrustful of much of the narrowness of many evangelicals. As he put it, 'Having come to Christ by the evangelical door, I had not been able thoroughly to harmonise my socialism with my Christianity.'[12] His socialism, as his faith, was heavily influenced by his still regular trips to France. He came into contact with Fourier, whose collective corporations, called *phalanstères*, he believed pointed the way to a more harmonious economic life, and on studying political economy in 1838 he found it to be a 'let-alone' philosophy that left humanity adrift on an open sea. In 1841 Pastor Vermeil had founded a deaconesses' institute in one of the poorest parts of Paris, the Faubourg Saint Antoine, and Ludlow was impressed by their work of visiting and working with the poor. Indeed, this lasting influence can be seen in Ludlow's permanent concern in later life to enlist women in the work of Christian ministry 'without the snare of perpetual vows' and his advocacy of crèches for working women. Similarly Ludlow was heavily influenced by an 1846 visit to Paris in which he met another Protestant pastor, Louis Meyer, who had founded the Société des Amis de Pauvres, a group of professional young men who visited the poor at home. Meyer pushed him to say what exactly he was doing for the poor, and on his return to England he was determined to set up a similar project in London. He approached Maurice, but had no joy of him, and so joined the Stranger's Friend Society, with whom he went visiting in the alleys and courts of London.

By 1846, however, two other significant events had occurred, for in 1843 he fell in love with his cousin, Maria Forbes, whom he much later married, and he started work as a lawyer in the chambers of the Whig Bellenden Ker, who, after serving on the Royal Commission of 1837 into the laws of partnership, was engaged by the Board of Trade to conveyance all charters of incorporation for joint-stock companies. In 1844 Ludlow helped Ker draw up the Joint Stock Company Regulation Act, thereby mastering the intricacies of parliamentary procedure and conveyancing.

Some English influences also came to bear on the young lawyer. As with Kingsley, he read and was impressed by Stanley's biography of Arnold. 'Arnold,' he said, 'showed me what I missed in my narrower evangelical friends, French as well as English, the combination of earnest faith, breadth of view and energetic action'.[13] Coleridge's *Remains* he valued, though the unsystematic approach irritated him: 'Why these huge blocks of thought and yet no temple?'[14]

At the start of 1848 Ludlow had perhaps the most secure political understanding of all the Christian Socialists. He had seen some of the early socialist experiments in Paris, he understood the British parliamentary system, he knew how associations could be framed in law and, above all, by virtue of his French upbringing he could maintain a degree of distance from the British political and ecclesiastical scene that meant he could study it without the concerns for preferment that tormented Kingsley or the instinct for appeasement that motivated Maurice. He was also the most austere of the three, more Puritan in his style, more analytical in his thinking, more clearly political, despite the fact that he voted only twice in his life, once to keep out a 'money-lender' in Finsbury and once to see how the new secret ballot worked.

So in February 1848 it was an excited Ludlow that visited Paris to witness the new Republic at first hand. He wrote to his uncle, Sir Charles Forbes, 'God has shown His power and His mercy in scattering the old government to the winds in a single day.'[15] On his return to London he instantly contacted Maurice again, conveying 'his conviction that Socialism was a real and very great power which had acquired an unmistakable hold not merely on the fancies but on the consciences of the Parisian workmen, and that it must be Christianised or it would shake Christianity to its foundations, precisely because it appealed to the higher and not to the lower instincts of the men'.[16] Now it was as if they met face to face: 'The veil between us was parted and it dawned upon me that the new friend [F.D.M.] I had made was the greatest man I knew.'[17]

*

On 10 April 1848 the two young men, Kingsley (twenty-nine) and Ludlow (twenty-seven), brought together by their mutual admiration for the older Maurice (forty-three) set off to Kennington Common to try to convince the Chartist crowds to move forward peacefully. By the time they reached Waterloo Bridge, however, they started to meet the first of the demonstrators returning from the disappointing event in a thick April drizzle. Barely a tenth of the expected numbers had turned out, and the Chartist leader Feargus O'Connor had urged the crowd to go home while he and the other leaders presented the petition to Parliament in a cab. Disillusionment was written on every face and was compounded days later when it was revealed that many of the signatures on the petition were false.

Kingsley and Ludlow decided to return to Maurice's house, where they talked and argued till four in the morning about the need for a genuine response to the day's events and what Christianity had to offer the challenge of socialism. By the morning they had produced a first placard, signed 'A Working Parson' and written in Kingsley's inimitable style. Its address to the workers was plastered all over the London hoardings: 'There will be no true freedom without virtue, no true science without religion, no true industry without the fear of God and love to your fellow-citizens. Workers of England, be wise, and then you *must* be free, for you will be *fit* to be free.'[18] Other placards were prepared, all betraying the authors' mixed feelings about political transformation and the working classes. Indeed, much of the first Christian Socialist writings seem no more than pious, paternalist but benevolent Toryism, with as much concern expressed about the leisure pursuits of the poor, and in particular the effects of drink, as about political change.

However, within three weeks the group of three had, at the suggestion of Hare, who visited Maurice later that week, set up a new weekly publication, *Politics for the People*. The first edition was published on 6 May, with Ludlow as editor and Maurice as a kind of editor-in-chief. Maurice wrote to Kingsley requesting an article: 'Could you not write a working parson's letter about the right and wrong use of the Bible – I mean, protesting against the notion of turning it into a book for keeping the poor in order?'[19] Contributors would not be paid, and the style would be similar to Cobbett's *Political Register*, though it would be published by Parker, who also published *Fraser's Magazine*. Early contributions included a series of articles by Maurice on 'Equality', 'Liberty' and 'Fraternity'. Ludlow on 'The People' and 'The Suffrage' and pieces by two successive archbishops of Dublin, Richard Whatley and Chenevix Trench, and a future dean of Westminster and Arnold's biographer, Stanley.

Maurice made it clear that the publication was not to be seen as the manifesto of any new party, and both Ludlow and Kingsley wrote of their distrust of political parties. Yet *Politics for the People* spoke directly of the need for Christianity to be concerned with the issues of the present world: 'Religious men have supposed that their only business was with the world to come; political men have declared that the present world is governed on entirely different principles from that.'[20] The aim of these writings was not to 'exact uniformity on any points' but to bring the teachings of Christ to bear on the politics of the age. So Ludlow wrote about Chartism in condemnation of the language of rights, 'We have duties to fulfil, and from those duties spring the rights of others, not as property in them, but as an obligation in ourselves.'[21] Kingsley, more radically, pointed to the specific concern of the God of the Bible for the poor, 'You say that the poor man has his rights, as well as the rich – so says the Bible; it says more – it says that God inspires the poor with the desire of liberty; that he helps them to their rights.'[22]

There was almost instant critical reaction, both from the Chartists to whom nearly all the articles had been addressed and from the more conservative reaches of the Church. Kingsley, who had hoped to secure a part-time teaching post at King's College, had its offer withdrawn. Maurice was also criticised by the college authorities and even had to defend Kingsley and Ludlow to Hare. He asked them to tone down their contributions, and, after some dispute, they agreed with the man they had started to call 'Master'.

By May the group had begun to meet weekly at Maurice's house to discuss the publication and put forward other ideas. Kingsley's college friend Charles Mansfield, who was then heavily involved in chemical experiments on how to extract benzol from aniline tar, came along. His almost equal obsessions, with mesmerism and with botany, he shared with Kingsley. Unlike him, Mansfield's theology was based more on a rationalist concept of a Divine Idea than on a clear Christian faith. When his father heard of his involvement in *Politics for the People* he immediately cut his allowance, and Mansfield adopted the vegetarian diet and simple lifestyle for which he became renowned. Mansfield also introduced others to the group: Dr Charles Walsh, a sanitation expert, and his own cousin, the architect Archibald Campbell Mansfield. Ludlow brought along a colleague from Ker's chambers, Frederick James Furnivall, who with Ludlow was to provide some of the most overtly political backbone to the growing movement.

By July *Politics* was selling at about 2,000 copies an edition, and special supplements had been produced, even including a print of Kingsley, but it was losing money, and the decision was made to stop publication. That same month Kingsley's first major novel *Yeast: A Problem*, started to appear in *Fraser's Magazine* under the pseudonym 'Parson Lot'. Critics instantly laid into it and Parker began to worry about the circulation of his more popular *Fraser's Magazine*. So Kingsley was asked to bring the novel to a swift conclusion, which explains the rather hasty final section of the novel. As George Eliot, in reviewing *Westward Ho!* in the *Westminster Review* put it many years later, 'Kingsley sees feels and paints vividly, but he theorises illogically and moralises absurdly.' None the less *Yeast* was Kingsley's first attempt to 'popularise' the ideas of Maurice and Ludlow, with its account of agricultural poverty and feudal indifference. All the Christian Socialist themes of sanitation, injustice, educational opportunities and Christian faith appear prominently, yet Ludlow asked him never to write another novel, and Mansfield called it no more than 'decorated lies'.

*

During that summer another popular Christian Socialist joined the group, although when Maurice announced he would be joining them, there was instant laughter. For Thomas Hughes had the reputation merely of a cricketer and boxer, not of a man in earnest. Yet Hughes was to become perhaps the most consistent of all the early Christian Socialists and undoubtedly one of its most likeable exponents.

Hughes at this stage was another young lawyer, born in the Vale of the White Horse of a middle-class Tory family. He had been sent to Rugby School, where he developed a profound respect for Arnold. At Oriel College, Oxford, he became a cricket blue, and met and fell in love with Frances Ford, whom he married in 1847. After college he started in the legal profession at Lincoln's Inn, where he was severely admonished by the beadle of the Inn for allowing some of the street urchins from the nearby slum to play on the Inn's green.

Hughes had spent 10 April as a special constable on duty at Trafalgar Square, where he was incensed by a series of Chartists' speeches. Somehow or other he managed to get into a fight and ended up being arrested himself for disturbing the peace.

Hughes joined the group at a vital point in its history. Maurice had been approached by the rector of St George's, Bloomsbury, who was particularly perturbed by a police black-spot in his parish at Little Ormond Yard. The group decided to set up a night school, primarily for men but open to all, and to staff the lessons in pairs. The school was a success in terms of the number of working men and women who came for lessons in everything from reading and writing to theology. It was also successful in that it bound the group in a common task, which fitted exactly with what Ludlow already hoped. In his autobiography he confessed his plan: 'My idea was to form what, in Nelson's life, he sought to make his captains before Trafalgar, a "band of brothers".'[23]

In December the format of the group's meetings was changed after a proposal from Ludlow. Starting on 7 December a new pattern was adopted, more akin to a Bible-study group than to a explicitly political meeting. Maurice presided, Ludlow generally played Devil's advocate, and the most wide-ranging discussions then ensued among the dozen or so who attended every Monday. Original suggestions for Bible texts had been the Gospels and the book of Revelation, but by the time of the first meeting it had been decided to start at the very beginning with Genesis.

Meanwhile the group had come to realise that though their aim had been to address the Chartists, and nearly all their publications had been written with them in mind, they still knew few of the activists themselves. So in April 1849, when Walter Cooper suggested that an open meeting be held with the Chartists at the Cranbourne Coffee House in London, Ludlow and Maurice quickly accepted the offer. On the day of the first meeting, on 23 April, Maurice wrote to Georgina Hare of his concern about the meeting to be held that evening:

A worthy bookseller, one of my Lincoln's Inn congregation, would have allowed the use of his rooms if we agreed to hold no religious discussions. These terms I could not consent to. I think it is very desirable that the poor men should feel the connection of politics with Christianity and that they should be allowed to state all their infidel difficulties frankly.[24]

Georgina was the sister of his friend the archdeacon, and he had recently formed a deep attachment to her, so it is not surprising that he was writing to her again the following day detailing how the 'meeting with my working-class friends went off very well'. Ever the clergyman, he goes on to explain perhaps his deepest motivation: 'Prayer is surely not asking God to love people and do them good because we love them better than he does; but offering ourselves as sacrifices to Him that He may fill us with His love and send us on His errands.'[25] The meeting was such a success that it became a regular fixture, though not all the meetings passed so smoothly. At one meeting Kingsley, who was up from Eversley for the day and had stayed over, was disturbed to see the meeting start badly, with evident suspicion on the part of the Chartists. He rose to speak, and in his incomparable way half-stammered and half-shouted that he was a Church of England parson and a Chartist. The announcement startled the meeting, which was suddenly prepared to listen to a clergyman despite the fact that for many the Church of England represented the worst elements of the establishment and they were more used to meeting Members of Parliament than clergy. Of a meeting in July Kingsley wrote to his wife: 'Last night will never be forgotten by many men. Maurice was – I cannot describe him – Chartists told me they were affected to tears . . . the man was inspired, gigantic, he stunned us.'[26]

So began the group's first real connections with the political movements of the day.

It is important to take Kingsley's announcement that he was a Chartist with a degree of caution, for he, along with all the others in the group, had profound reservations not only about the 'physical-force' movement within the Chartists but also about the Charter itself. Indeed, Kingsley's Chartism could only really be interpreted in the words of Alton Locke:

> If by a Chartist you mean one who fancies that a change in mere political circumstances will bring about a millennium, I am no longer one. But if to be a Chartist is to love my brothers with every faculty of my soul – to wish to love and die struggling for their rights, endeavouring to make of them not electors merely, but fit to be electors, senators, kings and priests to God and His Christ – if that be the Chartism of the future, then I am sevenfold a Chartist.[27]

Yet that summer Kingsley had met Thomas Cooper, the author of a Chartist poem in ten books, *The Purgatory of Suicides*, and had expressed to him his desire to get closer to working men:

> I am a radical reformer. I am not one of those who laugh at your petition of April 10th; I have no patience with those who do . . . But my quarrel with the Charter is that it does

46

not go far enough in Reform. I want to see you free, but I don't see how what you ask will give you what you want. I think you have fallen into just the same mistake as the rich of whom you complain – the very mistake which has been our curse and our nightmare – I mean the mistake of fancying that legislative reform is social reform, or that men's hearts can be changed by Acts of Parliament. If anyone will tell me of a country where a charter made rogues honest, or the idle industrious, I shall alter my opinion of the Charter, but not till then.[28]

The meetings with the Chartists, and the personal friendships that Ludlow in particular started to develop with individual Chartist leaders, came to have increasing significance in 1849. The Scottish tailor Walter Cooper introduced two watchcase finishers, Joseph Millbank and Thomas Shorter, to the group. A fustian cutter by the name of Lloyd Jones, who had opened a Co-operative store in Salford in 1831 joined the group, and both Feargus O'Connor and Bronterre O'Brien attended meetings.

Equally significant in 1849 were the damning articles on the poor of London published by Henry Mayhew in the *Morning Chronicle* and entitled 'London Labour and the London Poor'. They gave a shocking insight into the living conditions of the poor, the inability of working men and women to get fair terms or decent working conditions for themselves and, above all, the destitution and misery of many areas of the capital. In particular Mayhew wrote graphically of the area of Bermondsey known as Jacob's Island, where a cholera epidemic raged throughout the summer months, describing the water in the sewer of Mill Lane as 'solid as black marble, and yet we were assured that this was the only water the wretched inhabitants had to drink'. This was the area where Bill Sykes in Dickens's *Oliver Twist* (1838) had run to hide, and over the decade it had changed little. It was not the first such epidemic in Jacob's Island, and Kingsley was immediately fired up to organise a sanitation campaign in the area, travelling up to

London to visit the area with Mansfield and with Walsh, who had been appointed Superintendent Inspector to Southwark and Bermondsey. Together they purchased a clean water cart, from which they delivered water for several weeks until the cart was stolen.

At the same time Kingsley both published a polemical pamphlet entitled *Cheap Clothes and Nasty* in response to Mayhew, in which he laid bare some of the injustices of the 'sweating' system whereby West End tailors were having work done for them on piecemeal rates from people's homes instead of in their own tailors' premises, and started his next novel, *Alton Locke, Tailor and Poet*, which took sweated labour as its theme and again exposed the harsh lives and sheer inhumanity of much of London's working class. The novel was not finished and published until 1850, and some of its moralising elements strike us now as less than satisfactory. Much too of the immediacy of its message is lost, with Locke's discussions of political and religious matters too rooted in the dilemmas of the mid-nineteenth century to retain their urgency today. Yet *Alton Locke* reads as a book written with a keen sense of anger and of passion. The descriptions of Jacob's Island and the tailors' working conditions are still shocking, and while the final chapters occasionally lapse into cloying sentimentality, Kingsley manages to portray Locke himself with a rare degree of sensitivity. When compared with Disraeli's *Sybil*, which had come out in 1845, or Mrs Gaskell's *Mary Barton* of the year before, Carlyle's estimation is probably accurate: 'While welcoming a new explosion of red-hot shot against the Devil's Dung-heap I must admit your book is definable as crude. The impression is of a fervid creation left half chaotic.'[29] Yet the vitriolic vibrancy of *Alton Locke* is perhaps unmatched in the literature of the period.

Mayhew's articles did not inspire only Kingsley, however. Ludlow was also determined to do something about the miserable condition of the London poor and still visited the slums near Lincoln's Inn with his friend John Self. His Parisian visits had inspired him with the possibility of not just talking about but actually doing something that would make a difference to the lives of the poor, and he wrote an extensive article for *Fraser's Magazine* in response to Mayhew, arguing for a complete transformation of the Church, which he saw as the 'skeleton of a great army':

> The care of the sick, the reformation of the prisoner, the government of the adult pauper, the training of the pauper child, are all work which I am fully convinced can never be adequately performed either by mere mercenary skill or by solitary self-devotion, but require both a special religious vocation in the individual and the support and comfort of an organised fellowship. We must have Orders of nurses, Orders of prison attendants, Orders of workhouse matrons, workhouse teachers, parish surgeons, bodies of men and women that show forth in its purity the essential communism of the Church and leaven the whole of society with a spirit of self-devoted industry.[30]

Ludlow's involvement with the Jacob's Island project also convinced him of the need for a National Health League not only to pursue throughout the country major sanitation projects but also to argue the cause of clean water, clean air and a healthy environment. Ludlow drew up proposals, backed by Kingsley, in early November, and it seemed likely that this would prove to be the new task to which the whole group could dedicate itself. Maurice, however, was opposed, and though he described himself as only having thrown 'tepid water' over the plan, in effect he ruled it out altogether. For neither Kingsley nor Ludlow would go against the will of the 'Master'. Maurice's dread of 'societies, clubs, leagues' won the day over his desire to act, and while Ludlow was upset, he managed to contain his feelings, for other events in 1849 had changed his perceptions of the task ahead. Similarly a row had broken out over the suggestion that emigration was a possible answer to the 'problem of the poor', an idea that both Kingsley and Maurice supported and which Mansfield, quite rightly, condemned as offensive because he argued that the problem was not the poor, it was poverty. Ludlow, however, kept his counsel, for he had other plans.

For in 1849 Ludlow visited Paris again having recently met an older French radical, Jules St André Lechevalier. A new political refugee from Paris, elected in 1848 to the new National Assembly, he had helped set up Proudhon's People's Bank, and when Cavaignac decided to put paid to all socialist activities in June 1849 he was ordered to leave the country. When Lechevalier arrived in London he immediately made for Ludlow's house with a letter of introduction from Ludlow's brother-in-law, whom he had known in his native Martinique. Holyoake later described him as 'quite globular and when he moved he vibrated like a locomotive jelly';[31] but although he was the same age as Maurice, he already had a clear understanding of what socialism might involve, having worked with St Simon and Fourier.

Ludlow's Paris visit was, then, a direct attempt to understand and evaluate these socialist experiments. He wrote, 'It was the golden age of the *associations ouvrières*. Never before or since have I seen anything to equal the zeal, the self-devotion, the truly brotherly spirit which pervaded those workshops.'[32] Ludlow was converted, believing the French co-operative associations to be a new kind of society, heralding an economic order based on the fraternal feelings of those bound to one another by Christ. He was impressed that Proudhon's policy of 'mutualism' was being followed by the associations, with systems of direct exchange and credit being set up between them so as to avoid the middlemen and the banks.

So Ludlow returned to London determined to get the group to take on the task of promoting producer co-operative associations. When the National Health League plans were rejected by Maurice, he resolved with new vigour to pursue his idea of English working associations and arranged a dinner meeting in December to discuss the setting up of some co-operative workshops. As he put it, 'We could no longer remain content either with mere talk on the one hand, or with evening schooling and some individual visiting of the poor on the other.'[33] Maurice was not to be invited because of his recently expressed views on the National Health League.

In the event Maurice turned up anyway and wholeheartedly backed the new project. Whether out of guilt at having previously put such a sudden brake on the rest of the group or out of a radical conversion, Maurice took up the cause of the associations with vigour. On 2 January 1850 he wrote to Kingsley, 'Competition is put forth as the law of the universe. That is a lie. The time is come for us to declare that it is a lie by word and deed. I see no way but associating for work instead of strikes.' The workers' associations were to be the 'deed' that showed that competition was a lie, but Maurice was not interested in abolishing in every instant the relation of employer and employed. He felt the relation might be able to be made to work, but the present moral state showed 'that the payment of wages is nothing but a deception'. A 'hateful, devilish theory' had changed the real relation to an unjust one, and it 'must be fought with to the death'.[34]

Furthermore, the group had to take the political bull by the horns, and three days later Maurice argued to Ludlow that a series of tracts should be started with an explicitly Christian content: 'I see it clearly. We must not beat about the bush. What right have we to address the English people? We must have something special to tell them, or we ought not to speak. "Tracts on Christian Socialism" is, it seems to me, the only title which will define our object.'[35]

So within the space of a month the group iniated one of its most enduring projects in the new working associations and coined and adopted a new name, Christian Socialists. At the same time a split, which is rarely commented on, developed between the original group and the newcomers who helped to form the associations. In this latter group were Vansittart Neale and Charles Sully, neither of whom had any religious commitment, and it was primarily from this religious split that the final breach derived.

The first co-operative workshop, however, was to be a tailor's, and it opened in Castle Street in London under Walter Cooper's direction in February and soon had orders from a wide selection of the group's friends, including Samuel Wilberforce, the Bishop of Oxford, for a new set of liveries. Meanwhile the group held lengthy discussions on the need for a central board of managers for the new movement, and decided to form the Society for Promoting Working Men's Associations, which would have a 'Council of Promoters' embracing most of the group around Maurice. Charles Sully, another exile from Paris who had helped Ludlow draw up the Society's constitution, was appointed its Secretary, although the revelation in the *Red Republican* that Sully was a bigamist meant that he had to leave the country to settle in the United States, and Thomas Shorter was brought in to replace him.

Of course, co-operatives were not new in Britain. Robert Owen and others had had considerable success earlier in the century with a variety of co-operartive ventures. What was new, at least in Ludlow's view, was the determination to promote associations from a Christian base and thereby to transform the conditions of the working class: 'The principle of association appears to me the only effectual remedy against this fearful beating down of wages, against this fearful realising of capitalists' imaginary profits out of the starvation and degradation of the workman.'[36] The associations were each controlled by a Council of Administration and had a constitution that dealt in great detail with the overall management of the association and the divisions of profit. No Sunday work was allowed, and no working day was to exceed ten hours.

Almost immediately Maurice also invited Edward Vansittart Neale, a wealthy and successful lawyer who had expressed an interest in the associations, to join the inner group of twelve who formed the Council. Neale, who lived almost as long as Ludlow, was the nephew of the slavery-abolitionist William Wilberforce and had studied at Oriel College, Oxford, where he was tutored by John Henry Newman. He had read Maurice's *The Kingdom of Christ* but had little religious sensitivity. What he did have, though, was a considerable flair for organisation and for business.

Indeed, when he later set up a co-operative store in London and was sent some cornflour by a friend from India, he was the first to promote its use in England. Neale's wealth was to prove, throughout his long connection with the co-operative movement, extremely useful to the Promoters, despite the fact that several somewhat resented his generosity at first.

Meanwhile progress was swift in the establishment of other working associations. By the time of the first annual conference of the Society in the summer of 1852 there were twelve associations up and running, covering tailors, builders, shoemakers, pianomakers, printers and bakers. There were difficulties, though. Walter Cooper turned out to be a weak manager and absconded with some of the Castle Street funds. Other managers failed to keep their associations afloat, and there were constant requests for financial assistance from Neale. The commitment of the Promoters remained strong, however. Thomas Hughes wrote, 'I certainly thought (and for that matter have not altered my opinion to this day) that here we had found the solution to the great labour question: but I was also convinced that we had nothing to do but just announce it and found an association or two, in order to convert all England, and usher in the millennium at once, so plain did the whole thing seem to me.'[37] Yet not all the Promoters saw the associations in the same light. For Ludlow and Furnivall, as for Hughes, they were to be the prime engine of social change, altering the economic system for ever. For Maurice and Kingsley, however, they were simply part of the wider task of social transformation and represented a form of economic protest. Indeed, Maurice's disposition towards association was as much a conscious theological statement of his belief that all people were bound together in Christ and that isolation and individualism were a denial of that fact: 'Are we to live in an age in which every mechanical facility for communication between man and man is multiplied ten-thousandfold, only that the inward isolation, the separation of those who meet continually, may be increased in a far greater measure?'[38] he preached.

Other splits soon developed as well, with Ludlow and Neale

holding to very different ideas of what an association was. So in November 1850 Neale held an open meeting, with Henry Mayhew as speaker, to open a new co-operative store, thereby challenging the assumption that all associations had to be producer co-operatives rather than consumer ones. Hughes, Lechevalier and Lloyd Jones supported Neale, but Ludlow was furious, seeing it as a betrayal of the fundamental principles of the Society. After a year of quarrelling with Neale he presented, by proxy via Maurice, an ultimatum at the Promoters' Council meeting, that either they went or he did. Maurice refused to present the ultimatum, and Ludlow's resignation was averted only by some clever mediation.

In the meantime Maurice's *Tracts on Christian Socialism* had been superseded by the launch in November 1850 of Ludlow's magazine the *Christian Socialist*, the first of several periodicals to bear that title over the following 150 years. Acting both as a newsletter for the associations and as the official mouthpiece of the Christian Socialist movement, the *Christian Socialist* ran for a year before changing its title and content to become the *Journal of Association*, absorbing a large proportion of Ludlow's time and energy. It covered every topic imaginable within the field of national and ecclesiastical politics and preached the message of association through articles by all the major Promoters. Neale argued for his new London store, which was being managed by Lloyd Jones, and Kingsley wrote some of the lighter pieces.

At the same time there was a great demand for Christian Socialist speakers, and Kingsley and Lloyd Jones in particular had regular speaking engagements. At one such, when Kingsley had been asked to preach to the congregation of St John's, Charlotte Street, on 22 June 1851 on the subject of the Church's message to working men, he condemned all systems of society which favour the accumulation of capital in a few hands. The vicar, G. S. Drew, was so disturbed that he stood up at the end of the service to dissociate himself from the sermon. Dr Blomfield, the Bishop of London, banned Kingsley the following day from preaching in his diocese, although when Kingsley wrote to him and asked him to suspend his decision until he had read the text of his sermon, the ban was lifted.

Through 1851 the tensions among the Promoters grew. Ludlow was critical of Maurice, not least because he disapproved of Maurice's recent marriage to Georgina Hare. Maurice, in turn, was critical of some of the perceived 'excesses' of the *Christian Socialist*. Ludlow refused to publish a piece of Kingsley's on the Bible story of the Canaanites for its incipient racism. Mansfield, also suffering under Ludlow's criticism for taking up with a young working girl after the failure of his marriage, decided to leave for Paraguay. The row between the producer and consumer associations camps simmered and finally erupted in December.

In 1852, however, the most significant political row broke over a pamphlet written by a new recruit to the movement, Lord Goderich. Goderich, who was directly descended from Oliver Cromwell, had been born at No. 10 Downing Street when his father had briefly held the post of Prime Minister at Canning's death. He had read *Politics for the People* and had some broad understanding of Christian Socialism, though, living out of London, he had never become involved with the movement.

Meanwhile Goderich had been stimulated by the engineers' lock-out in 1851, and decided to seek a parliamentary seat. He drafted a pamphlet called *The Duty of the Age*, which he showed to Hughes and Kingsley, both of whom liked it. They agreed to publish it as a Christian Socialist tract and sent it off to the printers. When Maurice first saw it he suggested minor alterations, but when it had been printed without his say-so he was furious and demanded that it be suppressed. In particular he argued against its support for democracy. Goderich was somewhat taken aback, as were the others, but Ludlow was more specifically indignant at the non-egalitarian trend of Maurice's thinking. Hughes argued that Maurice's peremptory decision showed his great 'pluck' and kept the unopened pile of printed pamphlets in his study for many years, only surreptitiously allowing them into circulation. Later in the same year Goderich was elected MP for

Hull, describing himself as a Democrat and a Christian Socialist. A row over the disappearance of his election agent, one 'Citizen Bezer', meant that he had to resign his seat, but he was re-elected in another by-election a couple of months later, effectively becoming the Christian Socialists' first MP.

Of course, Maurice had never been a democrat. In *The Kingdom of Christ* he had supported the monarchy and the divine right of the Church of England. He held views similar to Coleridge's on 'the sovereignty of the people, in any shape or form', repudiating it 'as at once the silliest and most blasphemous of all contradictions'. He had a puritanical dislike of being liked by the majority and suspected that any fully democratic system would lead to either 'a most accursed sacerdotal rule or a military despotism'. He had not supported universal suffrage in 1848, and believed that the working classes needed to be fit to become electors before the franchise could be extended.

Here, then, was the first major ideological split between Ludlow and Maurice, for Ludlow supported universal suffrage. He saw that democracy 'must mean not the letting loose all the accumulated selfishness of the many, but the giant self-control of a nation'.[39] In correspondence with Maurice he stated that he had come round 'to the value of the principle of democracy for the safe practice of the art of partnership which we call Socialism'.[40] and he clearly saw public opinion as a potentially positive force in the political relationship between Parliament and people. Furthermore, there had been a split over the original cause of Goderich's pamphlet, the engineers' strike, for all the Promoters had supported the strikers except Maurice. Indeed, Ludlow had been much heartened by the Amalgamated Society of Engineers' new interest in co-operatives, which, prior to the strike had approved £10,000 for the setting up of associations under a board of trustees including Ludlow, Hughes and Neale. As a result of the strike the plans were dropped, but Neale did set up two co-operative workshops in Mile End and Southwark. Maurice was asked to preside at a special meeting with the engineers, but refused on the grounds that he did not think he had a case to put in the context of the strike. Neale took his place, effectively tying, for the first time, the trade-union movement and the Christian Socialist movement together. Simultaneously Neale opened up another rift within the movement by proceeding to launch his secular version of the Society for Promoting Working Men's Associations, entitled the Co-operative League. Ludlow later reviewed the League: 'although Neale did not see it, the Co-operative League was simply the setting up of non-Christian against Christian socialism. It never did anything substantial and vanished as soon as we were out of the way.'[41]

Although there were frosty exchanges throughout this period between the Promoters, the group still worked closely together. Most important, Ludlow had initiated with Hughes and Neale a campaign to reform the law regarding co-operative associations. In his *A Century of Co-operation* G. D. H. Cole pointed out that the co-operative associations had never suffered so severely under the law as the trade unions. None the less, co-operatives did not benefit under the law from many of the usual benefits of trade. Thus they could not enforce contracts or secure themselves against fraudulent or negligent officials. The closest to legal protection they received was under the Friendly Societies Act of 1793, which had been amended in 1834 and 1846 to allow for trading societies for the first time, but producer co-operatives were particularly vulnerable. In 1850 Hughes approached an MP by the name of Robert Aglionby Slaney, whose Select Committee of the House of Commons was to report on 'Investments for the Savings of the Middle and Working Classes'. The Committee heard evidence from most of the Promoters and came out in support of co-operatives. In June 1852 the recommendations of the Committee were taken up in the Industrial and Provident Societies Act, which gave real advantages to the associations. They were still denied the privilege of limited liability, but they were freed from much of the legislation regarding friendly societies.

In fact, this achievement, which required all the legal knowledge of Ludlow, Hughes and Neale, as well as their political nous and understanding of parliamentary procedures, was probably the

Promoters' most significant accomplishment, effectively enabling the co-operative movement for years to come.

It also meant that the Society had to change its constitution, and renewed disputes followed the first draft of the new constitution, which was finally amended by Maurice. A large part of the dispute hinged on a paper from Ludlow that seemed to deny any democratic principle within the Society, in contradiction of Ludlow's own views on Goderich's pamphlet. Mansfield wrote to Ludlow, 'If we are to have a monarchical executive, the monarch must not be interfered with,' effectively supporting Maurice's line on the new constitution. He continued, 'The whole thing is a china shop and you the bull at the present, it seems,' echoing sentiments of Hughes from the same period: 'You have the most aggravating way of finding fault of any man I know, which sets all the British lion within me up in arms.'[42] In July a first co-operative conference was held in the Promoters' Hall in Castle Street, which was attended by representatives from different associations around the country, including the Promoters, and with Maurice presiding. By the end of the year, however, he was keen to resign and attempted to hand over the presidency. The Promoters persuaded him to remain, partly because he alone could keep the secular and religious wings together and could avoid the split between the producer and consumer associationists, symbolised by the row between Neale and Ludlow. After all, it was Maurice who had persuaded Ludlow to accept the new constitution without resignation. So Maurice was still in the chair at the 1853 conference in Manchester. By then, however, the Society was disbanded, and its work had been taken over by two new organisations, the Association for Promoting Industrial and Provident Societies and the Co-operative Union, neither of which had avowedly Christian aims or objects, although many of the Promoters were involved in both. The conference was well attended, but Maurice's mind was already on other things.

By 1853 Maurice was facing a serious attempt to remove him from his professorship of Divinity at King's College because of his views on eternal life as expressed in the *Theological Essays* he had just published. The Principal of the College, Dr Richard Jelf, who had attacked Pusey's sermon on 'National Apostasy' in 1847, was worried that Maurice's views, which had attracted a great deal of criticism, might bring the College's reputation into jeopardy. Maurice felt that Jelf's belief that 'eternal life' meant a never-ending life in the hereafter, as opposed to communion with God, logically led people to believe that eternal life was a reward offered to those who had earned it by virtue of their 'upright' life. This was the doctrine that had been used to keep the poor in order, and Maurice was fundamentally opposed to it and refused to compromise. After lengthy internal wrangles Maurice was dismissed and almost immediately started the second most significant element of the early Christian Socialist crusade.

For in 1852 Mansfield had organised a successful series of lectures for working men at the Promoters' Hall. These were repeated in early 1853, and many of those who had attended the lectures came to a special presentation to Maurice on 27 December, following his dismissal. At the end of the meeting someone casually remarked that he hoped Maurice 'might not find it a fall to cease to be Professor at King's College and to become the Principal of a Working Men's College'.[43] By 10 January he had framed enough ideas to write to Kingsley regarding a series of 'Cambridge Tracts' he had planned, that 'my college . . . might come as a practical carrying out of the idea of the tracts'. The following day, at one of the regular Promoters' meetings, Neale read out a letter from the Secretary of the People's College at Sheffield, outlining its history. Maurice then drew up more concrete plans for a people's college that was to be founded in the premises of one of the failed associations at 31 Red Lion Square. In June and July a series of fund-raising lectures was given, and the college was ready for business in time for October, with a wide range of subjects and an interesting set of lecturers. The college was to be aimed specifically at the manual workers, and Maurice was to be the Principal. On 30 October the inaugural address was given in St Martin's Hall by an excited Maurice, while Furnivall gave out copies of the sixth chapter of John Ruskin's *Stones of Venice*, 'On the Nature of Gothic'. The meeting was packed, and by the end of a fortnight 130 people had been registered.

So began the Working Men's College, which later moved to Crowndale Road, further north in Camden, and which survives today as a centre for adult education. The early courses, which were attended by all sorts of men from a background very different from that of the Promoters themselves, were for the main part led by the Maurician team.

One of the first to join the venture, however, was John Ruskin. His wife Effie had recently left him and started nullity proceedings before marrying the young painter John Millais, and he was still smarting when Furnivall dragged him round to meet Maurice. Ruskin was by no means a conventional Christian Socialist. Indeed, some of his later thought was so apocalyptic in style that his contribution to the tradition of Christian Socialism is often ignored. Yet he proved in the 1870s and 1880s to be a significant link between the Promoters and their successors in the Guild of St Matthew and the Christian Social Union.

In 1854, however, he was renowned primarily for his artistic views, and it was as an art teacher that he joined the Working Men's College. He brought in the younger Dante Gabriel Rossetti, and the Art Department flourished. Mansfield had met a distant cousin of his in the street earlier in the year, the young artist C. Lowes Dickinson, and he was also forced to meet the famous Maurice. Within weeks he was teaching in the Art Department as well, to be joined a couple of years later by Ford Maddox Brown, whose famous painting *Work*, now in the Manchester City Art Galleries, includes a smiling late portrait of Maurice talking to Carlyle.

Other aspects of the life of the college now seem almost endearing. Regular walks at the weekend, sing-songs led by Hughes, debates about the opening of museums on Sundays, attempts to insist on prayers at the beginning of every class – all these smack of paternalism, yet the college was innovative in its accessibility to ordinary working people and in the breadth of its education.

The year 1854, however, was the one in which the Promoters really started to go their separate ways. Neale was still very much involved in the associations, and chaired the annual conference in Leeds at which he established the Co-operative and Industrial Union; but the row with Ludlow continued to simmer. Ludlow had meanwhile agreed to have a house built in Wimbledon, to be shared with Thomas Hughes and his wife. Called 'The Firs', with a communal library in which they would hold weekly prayers, it rapidly became a regular weekend retreat for students from the college. Kingsley, however, was largely out of action, working for a while in Devon, devoting time to natural history and writing a substantial piece on marine biology called *Glaucus*.

In the autumn the most significant political topic for debate was the Crimean War. Immediately a whole host of the Promoters stood up to support the cause, including Maurice, Hughes, Ludlow and Kingsley. Indeed, Kingsley was so keen that at Hughes's prompting he wrote a tract entitled *Brave Words to Brave Soldiers and Sailors*, which was distributed among the troops and immediately gained the rector of Eversley a new set of admirers.

In November, however, with Maurice's mind already firmly set on the establishment of the college, he proposed to the Promoters that the executive committee of the annual conference, on which several of the Christian Socialists sat, should now take over the duties of the successor to the Council of Promoters, the Society for Promoting Industrial and Provident Societies, and that the Society should be wound up. On 25 November the Society met for the last time and agreed to suspend its business. Ludlow was perplexed and angered, for gradually the closest Mauricians had devoted less and less energy to the associations, and though Hughes, Ludlow and Neale all continued working for associations in some form or other through to their deaths, the Council of Promoters was effectively dead by the Co-operative Conference of 1855. Ludlow was crushed and took Maurice's move towards education and away from associationalism as a personal slight, although in characteristic manner he internalised the whole debate. 'Mr Maurice never understood the crushing nature of the blow he had given me ... The Maurice I had devoted myself to was a Maurice of my own imagination, not the real Maurice. He was not to blame, I was.'[44] In his autobiography he tells of the difficult decision not to take the mantle of the Promoters on his own shoulders: 'I have never sought to draw men round me. More than once when I have perceived that someone was disposed to think too much of my judgment, to rely too entirely upon me, I have repelled him, thrown him forcibly back on himself, while pointing him to the source of all wisdom.'[45] It is hard to reconcile this image of ultimate sacrifice with the man whom his friends called 'Old Gruff', or, indeed with the apostolically zealous Associationist, but Ludlow swallowed all his anger and distress and let the Promoters die. Earlier in the year Mansfield had written to him: 'I dare not say you are too austere, perhaps it is your mission to be so, but it seems to me in excess, to my weak senses. Now I may only pray God may guide you, that if unhappiness has frozen the outside of you too much at any point, he may duly thaw it.'[46]

Indeed, the beginning of 1855 was a difficult time for the whole group. First Hare died in early January. Then Mansfield died from a horrendous chemical accident, which had left him horribly burned. Ludlow wrote of his profound affection for him in a letter to Kingsley: 'He came to me at a time when I never expected to have another intimate friend, and surpassed all conceivableness of intimacy. He was to me almost what a wife should be, a better and more delicate conscience.'[47] The others were equally distressed and the memorial service on 25 March was a sad event that they decided to commemorate every year. The following year they collected the letters they had received from him from Paraguay and published them with a foreword by Kingsley.

Historians have customarily argued that the end of the 'Band of Brothers' dates from Mansfield's death, that suddenly the group had lost one of its essential bindings. And it is true that apart from the Prophet he was the only person who had kept Ludlow,

Neale, Goderich and Kingsley talking. The regular meetings at Queen Square had indeed ceased, and the Council of Promoters was no more.

Yet to say that the Christian Socialist Movement died with Mansfield would be wrong. Most of the group were still engaged in joint projects, either through the life of the college or through continuing work for the co-operatives. Kingsley was out of London and writing a new novel, *Westward Ho!*, but he still went on regular holidays with Hughes and maintained an unceasing correspondence with Maurice. Furnivall had become the life and soul of the college, engaged in all the administrative work and seeing a real social challenge in creating a working educational community. Hughes was similarly devoted to the boxing class at the college and living at 'The Firs', next-door to Ludlow, who also taught at the college. Neale was still actively occupied in the work of the co-operatives and sat on several committees with Hughes. The work of the movement, and the basis upon which it had been founded, remained. All that had disappeared was the formal structure of the movement.

Indeed, although histories of the Mauricians have tended to focus on these first years from 1848 to 1853, their life's work was far from done. The Indian Mutiny in 1857 gave Ludlow, in particular, a new lease of life. Born in India and having many family connections with the colonial administration, he was ideally placed to give a series of lectures on India at the college, and these were published by Daniel MacMillan under the title *British India, Its Races and Its History*. Though the title would now seem aggressively imperial to us, Ludlow's tenet was essentially anti-colonial. He believed that Britain's role had been to bring Christianity to India and that the Indian Christians, though still in a minority, would eventually come to govern. He argued too that as Christianity was an essentially tolerant faith, there would be no violence, but self-rule should be granted soon and, indeed, would be the will of the working people of Britain. Ludlow also visited Kingsley at this time and was profoundly shocked by the rector's complete ignorance of India. Ironically enough, a few years later Goderich succeeded to the title of Lord Ripon and became Viceroy of India.

Meanwhile the literary endeavours of the group had grown dramatically. Kingsley had great successes with both *The Heroes* and *Two Years Ago*, though both echoed more a socially conservative nostalgia than an overt Christian Socilaist creed. His brother, the somewhat wayward Henry, returned from Australia and published one of the first great novels about that country, *The Recollections of Geoffry Hamlyn*, which had the same vivid pictorial quality to its writing as Kingsley's and outdid him in sharpness of characterisation. Hughes had also been writing and in 1856 produced, as a present for his son, *Tom Brown's Schooldays*. Originally appearing under the name of 'An Old Boy', it sold out instantly, and soon Hughes affixed his name to it. Dealing in a semi-biographical way with Rugby School, Hughes undoubtedly saw it as part of the Christian Socialist canon. The community spirit of the school, the hatred of the bullying Flashman and the intense respect for the Thomas Arnold figure all relate directly to Hughes's understanding of the concept of the good society, to which co-operation was the key.

The end of the 1850s was marked, however, primarily for the Maurice group, by a clear divergence between those who were to remain in the radical movement and those whose careers were to take them into the arms of the establishment. For on Palm Sunday 1859 Kingsley was asked to preach at Buckingham Palace for Queen Victoria and was subsequently made a Chaplain in Ordinary to the Queen. He had already gained a degree of respectability with his views on the Crimean War and a large number of Sandhurst officers attending worship at Eversley, but this was his first step on a path of preferment. Within a year Gladstone had recommended him to the post of Regius Professor of Modern History at Cambridge, and a year later he was appointed history tutor to the Prince of Wales. Though he retained some of his fighting spirit, inveighing against the mill-owners during the Lancashire cotton famine and exposing the plight of young chimneysweeps in *The Water Babies* in 1862, the main emphasis of Kingsley's life now became deeply conservative. In 1864 Kingsley also made one of his greatest blunders, when reviewing Volumes 7 and 8 of Froude's *History of England* in *Macmillan's*, for he peppered his review with anti-Roman Catholic remarks, specifically mentioning the new convert John Henry Newman. 'Truth,' Kingsley wrote 'for its own sake, had never been a virtue with the Roman clergy. Father Newman informs us that it need not, and on the whole ought not to be; that cunning is the weapon which Heaven has given to the saints wherewith to withstand the brute male force of the wicked world which marries and is given in marriage.'[48] A private subscriber complained, and Kingsley immediately printed an apology, but by then Newman had crafted a heavily satirical reply. Kingsley retaliated by sneering at Newman's belief in monks, nuns, the stigmata and celibacy, and promptly left for a holiday in Spain, only to return to Newman's expert *Apologia pro vita sua*, two sections of which dealt with Kingsley's assault and were omitted from later editions. Though neither party took permanent offence, the episode reveals Kingsley's ugly sectarianism, and it is difficult to sympathise with him, even though the Roman Catholic Church's then intense theological conservatism was emphasised by Pope Pius IX's publication of the *Syllabus of Errors*.

In 1866 Kingsley finally split with Ludlow over the case of the British Governor of Jamaica, Governor Eyre, who had reportedly killed 600 black citizens in suppressing an uprising. Ludlow and Hughes helped form the Jamaica Committee in criticism of Eyre's excessive violence, while Kingsley, along with Carlyle and Ruskin, took up the cudgels in defence of Eyre. Ludlow saw Kingsley's views, which were tantamount to a vicious racism, as anathema to Christian Socialism and resolved to sever connections with him, a view compounded by Kingsley's support for the South in the American Civil War. By 1869 he was effectively speaking only to Maurice, of all the group. In that year preferment came again, in the shape of a canonry at Chester, and in 1873 he was again elevated, to a canonry at Westminster Abbey, and he moved into No. 6 Little Cloister. The following year, although his health was not good, he travelled to America, where he was rapturously received. In November he preached his last sermon at Westminster Abbey on Advent Sunday, and he died on 23 January 1875.

In the intervening years Maurice had not exactly languished in the shadows. Freed, as he clearly felt, of the burden of having to lead the group of Promoters, he devoted his time to the twin tasks of theology and education. He lectured regularly at new working men's colleges in Cambridge, Manchester, Oxford, Salford, Ancoats, Halifax, Birkenhead and Glasgow, and was appointed rector of St Peter's, Vere Street, near Oxford Street in Central London. In 1866 he too was appointed a professor at Cambridge and took the Knightsbridge Chair in Moral Theology and Moral Philosophy, thus sharing nearly three years at Cambridge with Kingsley. Contemporary records show a marked difference between their lectures. Kingsley always had a packed room and fired off his enthusiastic talks with fervour and anecdotes, though many later questioned the accuracy of his facts. Maurice, meanwhile, had fewer attendees, spoke measuredly and, as in the group of Promoters, desperately sought to avoid becoming an authority. Increasingly Maurice left politics to others, agreeing to support John Stuart Mill's campaign for women's suffrage only on the understanding that he would not be able to do any public speaking. Maurice was also aware that he needed to cut down his activity, and in 1870, although he was entitled to retain both posts, he resigned from St Peter's, dedicating himself to Cambridge and assuming a small parish in the town. In 1871 he declined to take part in the new Church Reform Union, on the grounds that 'I fear I am becoming less and less fit for associations.' The following March he became seriously ill, and on Easter Sunday 1872 Maurice died. The funeral at Highgate was well attended, and even Kingsley and Ludlow managed to speak to each other.

While Kingsley and Maurice had been retiring from the political fray, however, Hughes was becoming more engaged in it. He had been almost the first prominent person in Britain to support the North in the American Civil War, and in 1865 he stood for Parliament as a Radical Liberal in Lambeth. Although a socialist as a matter of personal creed, he described himself as a Liberal with scant regard for parties. Indeed, there was no socialist party to which he could have belonged. He addressed a meeting in Norwich with the words, 'I stand before you as a Liberal politician,' and asserted his egalitarian principles, which most Liberals would not then have shared: 'there should be equality before the law for every institution, for every society, and for every individual citizen.'[49] Almost instantly he was perceived as the working man's representative in Parliament, a role he handed over to A. J. Mundella in the 1870s, by which time his fierce independence of spirit had isolated him politically from both the Radicalist Birmingham group and the Gladstonian Liberals. Hughes's interest in America was further strengthened in 1870, when he was invited on a lecture tour and made lasting connections with both writers like James Russell Lowell and the founders of the New York equivalent of the working men's college. He was also intimately connected with most of the work of the emerging trades unions, supporting the builders' strike in 1860 and the Sheffield strikers in 1866 and devoting a large part of his time to seeking legislative change for the unions. He served on the first Royal Commission on Trades Unions in 1866 and produced a minority report in support of the unions with Frederic Harrison, although he ended up voting for the piecemeal Conservative legislation in 1874. He was also considerably engaged in association work, supporting Neale in the Central Co-operative Agency and presiding over the Co-operative Congress in 1869.

Ludlow, in the meantime, spent most of his time on writing for a series of magazines, and in 1867 produced, with the Owenite Lloyd Jones, a masterful assessment of the political movements of his time, *Progress of the Working Class, 1832–67*. Starting with the Reform Act, the book charts legislative change relating specifically to the poor and highlights a series of 'questions for a reformed Parliament'. He argues forcefully for greater political reform on the basis of the social reform that has already been evinced, 'for we cannot reasonably suppose that political progress is inseparable from all other.'[50]

Two years later, however, Ludlow married the woman for whom

he had waited for two decades, his cousin Maria Forbes, and suddenly his lifestyle was transformed, heralding his own retreat from direct political work. In 1870, when the first Registrar of Friendly Societies, John Tidd Pratt, died, Ludlow seemed the ideal person for the job, but due to the political objections of the then Chancellor of the Exchequer, he was originally appointed only paid Secretary to a Royal Commission on Friendly Societies. The Chairman was Sir Stafford Northcote, and the report came out in 1874, prior to a general election in 1875 which made Northcote Chancellor. Ludlow was asked to draft a new Friendly Societies Bill, and was appointed Registrar, effectively becoming a civil servant. He continued as Registrar until his retirement in 1891, still deeply committed to the principles of voluntary associations and suspicious of statist interventions such as the emerging welfare benefits system in Bismark's Germany. When Hughes was setting up the Guild of Co-operators with Stewart Headlam, however, he declined to be involved, and one of his few late interventions came at the launch of the Christian Social Union, although his autobiography highlighted his own belief that he had become at one and the same time a fierce Radical and a Conservative.

In the meantime Furnivall had re-incorporated the college under the Companies Act of 1862 and helped found the Philological Society, out of which developed the Early English Texts Society. At his death in 1908 he was working on the *Oxford English Dictionary*, and had just completed the entry 'take'.

Goderich, who had become Lord Ripon and in 1884 been made Viceroy of India, adopting a pro-Indian position which had antagonised most of British and European opinion, returned from India to become First Lord of the Admiralty, and he held office in every Liberal administration until 1909, when he died.

Hughes had also spent a considerable amount of time and money on a project in Rugby, Tennessee, attempting to build an ideal community based on his belief that:

In the intoxication of this great materialist movement we English have somewhat lost our heads – have come to an alarming extent to acknowledge the heaping up of wealth to be the true end of all effort; and the hero, the man most worthy of admiration, the happy man, he who has succeeded best in business.[51]

In 1888 he completed with Neale an important *Manual for Co-operators* and wrote a sequel novel, *Tom Brown at Oxford*. He became a county court judge and eventually died in 1896.

Neale, the least avowedly 'Christian' of the group, had steadily worked away at building and developing co-operatives, working as General Secretary of the Co-operative Union and expending most of his wealth until he inherited Bisham Abbey a couple of years before his death in 1892.

It will always be difficult to evaluate the 'Band of Brothers'. For the temptation is to hold them up against later exponents of Christian Socialism and criticise either their innate personal conservatism or their distrust of systematic political change. Inevitably Maurice and his colleagues seem almost trivial in their socialism, focusing so narrowly on associations and education. Much of what several of the group believed is far from our understanding of socialism. Thus Maurice's monarchism and distrust of democracy, Kingsley's racism and sexual problems, Ludlow's refusal to vote or to accept widening the associations' work to include consumer co-operatives; all these provide problems for those who seek in them a perfectly formed Christian Socialism. Yet many of the later Christian Socialists, in every generation, have ascribed a very clear debt to the group. Thus Stewart Headlam acknowledged:

You, ladies and gentlemen, probably do not know what it is to have been delivered in the world of thought, emotion, imagination, from the belief that a large proportion of the human race are doomed to endless misery. You are freeborn – mainly through Maurice's work and courage. For myself I say that at a great price I obtained this freedom.[52]

Headlam was right, of course, to point primarily to the world of thought, for this was precisely where the Mauricians exerted their most lasting influence, forcing the Church to face up to the theological and political consequences of the Industrial Revolution. Maurice understood, above all else, the pernicious power of the pervasive belief that Christianity was exclusively about the salvation of individual souls. It was this false creed that led clergy to encourage the poor simply to accept their supposedly God-given lot and Mrs Alexander to write 'The rich man in his castle, the poor man at his gate, /God made them high and lowly and ordered their estate.' So for Maurice and Kingsley it was vital to rediscover the Christian faith and oppose the use of the Bible as a form of 'special constable's rule book'. The Sermon on the Mount and the parables of the sheep and the goats and the Good Samaritan indeed showed that Christianity was about practical, material concerns. The Atonement and the Incarnation both proved that all were already in Christ, so the aim of a Christian life must be to make that divine presence clear through the ordering of society. This did not necessarily require political change, for competition, selfishness, rivalry were the problems, not property or the employer–employee relationship. Social reformation, with concomitant personal transformation, was the key to the good society.

So the Mauricians' theology led ineluctably to a social critique that addressed the many concerns which enlightened Christians expressed about the horrors of industrial deprivation and rural decay. Sweated labour, the abuse of working children, the outrage of poor sanitation, the rights of women and the effect of harsh employers were Christian concerns as significant as gambling and alcohol. To the Church it argued that Christianity had to return to the person of Jesus to understand that the theological constructions of eternal punishment were not the essence of faith. To society it argued that 'let-alone' politics was not enough for a Christian with a lively moral conscience. The role of faith and of the Church in a society where the poor had been abandoned, and had in turn deserted the Church, lay not simply in individual piety but in the assertion that people needed to bind together, to associate for the common good rather than compete.

All these were philosophical achievements. Yet there were also concrete ones. The Industrial and Provident Societies Act of 1852, the legalising of peaceful picketing and the trades unions, the development of the Co-operative Union, the establishment of the working men's college are all directly attributable to the Christian Socialists. Indeed, if one includes the influence of Maurice on both Ruskin and Octavia Hill, the incipient environmentalist movements of the late nineteenth century and the National Trust itself have their origins in early Christian Socialism.

The best evaluation of the Maurician legacy, however, lies in Maurice's own words, written to Ludlow: 'My business, because I am a theologian and have no vocation except for theology, is not to build, but to dig.'[53] Maurice's work meant that for all who followed, the foundations were already well dug.

# 3

# *The First Socialist Organisation in England*

> The true perfection of man lies, not in what man has, but in what man is ... One's regret is that society should be constructed on such a basis that man has been forced into a groove in which he cannot freely develop what is wonderful, and fascinating, and delightful in him – in which, in fact, he misses the true pleasure and joy of living ... Individualism, then, is what through socialism we are to attain to.
>
> Oscar Wilde, 'The Soul of Man Under Socialism'

It has been traditional to see the Guild of St Matthew as the second wave of modern Christian Socialism, breaking almost unexpectedly upon a hostile shore. Yet in truth the first wave had never really receded in the late 1850s and 1860s. Hughes, Ludlow and Neale were still very much engaged in the practical elements of the co-operative movement, and Ruskin was still writing his socialist aesthetic theologies. Individual preachers and clergy were quietly preaching a radical Gospel throughout the 1860s and 1870s. James Fraser, the 'Citizen Bishop' of Manchester, was clear that there was a vital task of 'Socialising Christianity' to be done. Samuel Barnett was working in the harsh conditions of Whitechapel and initiating work that would later lead to the foundation of Toynbee Hall. In 1862 the ritualist fathers Mackonochie and Lowder were denouncing the sweatshops in the parish of St George's-in-the-East, to which the celebrated Fr Stanton was soon appointed and from which he welcomed the Paris Commune in 1871. Canon E. D. Girdlestone was fighting for the rural workers of Devon, and in 1873 Joseph Arch, a former Anglican who had left the Church of England to be a Primitive Methodist when he saw poor communicants having to wait until the wealthier parishioners had received their communion, founded the Agricultural Workers' Union. Even the profoundly conservative leader of the Oxford Movement, Dr Pusey, was preaching a radical message:

> Doubtless Dives encouraged the manufacturers of Tyre and Sidon, and the weavers of Palestine, while he bound not up the sores of Lazarus ... If he were uncared for, it was that there were not enough Dives to give employment to the poor. Miserable, transparent, flimsy hypocrisy. Were the employment of the poor our end, would they be less employed in manufacturing comforts for themselves than in weaving luxuries for us? ... A reckless, fraudulent competition, whose aim is to cheapen every luxury and vanity in order that those at ease may spend on fresh accumulated luxuries and vanities what they withhold from the poor, lowers the price we crave for by cutting down the wages of the poor.[1]

While Christian Socialism was alive and well, however, it is none the less true that by 1860 both Kingsley and Maurice were more interested in theology and Church polity than in Christian Socialism – and by the end of 1875 they had both died. In particular with Maurice's death it seemed that an era had passed.

Yet it was clear that the cause of socialism itself was not dead. In 1864 the International Working Men's Association, later known as the First International, was formed, and in 1867 Karl Marx published *Das Kapital* in German, although it was not translated into English until 1887. In 1868 the Trades Union Congress was formed, and three years later came the legal recognition of trades unions. In the same year the barricades went up again in France, and the Paris Commune waved the red flag for the first time.

The clergy of London were far from immune to the ferment of socialist ideas in the capital. Many feared that the Church, and especially the Church of England, would lose all connection with the working classes as the tide of socialism moved further up the beach. Others continued to be outraged, as Kingsley had been, by the worst excesses of Victorian industrial capitalism. Yet others were struck by the fundamental integrity of socialism or its ability to solve the problem of poverty. So it is in this context that the Guild of St Matthew has to be seen; the Guild's appearance was not independent from it. It was to be the first explicitly socialist organisation in Britain, beating both Henry Hyndman's Social Democratic Foundation and the Fabians to it with its adoption of socialist principles early in 1884, and so can claim to be a significant breaker on the shore. But it had already run for seven years before coming to socialism and was essentially part of a rising socialist tide. Its history was also deeply intermingled with the personal fortunes of one man, Stewart Duckworth Headlam.

Stewart Headlam was everything that Maurice was not. Extro-verted, radical in style as well as theology, High Church, eager to be the leader of a group of people, a 'joiner' of leagues and clubs, an aesthete with catholic tastes, a determined questioner of accepted social mores and the Church's hierarchy: in every regard he displayed a personal confidence and idiosyncrasy that made him one of the most original of all Victorian Christians. Whether in the field of the arts, of sexuality, of Church reform or of politics, he demonstrated a curious ability to tickle the funny-bone of Victorianism and jerk it into action.

Yet his background was respectable enough. He was born in Wavertree near Liverpool on 12 January of the year before the Chartists' demonstration in 1848, to a thoroughly proper family. His father, Thomas, an underwriter, took great pride in his evangelical faith and argued regularly with his brother who was a high-church curate in Liverpool. He also kept the family moving, to the Isle of Wight, to Surbiton, to Marlow and finally to Tunbridge Wells. In 1860 Headlam was sent to Eton, where he studied until 1865 under his housemaster the Revd J. L. Joynes, father of the later socialist colleague James Leigh Joynes, who travelled with Henry George.

In 1865 Headlam went up to Cambridge with no great intellectual pretensions and had as his tutor the King's College fellow, William Johnson. Johnson was a close friend of both Maurice and Kingsley, and Headlam's memories of Cambridge seem to focus almost entirely on the two Christian Socialists who were both lecturing at the time. He attended Maurice's 'at homes' and went to Kingsley's lectures, although his comments on Kingsley sound dismissive: 'At Cambridge in my time while not a dozen men attended Maurice's lectures on moral and metaphysical philosophy, all the horsey men used to crowd into Kingsley's lecture on history.'[2] What is clear is that Headlam was instantly taken with Maurice's theology. He wrote to his father that he stole an hour a week from 'the ancients' to go to Maurice's lectures and felt he had been emancipated by Maurice's radical thoughts on eternal punishment.

Headlam's father was not impressed by such straying from the strict evangelical path, and when Stewart managed to scrape through Tripos with a very poor third-class degree in 1868, he was packed off to a series of 'sound' clerics to cure him of his independent thoughts. First with Herbert James in sleepy Livermere, and then with Dr Vaughan at the Temple, he was drilled in orthodox Victorian evangelical doctrine, but it failed to take, and Headlam continued to articulate Maurician 'jargon about righteousness and peace'.

So, having been ordained deacon in 1869, Headlam found himself a new home as curate to the Revd Richard Graham Maul, the vicar of St John's, Drury Lane, another friend and supporter of Maurice. As a young curate he was immediately thrown into the parochial work of visiting parishioners' homes and workplaces. It was not a particularly poor parish, but it did include most of the theatre district of London, and from Headlam's rooms in Broad Court, off Long Acre, he soon built up a knowledge and experience of the theatre that was exceptional for a cleric of his time. Indeed, it was when Headlam recognised a couple of women who were members of the St John's congregation performing as dancers on the stage, and they begged him not to reveal their secret to anyone, that he realised the particular mission he was to develop to the theatrical profession.

Headlam also made the acquaintance of the then chaplain of the Savoy, Thomas Wodehouse, whose *Grammar of Socialism* had impressed him. In 1870 he had, as part of his preparation for ordination as a priest, to send some of his sermons to the bishop, who instantly objected to elements of his Maurician theology. Headlam was adamant that he would not alter his position, so Bishop Jackson delayed ordaining him until 1872. Maul took fright at such open oppositon to the bishop and demanded Headlam's resignation, which took effect in 1873. A close friend, Henry Wace, argued forcibly with him at the time about his rebelliousness: 'I don't ask you to hide your opinions, but surely you need not flaunt them without provocation in people's faces, especially while you are young and inexperienced.'[3] Yet the pattern of Headlam's life was by now well established, for he seemingly relished the opportunity to take the alternative route, the other view. He respected his father, and indeed spoke of his childhood in affectionate terms, yet throughout his life he was to find the whole concept of authority problematic, and the refusal to compromise his views was to become his trademark.

In 1873, however, he did manage to find a second job as a curate to the Revd Septimus Hansard at St Matthew's Church in Bethnal Green. Hansard was another friend of Maurice and of Dean Stanley, who that year welcomed Canon Kingsley at Westminster Abbey. He was also well connected with the local trades-union leaders and had worked hard for a new museum for working-class Bethnal Green. Hansard was committed to house-to-house visits throughout the parish, and Headlam was given a large chunk of the parish for his own. The visits were hard work, for Bethnal Green was then, as today, an area of extreme poverty. The 'sweating' practices that Kingsley had inveighed against in the 1850s were alive and well in the parish, and Headlam was genuinely shocked. He moved into a flat in a large block called the Waterlow Buildings, which had been designed to house working families, and rapidly became part of the local community, helping in the National School, running evening classes and visiting homes and workshops.

In 1873 he also joined a small group who styled themselves the Junior Clergy Society and met in the vestry of St Martin-in-the-Fields, Trafalgar Square. For the first time Headlam found himself part of a crowd who held similar radical ideas and declared allegiance to one another, and it was on the basis of this group that he was later to found the Guild of St Matthew.

His three closest colleagues were an interesting set. George Sarson, a friend of the champion of the Single Tax, Henry George, was the first curate at Holy Trinity, Westminster, and then later at St Martin's. He had graduated a year after Headlam, with a similar lack of academic distinction, and had taken straight away to a ritualist expression of Maurician theology. Sarson, known by his parishioners as 'I. G.' (Intellectual Giant), was probably Headlam's most intimate friend, and it was a source of great sadness to him that in later years his ill health meant he had to leave London for Orlestone in Kent and then Holy Trinity, Dover, where he served as vicar for sixteen years and managed to introduce a surpliced choir, candles, a weekly communion and radical politics.

Sarson's brother-in-law was also a member of the group. John Elliotson Symes, another Cambridge graduate, was the curate of St Peter's, Stepney, where his faith found a much less Anglo-Catholic expression. He too was later to leave London, for the north, where he took up an academic career in Newcastle and ended up as Principal of University College, Nottingham. Another supporter of Henry George, he served on the General Committee of the Land Reform Union, though he fell out with Headlam, as most of his friends did at some point, over the publication of his *Political Economy*, which Headlam saw as accepting the value of capital over labour.

The third member of the group was by far the most gifted

theologian of them all, despite the fact that he never attended college. Although Thomas Hancock suffered for much of his life the same fate as Headlam, namely unemployment, because of his controversial views on eternity, he was ordained in 1863 as the result of having come a very close second, to Joseph Rowntree, in a theological essay competition which Maurice had adjudicated. He served a series of curacies at St Leonard's in Buckinghamshire, at Leicester, at Westminster and at St Stephen's, Lewisham, but never managed to obtain secure employment. In 1884, however, he was finally given a post when his friend Henry Shuttleworth became rector of St Nicholas, Cole Abbey, in the heart of the City of London.

In the tradition of his mentor Maurice he held firmly to an understanding that all society was already in Christ and that the role of the Church, by which he meant the Church of England, was to help society discover that fact. Headlam and Sarson were out-and-out disestablishers of the Church, but Hancock was a decided denominationalist with an uncompromising attitude to the Nonconformists, 'They know at heart that the Church [of England] is much more liberal, radical and socialist than any of the sects is capable of becoming.'[4]

By nature Hancock was rigorously intellectual, exposing the incipient socialism of previous centuries: Archbishop Laud had fought the enclosures on democratic principles; Hooper and Latimer had both opposed the landlordism of their day and had stood up for the poor. He hated publicity and disliked theological vanity in others, especially Wesley, Booth, Manning and Spurgeon. He was also to provide the imaginative theological backbone to much of the *Church Reformer*'s social theology through articles like 'The Social Carcase and the Antisocial Vultures', 'The Magnificat as the Hymn of the Universal Social Revolution' and 'The Banner of Christ in the Hands of the Socialists', thereby developing a new, vigorous, metaphorical language for the movement.

As an activist, of course, Hancock was as deeply flawed as Maurice. He hated schemes and leaders because he thought they were illusory, and Conrad Noel was forced to admit, 'His hatred of schemes, a hatred based on his belief that we are already in God's scheme, seems sometimes to have confused the mind of a thinker generally so conspicuous for his clearness.'[5] He retained the Maurician contempt for party which also informed Headlam's hostility to Keir Hardie: 'The Ideal Commonwealth ... cannot be realised ... through the immoral and mechanical processes of any one party outwitting, outcrushing, outbribing, outvoting, confounding and crushing any other party.'[6]

Such idealism was deeply symptomatic of his age and it weakened his, and the Guild's, ability to effect change. Yet elements of his thinking went way beyond the contribution of any of his colleagues. His concept of the 'the world', for instance, not as irreligion or materialism but as the tendency to schism, provided a radically new basis to his brand of socialism.

> By the world, as opposed to the church we may mean any of the narrow and hollow fellowships, or the totality of those fellowships which men try to build upon the uncatholic or inhuman foundations of class or self, the world consists of those who mould and colour their lives as if they and their sort were independent centres and self-owners and not the children of God and members of his family.[7]

He held a profoundly historical faith.

> The theories of society [he preached in 1885] which are thought out by slaves under the lash of Egypt, by labourers sweating in the fields and workshops of the modern nations, and not those elaborated in the prudential councils of statesmen, or by comfortable professors of political economy, are those which exhibit the fullest reflection of the Kingdom of God's Son.[8]

Hancock's clarity of theological expression was to make him one of the most quoted Christian Socialists long after his death in

1903. At the time of Headlam's brief sojourn at Bethnal Green, however, Hancock was an unemployed cleric in search of a pulpit and had plenty of time, with the other three, to mount a robust assault on the portals of the Church. Throughout the 1870s they campaigned at meetings of the Church Congress, protested at secularist assemblies and demonstrated in favour of trade unions, while developing their own devotional life through increasingly High Anglican ritual, visiting both the high temples of Catholic ritualism, St Alban's, Holborn, and All Saints', Margaret Street, on a regular basis.

Indeed, it was through Headlam's evolving sacramentalism that he came to found, in 1877, the first truly socialist organisation in Britain. For Hansard had allowed Headlam to initiate a series of early-morning communions in the parish, so long as there were parishioners on every occasion. The stipulation was, in its time, not so curious as it may now seem, for eight a.m. communions were far from ordinary, even in ostensibly 'Catholic' parishes. One Sunday Headlam had had to cancel the early celebration because of lack of attendance, and he had reproached two of his most faithful young communicants. One of them, Carrie Hatch, then had the idea of founding a guild that would meet to encourage greater attendance, and by the time she had discussed it with one of Headlam's greatest allies, the schoolteacher Frederick Verinder, the idea had fledged and grown into the Guild of St Matthew (GSM) with a much wider set of objectives. Inaugurated on St Matthew's Day, it soon gained a membership of about forty, rising at its peak in 1895 to around 360.

Meanwhile Headlam had encountered a new set of troubles, for on Sunday, 7 October, he delivered a lecture at the local radical club, the Commonwealth Club. Entitled 'Theatres and Music-halls', it was an attempt to justify the theatre to a puritanical generation that still saw it as close to moral depravity, so much so that a bishop would not even dare to attend *Hamlet* unless incognito. Headlam preached against the 'sin' of dullness, cited even the Puritan Bunyan in his support and ended, 'above all, don't let us speak with scorn of the ladies who dance on the stage.'

The lecture was published. The bishop was livid. The rector was furious, and a week before his thirty-first birthday the curate was given his marching orders, ending the longest period of paid employment Headlam was ever to enjoy.

Within months, however, he had adopted a new role, to be pursued exclusively through the GSM. For as warden he transformed it into a general church guild, moving it to St Michael's Boys School in Shoreditch and transferring its annual meeting to Sion College by Blackfriars Bridge (where much of this book has been researched). In 1884 he also framed its objects:

1. To get rid, by every possible means, of the existing prejudices, especially on the part of the secularists, against the Church, her Sacraments and doctrines, and to endeavour to justify God to the people. 2. To promote frequent and reverent worship in the Holy Communion and a better observance of the teaching of the Church of England as set forth in the Book of Common Prayer. 3. To promote the study of social and political questions in the light of the Incarnation.

The GSM was, therefore, by its very nature, a two-faced organisation, first and foremost arguing theology with the secularists and the Church and, second, disputing the issues of the day with the politicians 'in the light of the Incarnation'. The early years of the Guild were concerned almost exclusively with issues of secularism, with Headlam attending meeting after meeting to confront the militant atheism of people like Charles Bradlaugh. Ironically enough, when Bradlaugh was elected MP for Northampton and deprived of his seat in two successive parliaments for refusing to take the oath, Headlam defended him and indeed campaigned for an end to the religious oath for unbelievers and a repeal of the blasphemy laws.

In 1884, however, the GSM took a more directly political tone and came to adopt, at one of its first open-air meetings in Trafalgar Square, Headlam's 'Priest's Political Programme'. The Guild declared:

> Whereas the present contrast between the great body of the workers who produce much and consume little, and of those classes which produce little and consume much is contrary to the Christian doctrines of brotherhood and justice, this meeting urges on all Churchmen the duty of supporting such measures as will tend (a) to restore to the people the value which they give to the land, (b) to bring about a better distribution of the wealth created by labour, (c) to give the whole body of the people a voice in their own government, (d) to abolish false standards of worth and dignity.[9]

The programme was in many ways symptomatic of its time, although most crucially it recognised a class distinction which few would have then acknowledged. Its chief policy, however, was based on the work of the American Henry George, whom Headlam met on each of his six visits to Britain in the 1880s. George had published his *Progress and Poverty* in Britain in 1880, and it had rapidly sold out. Because he saw the whole economic imbalance of society as stemming from the unequal ownership of land, he espoused one great Single Tax on its economic rent – not immediate nationalisation of the land but a more just, gradual taxation of its value until equality would inexorably come to pass.

Headlam, together with most of the Guild members, bought Georgeism hook, line and sinker. To it they added a keen commitment to democracy, which sharply differentiated them from the Mauricians. Headlam himself was not immune to snobbery – when others were arguing for Labour representation in Parliament he described it as 'utterly absurd' – yet he did have an understanding of the lives of ordinary people and he believed in an extension of suffrage. He was a man of private wealth, who could afford to decorate his new rooms in the smartest of latest fashions, yet he could speak readily to a working-class meeting, and throughout the Eighties he devoted himself to the task of building the GSM. Meetings were held in Preston, Northampton, Liverpool, Plymouth, Oldham and Wellingborough. A new branch was founded in Oxford, and regular meetings were held in Trafalgar Square. At the Leicester Church Congress in 1880 Headlam, with some personal investment, laid into the patronage powers of the bishops: 'At present the Bishop, by a stroke of a pen, without giving any reason, may deprive a curate of his position in the Church and it may be, all his means of getting his bread and butter.'[10]

In 1884 the Guild launched the *Church Reformer*, 'an organ of Christian Socialism and Church Reform', which came out on the fifteenth of each month and carried material on nearly everything that Headlam was interested in, especially the Guild itself and the Church and Stage Guild, which Headlam had also founded. In the 1885 general election the magazine published questions for candidates about their support for free education, the rating of unoccupied land and the land tax.

Of course, the Guild was not the work of Headlam alone. Frederick Verinder had come with him and provided the organisational gifts Headlam lacked. George Bernard Shaw used GSM meetings as a training ground for his own public speaking and became a close ally of Headlam throughout their years on the Fabian Committee.

The three most significant members of the Guild, however, were Henry Carey Shuttleworth, W. E. Moll and Charles Marson.

Shuttleworth was a Cornish man three years younger than Headlam who had become a minor canon at St Paul's in 1876 and who excelled at nothing so much as *bonhomie*. An extremely popular preacher, he had a persistent sense of fun and was reputed to be the 'first to combine chasubles before the altar with flannels before the stumps'. The jolly, back-thumping cleric Morell in Shaw's *Candida* may well be a very direct portrait of the man that Headlam later accused of forgetting that 'the priest's main work is to say the Mass and not to shake hands'.[11]

In 1883 Shuttleworth was appointed rector of St Nicholas, Cole Abbey, in the heart of the City, and made Lecturer in Pastoral and Liturgical Theology at King's, in the hope that preferment might calm his radical tendencies. Instead it confirmed him in them, as he gave Hancock a job, installed in the church a bar that was open to all and proceeded to write and preach a tough gospel: 'Poverty is not a mysterious dispensation of Providence, which, for some inscrutable reason, is the stern lot of the majority of our race; but an evil, brought about by causes which can be remedied.'[12]

Moll was very different. Graduating from Oxford in 1878, and a full ten years younger than Headlam, he served a series of curacies in London from 1879 to 1893, mostly around the area of Soho. A close colleague of Headlam, who frequently offered him an altar and a pulpit at St Mary's, Charing Cross Road, he was none the less a tougher, more robust character, little practised in the arts of polite society. Indeed, it was this down-to-earth quality that stood him in great stead when he moved to Newcastle in 1893, the year of the initiation of the first Independent Labour Party (ILP) in Bradford. For as vicar of St Philip's he came to be one of the foremost supporters of Labour representation, serving on the National Administrative Council of the ILP and taking a leading role in Labour politics in the north-east. He also trained a formidable list of Christian Socialist curates, including Marson in Soho and Percy Widdrington, Paul Stacey and Conrad Noel in Newcastle. Along with Headlam, he was in favour of disestablishing the Church of England, and took a sacramentalist approach to the Church's mission. In a paper to the English Church Union in 1885 he saw the Church 'not only as the guardian of theological truth . . . but as the social Emancipator of Europe, the inaugurator of its industrial life'. Arguing in similar vein to Shuttleworth he continued,

Why, again I ask, is there this poverty? Some say it is the will of Divine Providence and quote the text, 'the poor ye have always with you'. Surely the poverty is bad enough: but to fix it upon the Father of us all is possible only to men whose God is gold. This poverty, why is it once more? *Because they who toil have not had and do not get a fair share of the profits of their work.*[13]

One of Moll's curates, while he was in Soho, was the mordant Charles Marson, whom even his best friend, Francis Etherington, described as 'at no time an easy man to work with. He made great demands on the patience of his friends, for he never quite knew the weight of his own fist or the sharpness of his tongue.'[14] Twelve years younger than Headlam, Marson was born in Woking in 1859. His father, then a broad-church evangelical curate at St John's, Woking, and later vicar of Clevedon, insisted on Latimer for his middle name, though Charles was later to argue that he had inherited the bishop's incipient socialism rather than his low-church theological position. After studying at Oxford, he was ordained in 1881 and went to work at St Jude's, Whitechapel, in the East End of London, under Samuel Barnett, who was already establishing the phenomenal parish machine that later became Toynbee Hall. Already a member of the Guild, he moved, because of ill health, to another curacy in Petersham, from which he was thrown out because of his 'sedition'. After a brief stay as curate at St Agatha's, Shoredith, he took up the incumbency in Orlestone, which George Sarson had recently left. Within months of being an incumbent, however, his broad-church principles had changed to a fundamentally ritualist approach, which was not in keeping either with the views of the parish patrons or Bishop Parry of Dover.

By this time Marson had also taken a very active role in asserting that Christian Socialism was not an issue solely for the Church of England. He had become editor of the *Christian Socialist* in 1884, and through its pages he publicised the ideas of the layman Alfred Howard, who in October 1885 had argued for an organisation for Christian Socialists that would be open to 'non-sacerdotal Christians'. In support Marson wrote of the Guild that it was doing excellent work 'among those who see behind the drapery of the ecclesiastical letter and find comfort in symbolic teaching; but many followers of Jesus do neither'.[15] In March the Christian Socialist Society was founded with the explicit statement, 'The Society is independent of all theological views,' thereby enabling Nonconformists and broad-church members to participate in an organisation whose political programme was very similar to that of the Guild. Education for all; a system of production for use, not profit; the union of all in a universal brotherhood; public control of the land: all were core principles for both Guild and Society, and Marson was keen to see the success of both. While his own theology was sacramental, he could readily see the truth of the argument of Nonconformists like Philip Peach: 'I can conceive of nothing more mischievous . . . than the continued unfounded assertion that the Church of England in fact only consists of the baptised persons in England. Nothing could be more offensive or more likely to alienate the religious Nonconformist.'[16]

The Society's history was not to prove a lengthy one. Despite a healthy start, with branches in Bristol, Leicester and, most notably, Glasgow, its very uniqueness proved its undoing. Significant members such as the great Scottish Unitarian and ILP leader Alexander Webster, and the Liverpudlian leader of the Croydon Brotherhood Church, John Kenworthy, were a significant asset, but in the end denominationalism proved its strength. For several years the *Christian Socialist* was adopted as the Society's formal journal, though financial difficulties meant that it was given its independence again in 1887, and after limping on for a year through the sole effort of the Congregational minister T. A. Leonard from Colne, the Society was wound up in 1892.

Meanwhile Marson had decided in 1889 to take a post in Australia so as to accompany his invalid brother Frank, whose doctor had recommended a change of climate, and he set off for Glenelg in Adelaide only weeks after becoming engaged to Clotilda Bayne, who joined them a year later. The Australian stay did not diminish Marson's socialism, and within three years he had fallen out with his bishop, George Kennion, and his rector, Canon

French, most notably over the treatment of the Aboriginal population. After an extra year in Adelaide at St Oswald's, Parkside, at the insistence of the parishioners he and Chloe returned to England to a series of posts at Christ Church, Clapham, St Mary's, Charing Cross Road, under Moll, and St Mary's, Somers Town. The strain of the bleak decay of much of Somers Town, lying to the north of the Euston Road and between the railways, took its toll on his health, and in 1895 he was offered the living of Hambridge in Somerset by the Prime Minister, Lord Roseberry, much to the indignation of the new Bishop of Bath and Wells, the same George Kennion he had argued with in Adelaide.

Marson's return to England had also coincided with a second attempt at a non-denominational Christian Socialist organisation. The acclaimed Baptist John Clifford had started a 'ministers' union', which had brought together a radical set of clergy from all denominations, and in 1894 he founded the Christian Socialist League as an interdenominational organisation that would set up socialist demonstrations.

Clifford was by all accounts a remarkable man, born in 1836 to a working-class family in Leicester. He started work in a lace factory there before studying at the Baptist College in Leicester and moving to London, where he first preached in Paddington and then built the Westbourne Park Chapel in 1877. Fundamentally opposed to Spurgeon, who left the Baptist Union in 1887 over what he saw as an increase in liberal theology, Clifford was an avowed pacifist and a Fabian who quite simply regarded socialism as 'the plan of God'. Throughout his life committed to fighting for the underdog, Clifford was equally determined to see a secularist nation in which religion flourished, and to that end believed non-denominationalism to be vital.

Marson and Shuttleworth served on Clifford's executive, as well as Percy Alden, the Congregationalist who had studied at Balliol and Mansfield and was elected a Labour MP in 1906. The Vice-President, Bruce Wallace, was another Congregationalist who in the same year founded the Brotherhood Trust and whose 'tin tabernacle' off the Southgate Road was the home in 1907 of the exiled Fifth Congress of the Russian Social Democratic Labour Party with Lenin, Trotsky and Rosa Luxemburg. Again non-denominational Christian Socialism was not destined to last, and the Christian Socialist League folded in 1898, though a successor group, the Christian Social Brotherhood, which was founded at the Mansfield House Settlement in February 1898, managed to struggle through to 1903.

In many senses it was Marson's work within the Christian Socialist Society and League that distinguished him from his peers. Yet he also published in 1913 a significant volume in which he laid out the full historial background to his Christian Socialism, *God's Co-operative Society*. Insisting on Newman's belief that the doctrine of the Church could, and indeed should, change constantly for 'the past is the past because it was outgrown', he sought both a continuity of his beliefs with those of the early Church theologians and the vesting of them with a new dynamic. 'The Word,' he argued, citing St Basil, 'calls us to socialism (to *koinonikon*), brotherly love and obedience to Nature, for man is a political and gregarious animal.'[17] The early Church was a constant source of socialist texts, which he delighted in resuscitating. At the same time what passed for 'Religious Education' was in drastic need of change. 'While our clergy proclaims [sic] the glories of Huppim and Muppim and Ard the people are destroyed for lack of knowledge ... They know all about Abraham except the way to his bosom; all about David except his sure mercies; and all about St Paul except the Faith which he preached and which justified him.'[18]

In 1914 Marson's asthma, which had always given his voice something of a husky tone, took its toll, and he died just before the start of the war, to be recalled later by Gilbert Binyon as 'extremely attractive, an enchanting soul, a real leader'.[19]

While Marson was engaged in the life of the non-denominational organisations, however, he was also committed to the work of the Guild, and, as with most movements of the left, it too did not have a simple life. Indeed, its first major crisis came as a result of its very confessional nature, following Headlam's election to the London School Board in 1888. Some twenty years earlier, in 1870, the Forster Education Act had effectively split the English education system in two over the issue of religious education, for it had specified, in the Cowper–Temple clause, that no tax-aided schools should teach 'catechisms or religious formularies distinctive of any particular denomination'. This had meant that the voluntary church (of England) schools had been divorced, if they decided to maintain denominational religious education, from the main body of state education, while the Board schools had adopted a new pattern of religious education based entirely on the Bible. Headlam saw this as instituting a false two-tier education system, thereby effectively relinquishing the majority of children to the more self-consciously biblical teachings of the Nonconformists. In his election address in 1894 he argued, 'I do not believe that it is the duty of the School Board to settle what religion shall be taught to your children,' thereby calling for an end to church (of England) schools.

Consequently, he published, in the name of the warden of the GSM, a paper entitled *The Duty of the Clergy towards Board Schools and Elementary Education*. In it he called for the Church of England to withdraw from religious education and for a universal, single-tier system of secular education. The row that broke almost immediately was only to be expected, for many of the high-church clergy in the Guild were wedded to the work of the church schools and saw Headlam's ideas as playing into the hands of the secularists. Besides, Headlam had not warned any of the members of his paper before it was published. At the subsequent annual meeting of the Guild in September 1891 at Sion College, Shuttleworth, Sarson and Symes all opposed the paper that Headlam presented as a manifesto, and a vote was forced close to 11.10 p.m. Headlam won, but the Guild was presented in the press as divided and on the verge of collapse, especially when several of the clergy members objected that the voting had included several non-members.

The Guild did, however, survive and, indeed, moved into a new era of productivity. For in 1893 Percy Widdrington founded a new Oxford branch, and the following year Charles Marson opened a branch in Bristol. Several of the Guild's members were also now being preferred; Charles Stubbs, for example, who as vicar of Stokenham in Devon had run a semi-socialist 'Home Colony', was appointed Dean of Ely and then Bishop of Truro.

That was also the year, however, when the Guild had to take a formal position over the incipient Independent Labour Party. Headlam himself had joined the Fabian Society in December 1886, within three years of its establishment, and in 1887 had been one of the special committee of fifteen which had drawn up the 'Basis' of the Society. His involvement had started through the Land Reform Union, which had been founded by H. H. Champion and Lord Olivier in 1883. Olivier already knew most of the Fabians, Sidney Webb and Hubert Bland, and Headlam knew Shaw through the Guild, so it was an easy step for him to become an integral part of the embryonic Fabians. Yet the Fabians had in 1887 had to face the issue of their own party-political allegiance, whether to support the Liberals and act as a ginger group within the party or to push for a new party. Shaw's Tract *The True Radical Progress* in effect committed them to continued Liberal support, and in 1892 Webb joined the Holborn Liberal and Radical Association. Headlam and William Clarke supported him, but others, notably Hubert Bland, Joseph Burgess and S. G. Hobson decided to support Keir Hardie and the ILP.

The following year Webb and Shaw took a new tack in a controversial piece in the *Fortnightly Review*. Their article, entitled 'To your tents O Israel!', aimed at establishing an Independent Labour Party subsidised by the trades unions.

The call for Labour representation did not go down well with Headlam for a whole series of reasons. Partly there was little love lost between him and Hardie. When Hardie first visited Upper Bedford Place he confessed, 'As a Scotsman and as a Nonconformist I well remember the shock it gave me, that the leading member of the Guild divided his attention fairly evenly between socialism and the ballet.'[20] Furthermore, Headlam disliked the idea of party discipline in voting, and was keen to argue that the Liberals had done some good. Most fundamentally, however, Headlam refused 'to vote for a man simply because he is a carpenter and will try to improve the carpenters' wages'. He was axiomatically opposed to Hardie's belief in the ILP as 'a revolt against the assumption that working people are in any sense inferior, either mentally or morally, to any other section of the community'.[21] So in 1893 the *Church Reformer* came out against the ILP with a shrill attack by Headlam on the 'feeble Fabians' who were calling for fifty Independent Labour MPs. In 1895 he argued, 'The ILP is an logical impossibility . . . To form a little party [and to give it a big name] pledged only to vote straight away for the realisation of your ideal, and to keep out all others who would help towards realising it, is political suicide, immoral as all suicide is.'[22]

Not all the Guild agreed with Headlam, of course, as the later founding of the Church Socialist League was to evince, with its explicit support for the new Labour parties. Percy Dearmer was also far more critical of the Liberals than Headlam, arguing that they 'always looked at the working classes through bourgeois spectacles', and Moll took an active part in the ILP from its very inauguration.

The second major crisis of the Guild, however, centred not on a fundamental political difference so much as on one of Headlam's most impulsive acts. For in 1895 he was asked by a friend to stand bail for the Irish playwright Oscar Wilde, who had been accused of sodomy by the Marquess of Queensberry. Headlam agreed to pay half, the other half being met by Lord Douglas of Hawick, despite the fact that he hardly knew him. F. G. Bettany's biography of Headlam attempts to skate over this episode in Headlam's life, yet in terms of the life of the Guild it proved a crucial test. For Headlam had gone out on a limb. Wilde's name had been painted over on posters for his plays showing in the West End, the papers had lambasted him and Headlam himself attracted immediate condemnation. His housemaid even left in disgust. Yet Headlam's point was simple: 'I was a surety not to his character but for his appearance in court to stand his trial. I had very little personal knowledge of him at the time: I think I had only met him twice.'[23] So Headlam took Wilde to court each morning, and when he was released from prison two years later it was to Upper Bedford Place that Wilde came before seeking support from the Roman Catholic fathers at Farm Street, who refused to accept him, and before he eventually left for France.

Within the Guild Headlam met considerable anger. Members of the Guild had already been used to defending the apparently unconventional lifestyle of their Warden, as Headlam's wife had left him a couple of years earlier to live with another woman. So the annual meeting was dominated by semi-personal attacks and barely disguised homophobia. Marson referred caustically to the quotation from Blake that adorned the front of every copy of the *Church Reformer*, stating that he was 'all for building a new Jerusalem' but not for 'wading through a Gomorrah first'. Jimmy Adderley and others instantly resigned from the Guild, and a movement started to get rid of Headlam as Warden. The first attempt came in the *Church Reformer* in April 1895 with an attack by Marson on the 'sick state of the Guild of St Matthew' and a demand for a change of Warden without outright criticism of Headlam. Headlam responded by saying that if his opponents had the courage of their convictions, they would move a motion of censure of him. At the next annual meeting Marson moved that there should be a new Warden every year, and Headlam repeated his charge that this was a cowardly way to try to depose him. The vote went Headlam's way, but the air of personal acrimony was clear, Marson claiming the Guild wanted a Warden who 'would make it very clear that the Guild rejected doctrines subversive of Christian marriage'.

Within a few months Headlam decided to cease publication of the *Church Reformer*, claiming financial difficulties, but the truth was clearly that he no longer felt a great body of support within the Guild itself. The steam had gone out of the Guild in 1895, and in 1903 suggestions were made that it should be wound up. Many of its members had drifted over to the Christian Social Union, and several of the key figures had died, including Shuttleworth in 1900, Sarson in 1902 and Hancock in 1903. Headlam was reluctant to let it go yet, though, and the Guild persevered until 1909, by which time Moll, Marson, Noel and others had founded the equally radical Church Socialist League.

Meanwhile Headlam retained his commitment to education through the London School Board and the London County Council, to which he was elected as a Progressive in 1907. He also took an active role in the Fabians, following his Fabian Tract No. 42 on Christian Socialism in 1892 with a series of articles and pamphlets, all articulating the same basic political platform: universal free education; a minimum wage and maximum length of working day; land reform; housing improvements; female emancipation; and, more curiously, the nationalisation of public houses.

Shaw, speaking of Headlam's involvement with the Fabians, many of whose early meetings were held in his house, said that he 'kept tactfully to politics, letting the priest be seen and felt rather than heard',[24] and there is perhaps in this casual comment a hint of the key element of faith that bound the Headlam of the Anti-Puritan League with the Warden of the Guild of St Matthew, the Fabian and the founder of the London Shakespeare League. For, as the third article of the GSM pointed out, the aim was to study politics 'in the light of the Incarnation', and here lay Headlam's founding principle. The fact that the God had become flesh and dwelt among us meant that the material of this life was of significance. Indeed, there was no split between the spirit and the world. The Church was to be 'the great Secular Society', and the 'Kingdom of Heaven, of which Jesus Christ spoke, was not merely a place to which people were to go hereafter, but a Divine Society established in this world'.[25] The role of the Church, then, was to sanctify life not by separating itself from the world but by immersing itself in it. It was to be 'a great Co-operative organised institution for human welfare and human righteousness in this world',[26] and Christ was 'the social and political *Emancipator*, the greatest of all secular workers ... the preacher of a Revolution'.[27] In this theology the Mass and the music-hall could both point to Christ, for 'if human life is the most sacred and interesting thing possible, then the drama which interprets human life should have indeed the Church's support.'[28] Furthermore in the context of the 1904 Ritual Commissions, Headlam asserted that the Church should have better things to discuss than the legalities of liturgical practices, 'Whether I was right in making the sign of the Cross in the air, or in kissing the Altar are matters of infinitesimal importance compared with the fact that in the London diocese and the Canterbury province so many little children have no clean beds to sleep in ... so many are out of work, so many are overworked, so many are underpaid.'[29]

What was unique about Headlam was his ability to be reckless. More an impulsive artist than a considerate theologian, he managed to alienate many of his closest friends, yet at the same time he proved to be the first Christian Socialist to assault head-on the prejudices of the Church against the political might of the working classes. He could do so partly because he could afford to financially and partly because he sensed instinctively, and knew from his experience in Bethnal Green, the sweated agony of the poor. But above all he did so because of a deep inner confidence that was close to arrogance. Sidney Webb said of him, 'his ideas were seldom subject to modification under argument,' and it is clear from much of the history of the GSM that he enjoyed a confrontational style of debate. Yet he left a political inheritance many would envy, having been at the inception of so many of the elements of the modern Labour movement.

There were, of course, areas in which his views were flawed. In particular his suspicion of Hardie and the ILP, which was as much a hatred of Puritanism as a political judgment, left Christian Socialism for many years to one side of the political endeavour of the left. His distrust of ecclesiastical authority also tainted his understanding of political parties. Yet on the role of women, on theatre and the arts, on the emancipation of the poor, on the relevance of theology to social problems, he had an acute analysis that was decades ahead of its time.

The clearest expression of the paradox of Stewart Duckworth Headlam, the Socialist Individualist, lies in some words addressed to the Guild, for he saw as its aim:

> the greatest possible economic change with the least possible interference with private life and liberty. Spurious socialism, on the other hand, postpones the initiation of those reforms which are necessary to bring about the economic changes, but interferes with the individual in every possible way; and especially does it take delight to interfere with the pleasures and morals of the individual.[30]

# 4

# *The Army of Occupation*

Whereas it has long been known and declared that the poor have no right to the property of the rich, I wish it also to be known and declared that the rich have no right to the property of the poor.

John Ruskin, *Unto This Last*, Essay 3

We have used the Bible as if it was a mere special constable's hand-book – an opium dose for keeping beasts of burden patient while they are being overloaded – a mere book to keep the poor in order.

Charles Kingsley, *Politics for the People*

It is difficult to imagine an organisation more different from the Guild of St Matthew than the Christian Social Union (CSU). The Guild was founded in the heart of urban decay in Bethnal Green, while the Union started in the Chapter House of St Paul's. The Guild was driven by the work of young curates and an unemployed priest, while the Union had a bishop as its President. The Guild was devoted to hard-hitting social comment and action, while the Union was more committed to developing ideas. Even the aims of the two organisations seem divergent, with the Union far less certain than the Guild about any direct commitment to redistribution or economic socialism. Yet many of the Guild's members transferred *en bloc* to the Union, including Shuttleworth, Adderley, Donaldson and Moll, and even Headlam was prepared to welcome its inauguration in 1889: 'let us have no petty jealousy in this matter. We have laboured and they are welcome to enter into the fruits of our labours.'[1] Peter d'A. Jones, pointing to the inherently 'respectable' nature of the Union, has described the difference between the two groups: 'Stewart Headlam and his disciples were the shock troops of "sacramental socialism". The Christian Social Union was the army of occupation.'[2]

Some later Christian Socialists have also been highly critical of the CSU. Conrad Noel argued that it 'glories in its indefiniteness and seems to consider it a crime to arrive at any particular economic conclusion . . . An unkind critic has described it as forever learning but never coming to a knowledge of the truth.'[3] Yet the fact remains that at its height it reckoned among its 6,000 members sixteen out of fifty-three episcopal appointments; it reached deeper into the life of the Church than nearly any other Christian Socialist organisation; it scored real successes in establishing a social aspect to the mission of the Church; and it managed to harness the energies of more than one person. Whereas the Guild seemed to have room for only one leader, Headlam, the Union held together the talents of several – Henry Scott Holland, Charles Gore, Bishop Westcott – which meant that its effect could be that much more wide-reaching. Even Noel went on to recognise the Union's enduring legacy: 'Whatever its defects it has convinced a large mass of English church-goers of the importance of social questions. It has persuaded them that the Christian religion essentially involves social righteousness in some form or other.'[4]

The social, if not the political origins of the Christian Social Union lay in two groups, the Guild itself, from which many of its early members came, and the group of young clergy known as the 'Holy Party'. The real motor force behind the Union, however, was the work of Henry Scott Holland, a man now more generally known for his words oft-quoted at funerals, 'Death is nothing at all. It does not count. I have only slipped away into the next room,'[5] or the hymn 'Judge Eternal, throned in splendour', which he wrote as a Christian Socialist hymn for the Union's journal *Commonwealth* in July 1902. Gore acknowledged Holland's central role several years after his death: 'there is no doubt that Holland was the centre of the movement, and that the movement expressed a certain element of his mind.'[6] What is certain, above all, is that Holland was an outstanding speaker, instantly able to establish a personal rapport and maintain deep friendship. Many years after his death biographical memoirs were being written about 'Scotty', though his very personability perhaps detracted from his political effectiveness. 'I was sometimes tempted to wonder,' Gore admitted, 'whether his brilliant oratory and sparkling wit did not so delight his audience with a sort of physical joy as to conceal from them what severe doctrine and what unpalatable conclusions were really being pressed upon them.'[7]

Holland was born within a fortnight of Headlam in 1847, the son of a wealthy squire. His grandfather had been a senior partner at Barings Bank, and one of his uncles was an MP. He was sent to Eton, where he was tutored by the same William Johnson who taught Headlam and was a friend of both Maurice and Kingsley, and then on to Oxford: 'Eton over again, on a different stretch of the same river.'[8] At Balliol College he came into close contact with Thomas Hill Green, who taught philosophy in the college and was one of the few Oxford dons to be critical of the utilitarian school of John Stuart Mill. Although not an orthodox Christian, he was supportive of Holland's decision to go forward for ordination and provided him with a strong spiritual and ethical philosophy. 'Above all, Holland learned from Green a basic ethical stance, that one should not be overly concerned about one's own individual sanctity, that true religion must issue in a concern for social justice, and that all morality is at root a morality of citizenship and social responsibility.'[9] On graduation and ordination in 1871 he was awarded a studentship (the equivalent of a lectureship at other colleges) at Christ Church, Oxford. Here he framed the basis of his later political thought, reacting against the high-mindedness of the college high table and remaining deeply critical of utilitarianism. 'Imagine putting up a stained-glass window to Faith, Hope and Political Economy,'[10] he declared. He also ran Passion and Holy Week missions as St

Saviour's, Hoxton, in the belief that young Oxford dons should 'see what was really happening' in the depths of London's slums. 'It was intensely exciting, and, we were inclined to say, very successful. The crowd gathered in a moment, a real live dirty crowd of roughs and streety women; they followed us – they sang a bit; they listened with extraordinary intentness, and solemnity.'[11] More than merely evangelical mission, however, Holland was interested in the social relevance of these associations between the university and Hoxton, 'Do you think the association would lend itself to a scheme for organising a connection between Oxford and the socialistic spirit which springs out of the misery of our great cities?'[12]

As well as developing an embryonic Christian Socialism in this period, Holland cultivated his highly idiosyncratic linguistic style. He loved inventing words, especially adjectives, and would frequently turn a whole sermon or speech on a pun or a fragment of modern slang. He gained a reputation for his sermons, and through much of the CSU's history devised most of its campaigning slogans, using wit and linguistic dexterity rather than rhetorical or disputative techniques to win the argument. One of his favourite comments, to those who alleged that socialism championed the nanny or grandmotherly state, was that every man should be his own grandmother, personal and social responsibility neatly combined. By nature affable, with a rounded, jowly face and tiny eyes, he reserved his sharp temper for the political arena and the confrontation of what he saw as 'obscurantism'. Yet all his letters and addresses are striking for their colloquial feel, their bubbling enthusiasm and overt good temper.

During his time at Christ Church he also formed the closest connections of his life, in the shape of the group that Holland himself later dubbed, with a sense of irony, the 'Holy Party'. For after attending a reading party at Mortehoe in August 1875, Holland organised a series of annual meetings, the first of which was held at Brightstone. Holland described the Holy Party's intention: 'It was simply the habit of a gang of us young donlets to occupy some small country parish for a month, do the duty, read, discuss, say our offices and keep our hours together.'[13] Attendance was not the same every year – indeed, in 1881 Holland wrote to Gore, 'You asked me about the Brotherhood. I am the Brotherhood. You wanted to be told about the Holy Party. The Holy Party is entirely and wholly engaged at this moment in writing to you,'[14] for he was the only person to come.

The full list of regular attendees, however, is an impressive one: Charles Gore, later Bishop of Worcester, Birmingham and Oxford, and then a don at Trinity; Edward Stuart Talbot, later Bishop of Rochester, Southwark and Winchester, and then the first Warden of the new Keble College; John Richardson Illingworth, then a fellow at Jesus and, from 1890 to 1915, the host of the group at his rectory in Longworth; Arthur Lyttleton, then at Keble and later Bishop of Southampton; Wilfrid Richmond, the author of *Christian Economics* in 1888 and co-founder, with Holland and Lyttleton, in 1879, of the tiny Oxford-based Politics, Economics, Socialism, Ethics and Christianity; J. H. Maude; and Robert Moberley. The pattern for every day was identical: Communion at seven a.m., silence or study all morning, an afternoon walk, and the discussion of a selected book.

What is clear from all Holland's comments on the group is that the main aim was not to be excessively introverted and pious but to enjoy the fellowship of close friends in the context of a study programme. Its atmosphere undoubtedly informed Gore's later development both of the community at Pusey House in Oxford and the Community of the Resurrection (CR) at Mirfield. For several years the Holy Party was peripatetic, but when Illingworth was appointed rector of Longworth in 1890 the group settled there for its annual party, where 'Mr I.' and his wife played willing hosts for twenty-five years.

It was through these regular annual meetings that one of the most significant British works of nineteenth-century theology came into being, for in 1887 the Holy Party started to plan a book of essays on the religion of the Incarnation. The majority of the essays were written during 1888, and at a meeting in September at Holland's house in Amen Court in London, to which he had moved on being made a canon at St Paul's Cathedral in 1884, the texts were finalised. In November 1889 the volume was published under the title *Lux Mundi*, with essays by Holland on 'Faith', by Illingworth on 'The Problem of Pain', by Talbot, who was now vicar of Leeds, on 'History' and by Gore, now Principal of Pusey House, on 'The Holy Spirit and Inspiration'. The book was not intended to be controversial but instantly entered the theological bestsellers' list, not least because of fierce disputes over Gore's essay, which some saw as denying the divine inspiration of Scripture. Within a year Gore, as editor, was writing a special introduction to the tenth edition of the book.

In the meantime Holland had started another project in the form of the Christian Social Union. With Shuttleworth, he had been involved in drafting an encyclical, which was signed by 145 bishops at the Lambeth Pan-Anglican conference of 1888. This condemned 'excessive inequality in the distribution of this world's goods' and required clergy to show 'how much of what is good and true in socialism is to be found in the precepts of Christ'.[15] Later that year he also wrote to Wilfrid Richmond, whose *Christian Economics* had recently been published, 'We live in economic blindness down here, of the blackest kind. The world seems to have reacted into the mind of forty years ago. You would think that it had never talked democratic language. We are in a mad back-water, eddying furiously.'[16] Holland asked Richmond to deliver a series of lectures at Sion College, which lay close to St Paul's. The Lent meetings were to be chaired by Holland, Gore and others and would give a clear idea of whether there was room for a new society such as Holland envisaged. Richmond's talks were a great success, arguing that the laws of economics are not arbitrary and independent of moral considerations but the subject of constant ethical controversy. Two further meetings were held at Holland's house, and on 14 June he presided at a meeting in the Chapter House of St Paul's at which the new Christian Social Union was formed, with sixty-three members and an interim committee appointed with Holland as Chairman. The Union's offices were to be at Canon Mason's mission-house in Tower Hill, and a set of objectives was agreed:

> (1) To claim for the Christian Law the ultimate authority to rule social practice. (2) To study in common how to apply the moral truths and principles of Christianity to the social and economic difficulties of the present time. (3) To present Christ in practical life as the Living Master and King, the enemy of wrong and selfishness, the power of righteousness and love.

The difference between these objectives and those of the Guild of St Matthew could not be more immediately apparent, not least in the commitment to 'study' rather than 'to get rid, by every means possible, of the existing prejudices'. As Ken Leech puts it, referring to the Guild of St Matthew, 'It appealed primarily not to the intellect, as did the CSU, but to the conscience.'[17] Where the Guild had a political programme, the Union had simply a social commitment, and while Holland punningly referred to the Guild as 'Shuttlecock and Headlong', the Union's critics caricatured its style: 'Here's a glaring social evil; let's read a paper about it.' Yet the Union was determined to transform the Church as surely as it sought political change. Holland wrote to James Adderley, 'For the first time in all history, the poor old Church is trying to show the personal sin of corporate and social sinning.' Furthermore, Holland was clear that the whole purpose of learning and of theological endeavour was not pietist but rooted in practicalities:

> For all these years we have steadily voted against the tradition that to be a social reformer you must be shadowy in your creed. The old Broad Church man has made this superstition common. To care about drains was supposed to mean that you sat loose to the Creed; and we have upheld the counter-position all these years, that the more you believe in the Incarnation the more you care about drains.[18]

The new movement in political life had to be taken seriously:

> We believe that political problems are rapidly giving place to
> the industrial problem, which is proving itself more and more
> to be the question of the hour . . . It is the intolerable situation
> in which our industrial population now finds itself, that must
> force upon us a reconsideration of the economic principles
> and methods which have such disastrous and terrible
> results.[19]

Christianity had to reassert itself over the domain of economics
with consistency, as Holland further argued in his preface to
Richmond's lectures when they were published:

> We live as shuttlecocks, bandied about between our political
> economy and our Christian morality. We go a certain dis-
> tance with the science, and then when things get ugly and
> squeeze, we suddenly introduce moral considerations, and
> human kindness, and charity. And then, again, this seems
> weak, and we pull up short and go back to tough economic
> principle.[20]

So the parameters of the Union were clear. It was exclusively
Anglican but sought a broader base than the narrow sacramentalism of Headlam. In Adderley's words, its moderation was also to
be its key, for 'if the Church was not to be starved from inability
to retain its food it was necessary in the economy of Heaven for
the moderate physicians of the CSU to provide a diet.'[21] It was to
base its appeal on the force of reason as well as tradition, and it
was to subject socialism to tough but sympathetic theological
examination. As for its political stance, Gore wrote, 'so far as
socialism was a name for a particular theory or group of theories
involving the necessity for state ownership of the materials and
instruments of industry, it refused to be socialist.'[22] Appropriately
enough, it spent much of its time engaged in research, especially
through the work of John Carter, who ran the Oxford branch

from Pusey House almost as a direct continuation of the Oxford GSM branch. It also published a wide variety of articles, magazines and books. Thus in 1891 the *Economic Review* was started in Oxford and lasted until 1914. Jimmy Adderley also initiated *Goodwill* as a sort of 'parish magazine' in 1894 and from 1896 the monthly *Commonwealth* ran through to 1921.

There was the same emphasis on radical social *and* personal transformation that had also imbued much of the thinking of the Mauricians. In the context of the Union, however, it was given the added piquancy of a highly confessional form of Anglicanism. Holland, Gore and Talbot were all deeply committed to a sacramental, high-church understanding of the Church and worked as hard for a spiritual renewal of the Church as for the social renewal of the nation. Yet much of their work was not in-house theology but the development of practical measures. Thus in 1893 the Oxford branch drew up its first 'white list' of twenty local firms that had adopted trade-union wage-rates and encouraged members towards 'discriminatory purchasing', thus developing a model that was repeated in Leeds and in London and was the eventual precursor of the modern shoppers' boycott. Holland also helped to form the Consumers' League in 1890, with Clementina Black of the Women's Trade Union Association, and other campaigns were adopted to promote the 'leadless-glaze' technique in the potteries and improve the working conditions of several trades. The London branch's research committee also included the redoubtable Constance Smith and Gertrude Tuckwell, both of whom worked exhaustively on women's working conditions.

The first members of the Union came predominantly from the Guild of St Matthew, although it was not until 1895, and the serious rift over the Wilde affair, that the majority of Guild members transferred their allegiance. Throughout the Nineties the membership of the Union grew, and its campaigning activities focused on issues of deprivation and employment.

Within weeks of its foundation, however, the Union had to face one of the defining moments of the British Labour movement, in the form of the great dock strike. For in late 1888 the issue of the pay and conditions of the London dockers had started to come to a head. The Gas Workers' Union, which later became the National Union of Municipal Workers, had just won their battle for a change from twelve-hour to eight-hour shifts. Annie Besant had also helped the 700 match-girls at the Bryant and May factory to campaign successfully against their appalling working conditions. At the same time the twenty-eight year-old Ben Tillett, who had become Secretary of the Tea Coopers' and General Labourers' Association, on its inauguration at the Oak Tavern in July 1887, had become the spokesman for a workforce of about 100,000, mostly part-time and occasional workmen. There was much division between this group, which was largely unskilled and got work as and when it was available and were paid by the hour, and the skilled workers, who were represented by the crafts trades unions and did not want to see the casual workforce organise. Casual workers were on fivepence per hour and would frequently be hired for a single hour. Through the start of 1889 there was some co-ordination of the work of the other unions, with Tom McCarthy of the stevedores, John Burns and Tom Mann of the engineers, Bill Steadman of the barge-builders and Ben Cooper of the cigar-makers meeting with Tillett to consider possible action to improve the lot of all the dockers.

In August the men of the South-West India Dock agreed to strike action, and Tillett sent the Dock directors a three-point demand, calling for a pay increase to sixpence an hour and eightpence for overtime, an end to piecework and a minimum period of employment of four hours. The Chairman of the directors, Mr Norwood, a six-foot man of twenty stone, met with the diminutive Tillett but refused even to reply to the demands. On 14 August the strike began, with the whole of the London docks out on strike by the 20th, thanks to a campaign of military precision waged by Tillett, aided by the exceptional supportive strikes by the stevedores and the engineers. The strike committee drew immediate support from around the globe, with donations reaching £30,000 and coming in from as far away as Melbourne: and though the Government refused to take the situation seriously, the Churches were instantly determined to be involved. The Christ Church Mission at nearby Poplar, which Holland had helped to found, raised £800 through the work of Adderley; the Salvation Army in the Whitehall Road provided bread for striking families; and the then President of the Wesleyan Conference, C. H. Kelly, attended a free breakfast provided by the St George's Wesleyan Mission in Cable Street.

First on the scene, however, was the now eighty-one-year-old Cardinal Manning. Manning had been an early friend of Maurice and Kingsley and had been received, when an Anglican archdeacon, into the Roman Catholic Church, in which he also rose rapidly. Always radical in his support for the poor, he was involved in lobbying the Pope for a radical expression of social doctrine, efforts which were to prove fruitful later in 1889 with the publication of the papal encyclical *Rerum Novarum*. He also knew Tillett and had been quietly supportive when he had approached him in 1888. When the strike began, despite Tillett's Congregational background, he sought the Cardinal's support again. On 6 September Manning personally summoned a Committee of Reconciliation at the Mansion House, with the Lord Mayor and other City figures. Meanwhile the Christian Social Union had been determined that the Church of England should be equally involved, and Cyril Bickersteth had gone off to Dolgelly, 'without a rag of luggage', to drag a reluctant Bishop of London, Bishop Temple, back from his holiday to attend the meeting. The Committee proposed a compromise of a pay increase of sixpence to start in March 1890, which the strikers amended to January of that year. The directors then put further qualifications on the offer, which the dockers rejected, as their busiest time of the year was before Christmas, and they felt their demand was just. Temple promptly gave up and left for Wales, while Manning kept up the struggle. He met with each of the unions in turn, having persuaded the directors to let him negotiate on their behalf, and finally managed to broker a start date of 4 November for the pay increase. The strike ended as swiftly as it had started. Instantly Manning was hailed as the People's Cardinal, and the Labour movement came to look on the Church, and in particular the Church of Rome, as a friendly ally. Pope Leo was delighted, not least because Manning had managed to get to the very heart of the British social debate and had won a whole new constituency for Rome.

Of course, Manning was not the only cleric to be involved in the strike. Tillett was equally appreciative of the work of Adderley and the CSU people involved in Toynbee Hall in the East End, who had been active in finding financial support for the strikers. Gore later, controversially, chaired a meeting with one of the other dockers' leaders, Tom Mann, at Exeter College. The Bishop of London, who was later to be Archbishop of Canterbury and father of the far more radical William Temple, had been a great disappointment. Yet Holland defended him: 'The noble old chief sticks rather hard at certain points, and is rather stiffly economical in the older fashion of economy. But he is so great: and high: and square. And he is now working hard in the cause.'[23] Adderley recounted that Temple felt split: 'My head is with Mr Norwood, but my heart is with Mr Burns.'[24] Tillett did not agree and felt that Temple had been worse than useless, and Manning himself was swift to attack the lethargy of the State Church and the 'harshness' of Temple. Tillett was not blind to the combat of the Churches over the bodies of the dockers, however: 'the play of passion and personal interests was centred in the fight the square-jawed, hard-featured Temple put up against the ascetic and spiritual-faced Cardinal Manning; he would have sacrificed the whole dockers to win for his Church.'[25]

In the meantime the Christian Social Union was growing rapidly. In November the first annual meeting was held at St Paul's, at which Brooke Fosse Westcott was elected President. Westcott was soon to become Bishop of Durham, one of the most senior appointments in the Church of England, and was presently a canon at Westminster Abbey. Older than Holland (born 1825), he had taught Gore at Harrow, been a canon at Peterborough, the rector of Somersham in Hampshire and Regius Professor of

Divinity at Cambridge soon after Maurice in 1870, so Westcott's involvement in the CSU was considered remarkable by many. Headlam reckoned it showed the limitations of the new movement, for if established people like Westcott could join it, then it could hardly have much of a cutting edge. Yet Westcott's contribution to social unionism was dramatic. Very much the elder statesman of the CSU, he early on established both the acceptability of episcopal intervention in industrial matters by his successful mediation in the 1892 miners' strike and a case for socialism that set the tone of much of the Union's work. In true Maurician style, he held firmly to an incarnational theology that saw the mysteries of eternity in the practicalities of the material. In 1890 he addressed the Church Congress in Hull not on what he termed 'the paternal Socialism of Owen, or the State Socialism of Bismarck, the international Socialism of Marx, or the Christian Socialism of Maurice, or the evolutionary socialism of the *Fabian Essays*'.[26] Instead his interest lay in socialism as 'a theory of life', which was set fundamentally against individualism both in method and aim and which, in an age to come, would seem inevitable. 'Wage labour, though it appears to be an inevitable step in the evolution of society, is as little fitted to represent finally or adequately the connection of man with man in the production of wealth as in earlier times slavery or serfdom.'[27] He was adamant that 'God is calling us in this age, through the characteristic teachings of science and of history, to seek a new social application of the Gospel. We cannot doubt, therefore, that it is through our obedience to the call that we shall realise its Divine power.'[28]

The most significant of all the Union's members, however, was one of Holland's childhood friends and the 'Pope' of the Holy Party, Charles Gore. At the time of the founding of the CSU he was the head of Pusey House in Oxford, a centre for Anglo-Catholic study that had been opened in 1884 to house the library of the great leader of the Oxford Movement, Dr Pusey. Born on 22 January 1853 at Wimbledon, the youngest son of a civil servant from a noble background and the brother of the first

English Lawn Tennis champion Spencer Gore, Gore followed Headlam to Harrow, where he was taught by Westcott, to whom he attributed his vocation, having heard him preach in 1868 that 'a life of absolute and calculated sacrifice is a spring of immeasurable power.'[29]

In 1871 he followed Holland to Balliol College, Oxford, and started a period of eight years when he shared the world of academia with the man who was to be his closest friend, confidant, ally and adviser. It was a friendship that could not be overestimated. For each it provided a personal confidence and strength that they might otherwise have lacked and, equally important, rescued them from a loneliness which their self-enforced single lifestyle might have conferred. For years Gore would ask Holland's advice at every stage of his career, and Holland would send characteristically bubbling letters of support. Indeed, when Holland died, Gore acknowledged, 'For the last forty years and more, there was no question, speculative or practical, which has presented itself to my mind, on which I have not found myself asking, "What will Holland say?" and been disposed to feel that I must be wrong, if I turned out to be thinking differently from him.'[30] Gore took finals in 1875, the year of the first Holy Party and, as a result of his excellent first, immediately received a fellowship at Trinity College, where he taught until 1879, when he decided to serve as an assistant curate first at Christ Church, Bootle, and then St Margaret's, Prince's Road, in Liverpool. Later that same year, however, he was offered the post of Vice-Principal at Cuddesdon Theological College, where he would be training young clergy, and he moved back south to the tiny village outside Oxford where the Bishop's palace (now the Toc H centre) and college dominated the country scene.

In 1884, the year that Holland was appointed to St Paul's, Gore moved again, to the new Pusey House in St Giles Street in Oxford, which Holland termed, in his inimitable way, the 'Puseum'. Designed in memory of the celebrated leader of the Oxford Movement, Pusey House was in effect to act as a companion to Keble College, working in the university for the high-church

liturgy and theology that Pusey had espoused, and Gore's appointment as Principal Librarian, the titular head of the house, gave
him an immensely important new role in the Church, as unofficial
spokesperson for the Tractarian wing of the Church of England.
Gore was thirty-one and entered on an immensely productive
period of theological exploration, which culminated in both his
contribution to *Lux Mundi* and his immensely successful Bampton
Lectures of 1891.

Pusey House was also, however, a small community in its own
right with three celibate priests living and working together, and
Gore rapidly seized the opportunity of exploring the creation of a
religious community in a style very similar to that of the Holy
Party. Pusey was to become a regular home to many of the most
significant Christian Socialists. John Carter, the dynamic young
Canadian who had graduated from Exeter College in 1887 and
served a curacy in Limehouse, was assistant chaplain at Exeter
from 1890 to 1895 and stayed at Pusey, from which he started
the *Economic Review* in 1891. Stewart Headlam was an
occasional visitor, as, of course, were Gore's closest friends,
Holland and Talbot.

Gore's desire to build a religious community, however, was not
satisfied by Pusey House itself. In 1887 he took a further step,
with the inauguration of the Society of the Resurrection, at a
retreat at Keble on 4 October. Originally to be called the Society
of Christian Hope, Gore's ally Liddon had exhorted him to find a
more positive-sounding title, and Gore soon persuaded several of
those involved in Pusey to join. On 8 October twenty-one
members were professed, and Gore was elected Superior, a post
he was to retain until he was appointed Bishop of Rochester. In
1892 the Society formally became the Community of the Resurrection, with six members under a common vow of brotherhood;
nearly all of whom were Christian Socialists: Gore, Carter, James
Nash, George Longridge, Cyril Bickersteth and Walter Frere, who
was to succeed Gore as Superior and was later Bishop of Truro.
Gore himself detested unnecessary regulations and organisation,
so the brotherhood was to be simple, with all capital retained by

individual members but income placed in a common purse. Vows were to be repeated annually, with a commitment to celibacy and a holiday of at least four weeks. Gore also distrusted excessive hierarchism, so the Superior was to be elected for a period of three years, and though he was the only member of the Community not to be referred to by his Christian name, he always preferred the title 'Senior' to 'Superior'.

After a first year based at Pusey House in 1893 the Community decided, with Gore, to move to the village of Radley, where he tried a brief, and very unhappy, period as incumbent of the parish. From the outset the Community had a life of its own, made up, as it was, of extremely lively and able priests, but it was during the brief sojourn at Radley that the other members started to come into their own, and the lasting character of the Community was formed. At one point Gore suffered a major emotional breakdown and was sent abroad for six months. Frere, who had taken something of a deputy's role later said that during this period for the first time they had been able to 'have very free discussions, talk out many points of difference and do really a good deal at revising and adding to our ways and rule'.[31] Much later Frere wrote revealingly of Gore, 'much as I love him I have never yet been able to understand him. I do not think I have ever been quite at ease with him or he with me, though our relations have always been exceedingly cordial and affectionate.'[32] So in a sense it seems inevitable that though Gore was a vital catalyst to the formation of the Community, he himself was correct in assessing that it was only when he was absent that it could really take off. While he was away new probationers were also accepted into the Community, including the radical priest Paul Bull, who was later to play a dynamic role in the Community's support for the Labour movement.

On 7 December 1894 Gore was offered a canonry at Westminster Abbey, where he would come back into daily contact with Holland, who was across London at St Paul's, and Talbot, who in 1895 was appointed Bishop of Rochester, covering most of the south of London before the creation of the diocese of Southwark.

Gore vacillated briefly but was delighted at the prospect of re-entering the academic mainstream of the Church and accepted, despite the complicated position in which it put the Community. Most of the Community, in fact, stayed on at Radley, while two members, Frere and Bickersteth, joined him at Westminster.

This two-house phase was not, however, to last long. For several of the members, including Gore, had been keen to move to the north of England out of a desire to make a more radical engagement with the working classes. An approach had been made to the then Bishop of Wakeham, Walsham How, now better known as the author of the hymn 'For all the saints'. He suggested the possibility of Mirfield, an industrial town of some 15,000 people close to the major rail intersection Mirfield Junction, where his son was vicar and where there was a large empty house called Hall Croft. In August, while Gore was on an extended tour in America, Frere and Bickersteth visited Mirfield, and the Community agreed to take it on. On 20 January 1898 the first of the brothers moved in, and an inaugural mass was held on the 27th. There were six resident brothers, while two remained with Gore at Westminster. John Carter was to be based at both Pusey and Mirfield. The Community also started to develop its independent vocation and began to train ordinands, convinced that the present situation in the Church of England, where training could cost almost £1,000, made ordination impossible for those from poor backgrounds. One of the brothers, Paul Bull, argued forcibly, 'We have invented a class priesthood, with a money qualification,' and Gore agreed: 'Yes. We seem . . . to have patented a new form of simony.'[33] By the end of 1902 all of the Community bar Gore had left Westminster for Mirfield, and in 1901 Gore resigned as Superior, and Frere took over.

In the meantime Gore's politics remained radical, and he supported specific causes such as the Baptist preacher John Clifford's campaign for the Armenians to 'secure to industrious people the right to love peaceably in their native land'. He promoted the co-operative movement, speaking regularly at the co-operative Congress and buying much of his clothing from co-operative stores. He became a shareholder in a large London store simply so as to protest at the shareholders' meeting against its employment practices. In 1901 he provided the Jerusalem Chamber at the Abbey for a meeting of clergy and parliamentarians about the Factory Bill, which led to a series of meetings, under Gore's chairmanship, on the proposed Wages Board Bill, which the Christian Social Union advocated. He also became renowned as a supporter of women's suffrage in both Church and State, the *Churchwoman* of 6 March 1896 commenting with approbation on his views that women could no longer be held in the disdain in which medieval society had held them.

One of Gore's most pressing concerns, however, was that of South Africa. For with the routing of the radicals in the general election of 1895, the jingoistic Joseph Chamberlain had acceded to the Colonial Office. Despite Kingsley's and Maurice's fierce support for the Crimean War, other Christian Socialists had been deeply critical of most forms of fierce nationalism, and in 1886 Marson had lambasted British colonialism in the *Christian Socialist* as a campaign to 'dram, drug and syphilise' the population, 'Bible in one hand and gun in the other'. The CSU was far from united on the matter, and indeed one of the senior members of the Community, Paul Bull, went out to South Africa as a chaplain in the war, but the excesses of the Boer War established for the first time a rich vein of anti-imperialism within Christian Socialism. Gore and Holland, in particular, were more in tune with the Independent Labour Party, many of whom had adopted overtly pacific positions, than with the Fabians who supported the war. They berated the Conservatives for their arrogance, and Holland caricatured the proud English image of John Bull, preaching in St Paul's on the Siege of Ladysmith, that the 'twopenny patriotism of the "war-party" [was] beneath contempt'. Gore was wholeheartedly opposed to the Jameson Raid in 1895, and in 1899 preached in the Abbey against the cries for vengeance in the press for the British losses at Majuba Hill, which had happened a full eighteen years earlier. When the Boer War started in 1899 Holland found both a personal and a theological reason for his distaste for it:

We at home who risk nothing, who only tingle with the cheap fury of Fleet Street, could hardly have believed that we could fall so far from the memory of Jesus Christ ... We should humiliate ourselves for the blundering recklessness with which we entered on the war, and the insolence and arrogance which blinded us so utterly.[34]

Gore went on in 1901 to censure the Government in a letter to *The Times*, complaining about the appalling conditions of the Boers in British concentration camps, where 42,000 out of 231,000 died through bad sanitation and lack of food. And Holland, even on the night of peace in June 1902, was sickened by the revelling of the crowds: 'It was the utter abandonment which was so revolting. The faces lose human expression ... The hideous look comes, which marks the end of human nature.'[35]

In the meantime Lord Salisbury, much to the surprise of the press, had appointed Gore Bishop of Worcester and therefore the bishop covering Joseph Chamberlain's home city of Birmingham. The *Review of Reviews* commented at the time, 'Imagine John the Baptist appointed by Pontius Pilate to be bishop over Galilee when Herod was in his glory, and we have some faint idea of the nature of the appointment by which Lord Salisbury sent Canon Gore to be Bishop of Birmingham.'[36] It was a role in which Gore excelled, though his first act, his refusal to live in the unnecessarily vast and luxurious palace, antagonised many of his new charges. Immediately he set about masterminding the division of his diocese and the creation of the diocese of Birmingham, and then adopting the life of the city as his task.

The work of the CSU was practical as well as academic, its detractors notwithstanding. In 1898 the London branch started to lobby Parliament on the issue of the Factory Acts, a campaign it pursued through its Members of Parliament (H. J. Tennant, Sir Charles Dilke and Talbot's son, J. G. Talbot) through to the Trade Boards Act of 1909. In 1897 the Cheltenham branch formed a Society for the Improvement of the Housing of the Poor, which bought up slum property and tried to act as a model landlord.

In 1905 F. Lewis Donaldson, the vicar of St Mark's, Leicester, and a member of the CSU's executive, adopted a more urgent political style, reminiscent of the work of the Guild. The previous winter had been very harsh in Leicester, and Donaldson's socialism was uncompromising. 'Christianity is the religion of which socialism is the practice,' he asserted,[37] and he believed that the exigencies experienced especially by the large number of unemployed in the city were the direct business of government. The State should provide employment 'if the agencies of ordinary commerce fail for lack of discipline',[38] and if unemployment were rife, then the Government should be forced to recognise its duty. Consequently, in April 1905 an 'Unemployed Committee' had been formed in the city, and on 5 June Donaldson addressed the 440 unemployed men who were to march to London to petition King Edward. In fact, he not only spoke but actually led the men on their march with the Tractarian hymn 'Lead, kindly light'. In the event the march had chosen the wrong week to arrive in London, for it was Whitsun and Parliament was in recess. London was quiet, and even the Archbishop refused to see them. None the less Donaldson was convinced that the march had served a vital purpose, having 'profoundly affected the imagination of the nation'.[39]

By 1906 Gore was beginning to think that 'the CSU has done its bit'. The general election had brought very real advances for the Labour and Liberal/Labour candidates, and even the Church of England had initiated a near-universal system of Diocesan Social Services committees. The Church seemed to be changing, and the Socialists seemed willing and able to take up the baton. Yet the real effect of the Union was only to be felt in 1908, at the Pan-Anglican Congress, followed by the decennial meeting of the Lambeth Conference of Bishops, which represented a singular triumph for Gore's personal style. Curiously, for a bishop who was at the heart of the Church of England for upwards of thirty years, this was the only Lambeth Conference Gore ever attended, and he nearly missed it due to an emergency appendix operation. He had supposed that his usual position of being in opposition would be repeated at Lambeth but found instead that many of the foreign bishops held him in great regard. Gore addressed the Conference twice, arguing for the adoption of a radical political agenda: 'The socialistic movement is based upon a great demand for justice in human life ... The indictment of our present social organisation is indeed overwhelming. And with the indictment Christianity ought to have the profoundest sympathy. It is substantially the indictment of the prophets.'[40] Gore had always held the Maurician view that any political transformation must require both social and personal reform, and he took an overtly penitential tack throughout his speech. The Church must welcome socialism because it had so patently failed society, and it must do so promptly: 'Penitence must lead to reparation while there is yet time, ere the well-merited judgments of God take all weapons out of our hands.'[41] Furthermore, 'there is nothing in the socialistic idea of the constitution of society which is antagonistic to society and ... its main idea is closely allied to the Christian idea.'[42] John Carter also spoke, urging three core 'socialistic principles': ethically, the principle of each for all and all for each; politically, the concepts of Green's positive state; and, economically, the principle of co-operatice organisation. The conference, which Percy Dearmer and others of the CSU also addressed, almost unanimously approved the Union's resolution, and when, in 1910, a major Missionary Conference was held in Edinburgh, Gore and Talbot again argued a radical social commitment as a core element to the Church's mission. Here was a new departure. Christianising the heathen could no longer mean Europeanising them, but introducing the leaven of Christianity to work in the native dough. The old-established communions and Churches would have to work together unless they were to confound their best efforts and for fear of creating German, English, Scottish Churches in foreign climes rather than genuinely native Churches. It was from this combination of social teaching and interdenominational concern that the modern ecumenical movement sprang.

Meanwhile the Union was beginning to lose energy. Gore had devoted much of his spare capacity to defeating the Liberals' 1906 Education Act, a process which split the secularist socialists from the Christians over the same Cowper–Temple clause that had so exercised Headlam. In the end Gore's intervention in the House of Lords, allied with the work of Clifford and others, meant that a constitutional crisis was provoked over the Lords' refusal to pass the Commons' legislation.

The formation of the Church Socialist League in 1906 had syphoned off many of the Union's more radical members, and when others, such as Adderley, left in 1908, it felt as if the time had come to wind up or at least reorganise. In 1910 a major reorganisation was undertaken, and Gore handed over the reins to others immediately prior to being offered the diocese of Oxford. Almost simultaneously Holland moved to Oxford as a canon at Christ Church and Regius Professor of Divinity, and Talbot was translated to neighbouring Winchester. Gore's last episcopal charge was far from uncontroversial, however. In 1911 he supported the dispute at a large industrial works in Reading and, a year later, took the chair at a crowded meeting in support of women's suffrage. He also played a leading role in the development of the Interdenominational Conference of Social Service Unions and became the first President of its successor, the Council for Christian Witness on Social Questions, which in 1913 published a searing manifesto on the principle of the living wage, with especial reference to the miners. Later that year, in the debate over the disestablishment of the Church of Wales, Gore argued that the Church of England had 'not succeeded in becoming the Church of the poor as is the Roman Catholic Church in so many parts of Europe, or the Salvation Army, or Primitive Methodism'.[43]

The First World War, as we shall see in the following chapter, hit all Christian Socialists hard but none more so than the CSU, for whom it effectively dealt the final blow. By 1914 membership had already dropped significantly, and even Gore and Holland had expressed their desire for more direct political intervention.

When Holland died in 1918, just before the end of the war, it was inevitable that the Union would wither. Within a year it was wound up and subsumed, together with the Navvy Mission, into the Industrial Christian Fellowship, under the aegis of an army chaplain just returned from the war known as 'Woodbine Willie', Geoffrey Studdert Kennedy. Gore, aged sixty-six, soon resigned from the diocese of Oxford, and went to a semi-retirement at King's College, London, where he mixed teaching with preaching at Grosvenor Chapel. Allegedly he resigned over the Church's decision to make baptism rather than confirmation the condition for membership of the new church electoral rolls, but in January he wrote to William Temple, 'It is partly that Broad and High and Low and Conservative are all against me . . . Also I'd like to join the Labour Party.'[44] Gore died thirteen years later in 1932.

It has always been easy to be condescending about moderate organisations, and many of the Union's Christian Socialist successors have passed censorious judgments on its ambivalence, its donnishness and its air of extreme respectability. Certainly it is true that the Union was an overwhelmingly patrician affair, dominated by wealthy, landed clerics, well-entrenched in the establishment. And for all their commitment to the rise of Labour, none of the major protagonists of the Union had any real experience of the working masses.

Yet Holland, Gore, Talbot, Westcott and the rest did manage to sustain a lengthy period when the Church had no choice but to take the issue of socialism seriously, setting the scene for the dramatic advances that William Temple and others would be able to make in the 1920s. Indeed, they were so successful at capturing the mind of Anglicanism that when the Church of England set up a Committee on Social Issues in 1905 all five bishops were CSU members: Gore, Talbot, Percival (Hereford), Hoskyns (Southwell) and Harmer (Rochester). It comes as little surprise that the Committee's report argued that property was not absolute but held in trust and that a living wage was a basic Christian principle. What is surprising, considering the modern Bench of Bishops, is that the report was agreed without opposition by the House of Bishops. Even Randall Davidson, the Archbishop of Canterbury from 1903 to 1928, was a Christian Socialist-in-law, as his wife played a minor role in the Union. The Union also confronted, for the first time from a Christian perspective, imperialism and the role of industry in warmongering. Through the *Commonwealth* Holland in particular challenged the assumption that the Church of England had to be on the side of Conservatism and capital, reserving some of his wittiest prose for his attacks on the ethics of individualism:

> Life was for the adventurous, for the independent, for those who could launch out alone and tempt the dangerous flood. Everything conspired to invoke into play the vigour and daring of individual initiative. A man was asked to fling behind him the worn-out familiar customs of social activity, on which lay already the dust of earth, and to let himself go, out of sheer trust in his own soul, to discover what novel experiences might unfold their secrets under the conquering force of his own personal attack.[45]

Gore's enduring contribution lies, of course, not only in his Christian Socialism, nor even in his inauguration of the Community of the Resurrection, out of which was to spring the Church Socialist League, but in his immense theological and episcopal work, editing *Lux Mundi*, taking the Anglo-Catholic gospel out from behind its liturgical obsession and forming the diocese of Birmingham. After 1905 he too started to be frustrated with the political ambivalence of the CSU and became one of first Anglican bishops to become directly involved in industrial disputes.

Summing up the political and theological core of the Union's work is difficult, for so many of its members came with varying perspectives, but what united it above all was a perception that the social issues of the day, often referred to as the 'industrial question', had to be addressed by the Church, both because Christianity had a vital contribution to make and because otherwise the Church would remain a dwindling irrelevance. For many in the Church wages might seem a purely political matter, but for Holland, 'The market ought to recognise an adequate minimum ... It is vital that this should be seen to be the question at issue. It is human, moral "Christian" to ask for this. A Bishop might speak out on this.'[46] Besides, individualism was a denial of Christianity, for, again in Holland's words: 'There is no such thing as a solitary isolated person. A self-contained personality is a contradiction in terms ... Society is, simply, the expression of the social intercommunion of spirit with spirit which contributes what we mean by personality.'[47] In order to be truly persons humans, then, must recognise their relation to others, their dependence upon others and others' reliance upon them. Property was a human right but not an absolute one, for 'if it appears that the condition of property-holding ... sacrifice the many to the few ... there is no legitimate claim that property can make against the alteration of conditions by gradual and peaceable means.'[48] Redistribution, then, must be a condition of good govenment, for

> the success of a civilisation for us must be measured not by the amount and character of its products or material wealth, nor by the degree of well-being which it renders possible for a privileged class, but by the degree in which it enables all its members to feel that they have the chance of making the best of themselves.[49]

As for how socialist the CSU was, there are conflicting messages. Gore wrote in his appraisal of Holland that 'in the general sense of the term "socialist", in which socialism expresses the antithesis to the individualism of the *laissez-faire* policy, it could not escape the charge of socialism,'[50] and goes on to say, none the less that it never supported any 'particular platform of reconstructive politics'. Yet Gore and Holland took clear positions on a whole host of issues, and Gore and Talbot were instrumental in pushing twelve of the bishops through the Liberal Government's lobby in the 1909 budget debate, when the Government would have lost without them. Their support for trades unions and their concern for justice may not have led them to dialectical materialism, but then few socialists in Britain of the time were urging even collectivism beyond a vague understanding that in working collectively society could achieve more than as individuals.

Finally it would be impossible to assess the work of Gore, Holland and Talbot without acknowledging the overwhelming impression of their deep personal friendship. Each relied upon the other for advice and support, and in particular the two single clergy, Holland and Gore, embodied exactly what they preached, that 'A personality is what it is only by virtue of its power to transcend itself and to enter into the life of another . . . Its power of life is love.'[51]

# 5

# A New Jerusalem

One day, thou say'st, there will at last appear
The word, the order, which God meant should be.
– Ah! we shall know that well when it comes near;
The band will quit man's heart, he will breathe free.

Matthew Arnold, 'Revolutions'

Let every Christian, as much as in him lies, engage himself openly
and publicly, before all the World, in some mental pursuit for the
Building up of Jerusalem.

William Blake, 'Jerusalem'

On Saturday, 5 May 1906, in a disused Yorkshire quarry the fifty-
year-old Scottish Labour MP Keir Hardie addressed a large open-
air gathering of clergy and socialists on the subject of the Labour
Party's recent dramatic general-election successes and the basis of
his political credo. His speech was the highlight of a day-long
meeting called by two prominent members of the Community of
the Resurrection, Walter Frere and Paul Bull, at the Community
house at Mirfield. The ex-miner and stone-quarryman, in the
words of the *CR Quarterly*, 'notwithstanding his red tie, might
have been a Bishop speaking in the loftiest vein in his Cathedral.
Keir Hardie's Cathedral was our Quarry.' The striking image of
the bearded radical, by far the most famous working-class politician of his time, claiming the Sermon on the Mount and the Ten
Commandments as the basis for his political stance, and in a tone
evidently both impassioned and sincere, made many of those

present who had stood on the sidelines of political organisation see things afresh. Again the *CR Quarterly*: 'Churchmen went away with a new sense that even the political side of the new Social agitation is really after all one of the manifold ways in which God is working out His purposes.'[1]

So began a vital new episode in the life of Christian Socialism, which would take it dramatically away from the dilettantism of the Guild and the almost suffocating respectability of the Union.

For if there is one thing Keir Hardie was not, it is respectable, at least in the terms of Edwardian society. Born out of wedlock, sacked as a miner for agitation, a pacifist opposed to the Boer War, a supporter of the suffragettes, he even had the temerity to turn up for his first day as an MP in 1892 dressed in working clothes and a deerstalker rather than the more usual gentleman's attire of frock-coat and silk top hat. Within a year of his election he had further antagonised the establishment by questioning the fact that Parliament seemed more interested in the birth of a child to the Duchess of York than in the loss of 260 lives in the Albion Colliery explosion in Cilfynydd.

So the man who stood and addressed the clergy with such power in 1906 was a deeply controversial figure, but he was also the indubitable father of the Labour movement.

His upbringing in Lanarkshire, where he had been born in a one-room cottage in Legbrannock on 15 August 1856, had affected his politics most profoundly. By the age of seven he was at work at a bakery, where he gained his first experience of the hypocrisy of much that passed for Christianity. For he was sacked by the baker, a church-going 'pillar of the community', for turning up half an hour late for work on two subsequent days. His brother was dying, his mother Mary Keir was expecting a child and his odd-job man stepfather was away. Yet the young Keir's excuses did little to impress the baker, who summarily dismissed him and refused even to pay him for the week he had already worked.

Much of Hardie's early life, however, was spent down the mines, where he acquired both a sense of respect for those who laboured in abominable conditions where life was held cheap and a determination to improve his own, and others', lot. Hardie saw that the only hope of change lay through collaboration with others, and he set about trying to unionise the pit in Hamilton. Motivated equally by his sense of injustice and by his new-found Christian faith, to which he was converted in his teens, he was an earnest and resolute young man. He later ascribed his political energy to his faith: 'The impetus which drove me first of all into the Labour movement and the inspiration which has carried me on in it, has been derived more from the teachings of Jesus of Nazarath than all the other sources combined.'[2]

Unfortunately, his politics soon earned him, and his two half-brothers, the fate of many trade-union organisers of his time. In 1879 he was sacked and blacklisted by the pit managers, effectively depriving him of any chance of local work. Over the coming years he managed to patch together a living from occasional payments for articles for local papers and a small salary from some of the growing trades unions, but in essence he was unemployed and poor. His political affiliation during this time, as with many radicals of the period, was Liberal, although he was acutely critical of their *laissez-faire* belief in the market to rectify the exigencies of life. There was also, of course, a cutting edge to Hardie's politics. He believed that the hierarchies of the class system were wrong, that miners deserved to be represented not by landed gentry of another class but by their own kind. So when in 1888 a Liberal MP resigned his seat in Mid-Lanarkshire Hardie argued with the local party that, as the seat was a mining constituency, it should have a miner as its MP. The previous year he had stood as a National Labour Party candidate for the North Ayrshire seat and had lost. This time he was prepared to stand on the same ticket again or to be supported by the Liberals. They, however, in the shape of Sir George Trevelyan, tried to buy him off with the offer of another safe seat if he stood down. Hardie found the offer offensive, was hardened in his resolve to stand and came third.

By this time Hardie was clear, as were many of his colleagues around Clydeside, that the Liberal Party could not be a sufficient vehicle for the political change they sought. It was too wedded to the market and the establishment. So on 25 August 1888 the Scottish Parliamentary Labour Party was formed, in the Waterloo Rooms in Glasgow, with the express intention of seeking the return of working-class MPs to Parliament, bringing together the ex-Radical MP and Latin American traveller R.B. Cunninghame Graham as President and J. Shaw Maxwell as Chair. The title 'socialist' was eschewed as being too controversial, and Hardie, as the new Secretary, argued for an approach to parliamentary politics that was essentially evolutionary and moral, rather than ideological. In his book *From Serfdom to Socialism* he wrote, 'Socialism, like every other problem of life, is at bottom a question of ethics or morals. It has mainly to do with the relationships which should exist between a man and his fellows.'[3]

In the meantime, as we have already seen, the Labour Movement was gaining pace outside Scotland too. In 1881 Hyndman had founded the Democratic Foundation, which in 1884, soon after the Guild of St Matthew, adopted a clearly socialist agenda and changed its name to the Social Democratic Foundation (SDF). The Fabians had formed, and were beginning to articulate socialist ideas, although in the context of a class background very different from Hardie's, and in 1888 and 1889 significant Labour disputes in London and elsewhere transformed the 'New Model Unions' from the friendly-society role into clearly political bodies with a determined programme. What was lacking, as yet, was a parliamentary breakthrough.

In the general election of 1892, however, several candidates stood under a loose Independent Labour banner. Three were elected: John Burns in Battersea, who later joined the Liberals; Havelock Wilson in Middlesbrough, who was interested primarily in the seamen; and Hardie, who was elected for West Ham South in the East End of London, where the Liberals had decided not to put up a candidate. Hardie defeated the Conservative, Major Barnes, by 1,000 votes – 'the miner beating the Major', as the papers put it. Despite a summer election, Parliament was in recess until February 1893, so Hardie and others used the time constructively. On 12 and 13 January a special conference of sympathetic people was called in Bradford with the express intention of forming a new political party. Representatives from Scotland argued that the name should be the Socialist Labour Party, a view which was defeated in preference for Ben Tillett's suggestion of the Independent Labour Party. Policies were adopted: an eight-hour day, the abolition of piece-work and child labour, democratic change, provision for orphans and non-sectarian education. A committee was set up, with several of the old Guild of St Matthew and Christian Social Union members involved, including Moll. Soon Ramsay MacDonald, Philip Snowden and Tom McCarthy joined, and within a year Hardie had transformed the *Miner* into the *Labour Leader* and was editing it as the new mouthpiece of the party.

In effect Hardie was on his own in Parliament at this stage, and many of his contributions to debates left him even more isolated, yet he remained until the general election of 1895, when all the radicals, including the progressive Liberals, were routed. Hardie decided to devote all his efforts, as before, to an indefatigable, near-evangelical tour of the country while still editing the *Labour Leader*.

In 1900 the Trades Union Congress, which until now had remained unconvinced by the need for the new party, decided through its Parliamentary Committee to summon a meeting of co-operative and socialist organisations at the Memorial Hall in Farringdon Street on the edge of the City of London. The Fabians, the Social Democratic Foundation and the unions were well represented, as was the ILP, and it was agreed to establish 'a distinct Labour group in Parliament, who shall have their own whips and agree on their own policy'. To be called the Labour Representation Committee (LRC), the new executive took five out of twelve of its members from socialist societies and appointed Ramsay MacDonald as its Secretary, thereby stepping closer towards a socialist rather than a purely working-class agenda while still rejecting the SDF's campaign for an overtly socialist party.

In September 1900 the 'Khaki' election was fought over the Boer War. The LRC fought fifteen seats, and, through a complication over his nomination, Hardie stood in both Preston and Merthyr Tydfil. Fortunately, Merthyr's election was held the day after Preston's, and, having lost there, Hardie managed to get to the hustings and was elected the second of two MPs for the Welsh constituency, which he was to represent until his death in 1915. The following year the ILP had a further success when David Shackleton won a June by-election, to be joined a year later by another Christian Socialist, Arthur Henderson, who was elected for Barnard Castle. Hardie moved back to London, leaving his wife Lillie and their three children in Scotland while he engaged in the work of the House of Commons from his flat in Fleet Street.

In 1905 Hardie challenged the clergy in the *Labour Leader* to support the party in the impending general election, and many did, including Bull and Frere, who both spoke on platforms in favour of ILP candidates in Leeds and Dewsbury. In January, only ten years after the disastrous Conservative landslide of 1895, the unimaginable happened, with twenty-nine out of fifty LRC candidates joining twenty-two Lib/Lab MPs in the new House of Commons. The LRC was swiftly renamed the Labour Party, and Hardie elected its first Chairman and Leader of the party. He received a letter of congratulations from 165 clergy, including Holland and many of the CR.

Most early biographies of Hardie were hagiographies, referring to his prophetic energy, his moral steadfastness and his absolute determination to change society. Yet as a man he was lonely and often confessed to having few friends. He did not last long as Leader of the party because of his long absences from the House and his tendency to pursue his own issues rather than work with others, firing off at random and losing his colleagues' confidence. He disliked London and was described by the journalist A. G. Gardiner as 'the Knight of the Rueful Countenance'. His politics, of course, had been forged in a stern and unforgiving environment, under the oppressive regime of the pits and with the Calvinist theology of Victorian Presbyterianism. It comes therefore as

127

something of a surprise that he entered in 1906 into an affair with the twenty-two-year-old Sylvia Pankhurst which lasted for several years. Yet the energy with which he approached campaigning against unemployment, against unjust wages and poor working conditions and for women's suffrage all betoken a passionate man. A stern Old Testament prophet inspired by a biblical vision, who smoked too much, worked too late into the night, with little personal inclination to friendship, he was none the less an outstanding campaigner outside Parliament and an essential element in establishing the Labour Party's moral argument and electoral success.

The man who spoke in the quarry to a mixed group of clergy and local socialists was a renowned figure from a social and political world very different from the semi-aristocratic atmosphere of the CR. Yet within a few days Frere, Bull and another member of the Community, Samuel Healy, together with a range of other members of the Union and the Guild, had taken his challenge further and issued an invitation to a conference to be held at Morecambe on 13 June to consider the inauguration of a new Christian Socialist group. Conrad Noel later ascribed the impetus for the meeting to himself, W. E. Moll and Percy Widdrington, but, whoever was responsible, the important difference was that this was to be the first Christian Socialist group to consider itself politically aligned in the knowledge that there was significant Labour representation in Parliament.

The Church Socialist League (CSL) was founded at Morecambe, yet again as an Anglican organisation, with much of its membership focused in the north, where the ILP and now the Labour Party was strongest. An executive was set up comprising Lewis Donaldson; Algernon West, who chaired the Morecambe conference and was the CSL's first President till 1909; Moll; Bull; R. S. Greane of Workington; and J. S. Harold Hastings of Halton as General Secretary. The tenor of the League was clearly northern and socialist. West told the Church Congress later that same year, 'The League stands for economic socialism. It exists to further the socialism of the ILP and SDF among Churchmen.'[4] It was also to be more radical than the Union, whom Ruth Kenyon had caricatured in 1904 as 'a mere bread-and-butter, gas-and-water movement; a socialism sans doctrines, or rather perhaps a socialism depending upon the remains of its old doctrines to work out their practical corollaries'.[5] Noel wrote in his autobiography of the CSL's socialism,

> Its basis was the belief that the Catholic Faith, as held and taught by the Church of England, finds its expression and application on the economic side in a Christian Socialism, which is not, as some appear to think, a particular variety of Socialism, milder than the secular brand, but economic Socialism come to by the road of the Christian faith and inspired by the ideas of the Gospel.[6]

Indeed, the formal aims of the League take it closer to the language of party politics than any other of the Christian Socialist movements:

> The Church Socialist League consists of Church people who accept the principles of socialism, viz.: The political, economic and social emancipation of the whole people, men and women, by the establishment of a democratic commonwealth in which the community shall own the land and capital collectively and use them for the good of all.[7]

This was stronger fare, certainly, than the nascent Labour Party could stomach until it adopted its reformed constitution in 1918.

At the same time Free Church ministers, like the Congregationalist R. J. Campbell, were welcoming socialism with arms open as for the Messiah: 'The practical end which alone could justify the existence of the Churches is the realisation of the Kingdom of God, which only means the reconstruction of society on a basis of mutual helpfulness instead of strife and competition.'[8] Mirfield held a second conference that April, with a large number of women present, including Emmeline Pankhurst, whose suffragette movement both Bull and Healy supported. Resolutions were passed on unemployment, the minimum wage and working conditions, all of which were denounced in both the secular and the religious press. Bull also set about writing and editing a lengthy series of 'Manuals', which were in effect Christian Socialist tracts, articulating a belief in humanity's social nature 'When Jesus Christ, the son of God, became Incarnate and was made man, he did not write a book. He founded a Society'; a sense of God's involvement in all of life, 'God is not shut up in a Church. He is in the home and school, the office and workshop, the mine and factory and mill'; and the need for radical change. 'The economics of the last century taught that social life can only be based on self-interest. Christ teaches that it can only be based on self-sacrifice.'[9]

For all its radical commitment to the working classes, however, the League could barely be considered a working-class movement. Its Organising Secretary, certainly, was far from working-class. Conrad le Dispenser Roden Noel (1869–1942) was, in fact, the grandson of a lady-in-waiting to Queen Victoria, Lady Gainsborough, and was born in a royal grace-and-favour house because his father was a Groom of the Privy Chamber. After a very inauspicious academic start, being sent down from Corpus Christi College, Cambridge, for heavy drinking, he went to Chichester Theological College and worked in Portsmouth with the ritualist Father Dolling. The Bishop of Exeter then refused to ordain him because of his 'pantheism' and his extreme Catholic practices, which were still illegal according to canon law. He then moved to London, to live just off the South Lambeth Road, where he met both Percy Dearmer and 'Brother Bob' Morris, the vicar of St Ann's, Vauxhall. By now a convinced socialist, he was ordained in 1894, in the same year as his marriage, which was celebrated by Dearmer. After another period of unemployment, when even Bishop Westcott refused to ordain him because of his high-church practices, Gore managed to land him a job at St Philip's, Salford. By the time of the Boer War he was working as Moll's curate in

Newcastle, where he preached a notable sermon against war, despite the fact that a large proportion of the congregation were munitions workers. One of them complained to Moll, threatening to blow the church up unless Noel's preaching was forbidden. Moll told Noel, 'by all means let it go on as it is the truth, and if we lose our church, which is the ugliest structure in Newcastle, we can build a new one with the insurance money.'[10] Meanwhile, having been a member of both the Guild and the Union, he had developed relations with nearly every notable Christian Socialist, and most of the secular socialists in the land, so that his appointment as Organising Secretary for the new League seemed fortuitous.

Noel did not stay long at St Philip's, however, and spent a further four years as a form of clerical nomad, working in Boulogne and Paddington Green before deciding to settle at one of his family's houses, Paycockes in Essex, now owned by the National Trust, where he set about writing the first real history of Christian Socialism, *Socialism in Church History*.

In the year that the book appeared, 1910, he was offered, miracle of miracles, a living by Lady Warwick, who had been converted to socialism in 1895, when a costume ball she had held at Warwick Castle had been criticised for its lavishness in Robert Blatchford's radical newspaper *Clarion*. She had stormed into his office to demand the meaning of this affront and had left a convinced socialist, who wrote to one of her friends, 'Socialism is the one religion that unites the human race all over the world, in the common cause of Humanity, and it is very, very wonderful, and it is growing as mushrooms grow, and nothing can stem the tide.'[11] In January 1910 she held a large gathering of the CSL at Warwick Castle, with Arnold Pinchard, the vicar of St Jude's, Birmingham, who had spent several years working in Latin America, Widdrington, Dearmer and Noel all speaking over the course of the two days. During the meeting Dearmer confided to Noel that he was on the verge of giving up his work as Secretary of the CSU so as to join the League, and within a few weeks Lady Warwick offered Noel the vacant living of Thaxted in Essex, of which, through the arcane hereditary system of the Church of England which Noel much deplored, she was patron.

So began a passage of thirty-two years when Noel had the luxury, for a radical, of a safe clerical seat.

In 1906, however, Noel was at the very heart of the League. Like the Union before it, it grew fast, absorbing many of the Guild's and the Union's more radical members. Its theological position was deliberately broad, as it was resolved that, in contrast to the Guild, the League would 'not risk the rejection of its socialist propaganda by announcing on other points ... indifferent to socialism and controverted among good socialists – a deliberate dig at Headlam's support for Oscar Wilde. By 1909 it had 1,000 members, with branches throughout the north and in Bristol, Leicester and London. During Noel's various stays in London he had come to know G. K. Chesterton, whose brother Cecil he had prepared for confirmation, the poet Francis Thompson and the artists Augustus John and William Orpen, so when in 1909 the *Optimist* was taken over by the League and renamed the *Church Socialist Quarterly* it had a ready set of writers, several of whom had already made a name for themselves in other fields.

All was not plain sailing, though. For a rift steadily began to widen within the CSL between those who wanted to see a direct identification of the League with the budding Labour Party and those who wanted to maintain a more distinctly theological line. West, as President, proposed at the annual conference in 1909 that there should be three core principles to Church Socialism, 'adaptation, assimilation and permeation', and argued for affiliation to the Labour Party, despite the fact that he would prefer it to proclaim itself more clearly 'a purely Socialist Party'.

Some of the scepticism about the Labour Party related to the specific instance of the Victor Grayson affair. Grayson had been elected as an SDF MP for Colne Valley in July 1907, with some support from the Churches, including a local curate and various League members. Grayson was a dramatic figure and soon gained a reputation for fiery speeches and impassioned pleas. Indeed, when Labour's Right to Work Bill was defeated by two to one Grayson was incensed and, at successive meetings of the House of Commons, insisted on raising the issue of employment. When finally he lost his temper and was ordered from the Chamber by the Speaker, calling the Commons 'a House of murderers', he did not spare the Labour Members his scorn. They in turn decided to vote for his expulsion. Lenin, who was in London in 1907, referred to Grayson as a 'fiery Socialist, without any principles and given to mere phrases', and Hardie had little regard for him because of Grayson's unhidden disdain for his puritanical attitude to politics. Later history, following Grayson's losing his seat in the 1910 election, his heavy drinking and his complicated sexual infelicities, does not endear him to modern readers. Yet many socialists in 1908 retained a suspicion that Labour had failed to support one of its own, and many League members, especially those who had been involved in his election campaign, were sceptical of the party's radical credentials. Certainly it is important to remember that even at this stage few Labour politicians had read Marx or had an advanced theory of capital, and many had learnt their oratorical skills in Methodist chapels rather than at universities and had acquired their passion for social justice from the works of Isaiah and Amos rather than Engels. As Arthur Henderson put it, describing the new Labour intake in 1906, most MPs owed more to the Bible than to Marx. While this might have bound Labour and the League more closely, in fact it left many Church Socialists more certain of their political agenda than many in Parliament. Further reluctance undoubtedly stemmed from the different social backgrounds of the League. So that while the message might sound the same, typical members of the parliamentary party and the League were so different in style that a real identification was always going to be unlikely.

A typical member of the parliamentary party was the disabled MP Philip Snowden, who was first elected in 1906. The son of a Methodist weaver, born in 1864, he rose to the rank of Chancellor of the Exchequer in both 1924 and 1929–31, yet much of his political basis, as expressed in his work in the CSL, the Free

Church Socialist League and the League of Progressive Religious and Social Thought, for whose magazine *Christian Commonwealth* he wrote, was straight theology. 'Personal Salvation and Social Salvation,' he argued, 'are like two palm trees which bear no fruit unless they grow side by side.'[12] In 1903 Snowden, whose wife Ethel was the local Sunday school teacher, published under the ILP's aegis a direct appeal to Nonconformists, *The Christ that is to be*. For Snowden Christ was 'the greatest influence in the world's history' and differed 'in degree but not in kind from all great teachers'. The religion of the future would be a 'political religion . . . which will seek to realise its ideal in our industrial and social affairs by the application and use of political methods.'[13] Snowden ends with the language of the Chapel: 'the only way to regain the earthly paradise is by the old, hard road to Calvary – through persecution, through poverty, through temptation, by the agony and bloody sweat, by the crown of thorns, by the agonising death. And then the resurrection to the New Humanity – purified by suffering, triumphant through Sacrifice.'[14]

The League, by contrast, was typified by one of its most effective slogan-writers, the Honourable and Revd Jimmy Adderley, who had also been a member of both the Guild and the Union. As the younger son of the first Baron Norton, a celebrated Gladstonian Liberal who had worked in penal reform, he was born in 1861 and was originally brought into the Christian Socialist circle through his membership of Headlam's Church and Stage Guild. The 1883 Congregationalist pamphlet *The Bitter Cry of Outcast London* had dramatically affected him, and from 1885 he spent his working life in the slums, first at the Christ Church Mission in Poplar and then as vicar of Saltley in Birmingham. A successful novelist in his spare time (*Stephen Remarx*, 1893), he had a keen eye for a religious caricature and a hard economic point: 'True, Lord, I denied myself nothing for Thee . . . I did not feed Thee when hungry; political economy forbad it: but I increased the labour market with the manufacture of my luxuries.'[15]

Labour and the CSL spoke a similar language, then, but the apparent social and political differences between them meant that it is hardly surprising that direct support was as often as not reluctant. Furthermore until Arthur Henderson's reforms in 1918 it was impossible to be an individual member of the party, and it was only through affiliation that CSL members could have become Labour Party members unless they were elected to Parliament. Formal affiliation would have committed all of the CSL to the party.

So, despite Moll's membership of the ILP administrative committee for several years, the tack that Percy Widdrington and Arnold Pinchard took at the 1909 League Annual conference was to oppose affiliation to the Labour Party in the belief that the role of the League must lie in developing a 'Christian sociology' rather than make all its members subscribe to the party. West lost the vote, and resigned as President, to be replaced by Pinchard with, strangely enough, George Lansbury, who was later to be Leader of the Labour Party, as Vice-President. Pinchard wrote in the subsequent edition of the *Church Socialist Quarterly*, 'We are a society of Socialists of various shades of Socialist opinion, and our common platform is not that of the ILP of the SDF but that of the Church of God. Our business is to convert Churchmen and make them Socialists, but the particular tint which may colour their Socialism is no concern of the League.'[16] West's original intention at the inception of the League was thus effectively overturned.

Consistent with Pinchard's position, the League decided not to support any particular party in the two general elections of 1910 and instead urged people to vote for candidates who would abolish the hereditary principle in all legislation; democratise the House of Commons by extending suffrage to women; abolish taxes on food; establish a National Labour Department to organise industry; introduce a minimum wage and forty-eight hour week; and raise the school-leaving age to sixteen.

All of this, of course, was tantamount to supporting the Labour Party, and just as the 1907 by-election at Jarrow had seen many League members in the north rallying to the support of the ILP candidate Pete Curran, many others, including Donaldson, Egerton Swann and Healy, worked hard for Lansbury in his two campaigns for Bow and Bromley. At the second attempt the Vice-Chair of the League was elected MP.

George Lansbury was born the son of an itinerant navvy when the man was working on a job in a toll house in Suffolk on 21 February 1859. Both his parents drank heavily, and his early life was unstable, to say the least. By the age of nine, however, his family had settled in the East End of London, and by eleven he was working at a coal merchant's. After briefly running away from home to Herefordshire, where he worked (most ironically for the subsequent teetotaller) in a public house, he returned to London and to school at St Mary's, Whitechapel, where he acquired a reputation as an agitator, campaigning for extra playtime for his colleagues. At the age of fourteen, however, he left school to work with his father and brother James, unloading coal from trains and barges, a job he retained when he took over the contract on his father's death two years later.

Very soon afterwards he came into contact with the vicar of Whitechapel, Fenwick Kitto, who prepared him for confirmation and involved him in running breakfasts for tramps and the Sunday school. It was there that he met Bessie Brine, whom he married in 1880 after a debilitating and impoverishing period of illness. In 1884 George and Bessie, together with their three children and his two younger brothers, whom they had adopted when Lansbury's mother died, decided to emigrate to Australia and set sail on the *Duke of Devonshire*. After a disastrous year in Brisbane, where employment was very hard to find, the family decided to return to England.

Whether anger at the emigration authorities' raising of false expectations or the experience of grinding poverty in Australia most kindled Lansbury's political fire is uncertain. What is clear, however, is that on his return he immediately engaged himself in politics, organising demonstrations against emigration and acting as agent for the Liberal MP Samuel Montagu in the 1886 election.

Montagu was a progressive Liberal who supported an eight-hour day, and Lansbury, like Hardie, was content to work for change within the Liberal Party from its progressive wing. His connections with the SDF and local trades unions, however, was much stronger than Montagu's, and he started to feel increasingly ill at ease with the Liberals' mixture of good works and unabated industrialism. When he finally broke with Montagu he described his socialism in terms that could no longer fit with Liberal philanthropy: 'We do not believe in rich and poor and charity. We want to create wealth and all the means of life and share them equally among the people.'[17] Montagu's response was to offer him £5 a week until a safe seat could be found for him, at which Lansbury took immediate offence and decided to leave the Liberals for the SDF, setting up a Bow and Bromley branch and standing throughout the 1890s on their ticket.

The SDF was to be Lansbury's political home, however, only through to 1903, when he split with Hyndman over the latter's insistence that only violent revolution would bring about the radical transformation that Britain needed. Lansbury, by contrast, had always been a pacifist with a radical but far more evolutionary creed. So in 1903 he stood for, and was elected to, the Poplar Metropolitan Borough Council under the much broader LRC banner.

Already Lansbury's connection between his politics and his faith was clearly set. Of his socialism he wrote, 'I am a socialist pure and simple . . . I have come to believe that the motive power which should and which *will*, if men allow it, work our social salvation is the power which will come from a belief in Christ and His message to men.'[18] Furthermore, political life was to be about service not self-interest:

> go back to the lonely Nazarene, learn of Him and, learning, understand that wealth and power, majesty and glory are no worth, that no lasting happiness comes from great possessions, but instead that today, yesterday and forever the only gospel whereby man can be saved from the power of evil is contained in the words, 'He who would be the greatest

among you must be the servant of all' – and not the servant in order to rule but to serve.[19]

Lansbury's concerns were wide-ranging: the conditions of the poor, education, Home Rule for Ireland and India, votes for women – all these national issues he campaigned on. Yet perhaps the most significant aspect of his political career is the fact that he never lost an intensely local, even parochial, edge to his politics.

A classic instance of this is his work as a Poor Law Guardian. The Poor Law, which was only finally abolished after the Second World War, stemmed from the Elizabethan Relief Act of 1601 and had been adapted by the Poor Law Amendment Act of 1834. In broad outline it provided a national network of workhouses where the destitute could live and work, segregated by gender and often subjected to extremely harsh 'corrective' regimes. There was a national body, the Local Government Board, and locally elected Boards of Governors who ran the local institutions. These were the Guardians who, at least in theory, were prevented from providing relief to any except those who declared themselves destitute and were therefore housed in the workhouse. In practice a few of the more socially concerned Boards saw the wisdom of providing 'out-relief' to poorer families in the parish, thereby preventing them from having to go to the workhouse.

In 1892, now working in his father-in-law's woodyard, Lansbury was elected for the first time and slowly and painstakingly set about reform of the local workhouse with his fellow Guardian and friend Will Crooks. In the face of considerable opposition they tackled corruption among the officials, rat droppings in the food, the segregation of parents and children and, most important, the provision of 'out-relief'. At the same time as engaging with the system as it was, however, Lansbury campaigned for an end to the Poor Law itself because, rather than relieving poverty, it exacerbated it, forcing the poor to a point of complete destitution. He served in 1909 on a Royal Commission that produced a minority report in favour of abolition, which he publicised assiduously, together with one of its co-authors, Beatrice Webb.

In 1911 he published *Smash the Workhouse* and argued again and again, with genuine practical insight, for real local-government powers to tackle poverty.

At the same time Lansbury took a significant role in the CSL. At the first meeting he was elected Vice-President and then President, doubtless helped to prominence by the fact that he, unlike nearly all the other members of the executive, was a layman. When he was finally elected to Parliament in 1910, he instantly took his place as one of the leading Labour figures. In 1912 he organised and led a special march to see the Archbishop of Canterbury at Lambeth Palace to complain about the drastic effects of unemployment. His parliamentary career, however, was a stormy one. For that same year he lost his temper in a Commons debate when the Prime Minister, Herbert Asquith, was questioned about the imprisonment and alleged torture of several of the most prominent suffragettes, many of whom were close friends of the Lansburys. He was reprimanded by the Speaker, and briefly suspended, but in his fury at the Government's response he decided to resign his seat so as to stand again on a single-issue manifesto of votes for women. Brave and courageous it may have seemed at the time, but Lansbury afterwards regretted it, not only because he lost his seat and only regained it ten years later but also because he realised that he had succumbed to the worst form of gesture politics.

Curiously for one who cared so deeply about international issues, Lansbury's political work was confined throughout the First World War to the Poplar Guardians, the CSL and the pages of the *Herald*. When Britain declared war on Germany on 14 August 1914 the League, like most Christian Socialist organisations, found it difficult to agree over the issue of war itself, let alone this war. At the Coventry annual conference Lansbury, Dick Sheppard, who was then vicar of St Martin-in-the-Fields, and Mary Phelps, who was later editor of the *Church Socialist*, spoke forcefully for a pacifist position, rejecting the whole concept of a just war. Lansbury wrote with sadness in his autobiography:

'Then came the War, and Church Socialists became as divided as materialist Socialists. Our God of the human race became . . . the God of the British.'[20] Others, including Noel, felt that war could be justifiable and, indeed, on this occasion, was the only way forward. In a derisive note in his autobiography, he commented, 'Many of its [CSL] members, too, were pacifists, and it is impossible for activists and pacifists to work together in the same body.'[21] Egerton Swann, by contrast, nurtured a fairly extreme hatred for the Germans, while Maurice Reckitt, a new member of the League who was later to play a vital role in chronicling Christian Socialism, felt that the war was the only way to preserve social democracy. Bull, who had served in the Boer War, took by far the most militaristic line, with a book entitled *Our Duty at Home in Time of War* which rivalled Kingsley in its support for the British troops. His colleague at Mirfield, J. Neville Figgis, wrote, 'I believe that at this moment no man is more truly working for the cause of God in the world than the soldier in the trenches.'[22]

Outside the League, Holland, now at Oxford, was as much opposed to the war as Lansbury, writing at the outbreak of hostilities, 'I will not allow that all the weary idiots have been right. My one comfort now is to remember that I never insisted on war as inevitable, never shouted Armaments . . . It is just this which I denounce in the Germans. By talking like this they have made war inevitable.'[23] Gore, now Bishop of Oxford, similarly wrote a courageous pastoral letter to his diocese in 1914, saying, 'Truly war is not a Christian weapon . . . Nevertheless there are circumstances when the safety of our own country and our obligations to sister countries compel us to go to war.' He concluded, in the face of the intense jingoism of Kitchener's campaign, 'The Bible is full of patriotic emotion; but even more conspicuously the Bible is full of a great warning against the sufficiency of patriotism.[24]

Yet the greatest heart to break over the war was that of Hardie, who was still MP for Merthyr Tydfil but had handed over the leadership of the party to Ramsay MacDonald in 1907. Devastated by the war, he found it impossible that working men could raise arms against other working men and argued in Parliament that Britain should have remained neutral. In September 1915 he died while the battles were still raging.

The effect of the war on Christian Socialism cannot be underestimated. Not only did the pacifist witness that ascribed the full horrors of war to rampant imperialist capitalism take its first true hold on the political imagination of the Christian left, but it also shot to pieces the overwhelming optimism that characters like Holland and Gore had brought to their interpretation of the rise of socialism. It also put an effective end to the Church Socialist League, for by the end of the war Noel, who had handed over the role of Organising Secretary to Donaldson's curate at Leicester, Claude Stuart Smith, had left the League in 1916, together with some of its more radical members, to found the more theologically precise Catholic Crusade in 1918.

To give it its full title, the Catholic Crusade of the Servants of the Precious Blood to transform the Kingdom of this World into the Commonwealth of God; the Crusade was never intended to be a popular movement and, indeed, at its peak had a membership of only 200 loyal adherents. It was founded at a small meeting of twelve at Thaxted, on the anniversary of the Chartist rally at Kennington, on 10 April 1918. Focused very narrowly on a particular Anglo-Catholic sacramental theology, it inherited much of the maverick character of its founder, who in turn seemed to style himself in part on Stewart Headlam, although he dismissed him as 'more valuable as a theologian writing on behalf of social justice than as a politician under the influence of the land reformers'.[25]

The Crusade's distinctiveness, however, lay in its strongly apocalyptic tone. Others, of course, were ready to interpret events as evidence of the end of time, but Noel in particular took an almost anarchist attitude to the political endeavour. The role of the Crusade was 'to shatter the British Empire and all Empires to bits', and the Church was 'the organ of the Coming Age, the nucleus of the universal Kingdom wherein dwelleth righteousness, the midwife of a new world in the pangs of birth'.[26] It seems appropriate that the Catholic Crusade was the first socialist organisation to welcome the Russian Revolution.

Noel's theology was undoubtedly extreme, yet it retains a fascination, not least because of the dramatic combination he achieved in his parish life in the depths of rural Essex. Thaxted rapidly became a centre of high-church worship with a radical political edge. Both the international red flag of socialism and the green flag of Sinn Fein were flown from the church tower. The old private box-pews were dispensed with. Morris dancing and carolling became central parts of church life, and the choir was transformed with the help of Gustav Holst, who lived in the parish. Shrines to the martyrs of the people, John Ball and Thomas à Beckett were set up and prayers offered for the conversion of the Bishop of Chelmsford to the true faith. Regular processions through the village were held to commemorate Beckett or Corpus Christi. Like Headlam, Noel saw the sacraments as pointers to Heaven and argued that all the rest of creation was an 'effectual sign of the presence of God who prevents and follows and enfolds us, as the waters cover the sea'.[27]

Yet Noel was a controversial figure. He could be waspish and unforgiving, and was prone to exaggerate his opponents' folly. His critique of the industrial era also smacks somewhat of a snobbish distaste for manual labour, harking back to a golden age of craftsmen. His politics veered dramatically from near-anarchism to extreme communism. Yet his legacy is perhaps more secure than that of most. After his thirty-two years at Thaxted he was succeeded by his assistant Jack Putterill, another Christian Socialist, and much of the beauty he tried to evince from the church still survives, not least because he was perhaps the first great priest to realise that you enhance the beauty of most churches by taking things out rather than putting things in. He died in 1942, after nearly twenty years of diabetes and several years of blindness.

*

Noel's split with the League had been founded on a conviction that a clearly enunciated Catholic theology was the key to lasting socialism. Yet the inauguration of the Catholic Crusade had hardly presented a serious challenge to the viability of the League. Two other splits were to prove far more significant, and both focused on the complicated figure of Percy Elborough Tinling Widdrington.

Widdrington had been born on 5 June 1873, the eldest son of a customs inspector at Southampton. After being educated by a mixture of private tutors and Glasgow Academy, he spent three years working in a merchant bank in the City, which he later described in semi-purgatorial terms. In 1893, already a member of the GSM, he decided to study for ordination, starting at St Edmund Hall in Oxford and experiencing, along with Frank Weston, the then Chair of the Oxford GSM, some of the open hostility to socialism that many undergraduates were happy to vent.

In the noble tradition of Headlam, Widdrington's main interests were not academic – he joined the Fabians in 1895 – and when he was sent down for two terms he spent all his energies on Ramsay MacDonald's by-election campaign in Southampton, where he met the already well-known Enid Stacey.

In 1896 he spent some time studying with another of the veteran Christian Socialists, Charles Marson, at Hambridge and, the following year, secured a job as curate to Moll at St Philip's in Newcastle, where Noel was to arrive a year later. By then he and Enid had married, and Enid was becoming ever more involved in the Labour movement and the campaign for women's votes. One of the churchwardens, indeed, who also happened to be the chief clerk of the Elswick works, complained vociferously to Moll about his curate's sharing a platform with Hardie and Enid in support of the local engineers, whom he had recently locked out. Moll, of course, was as impervious to such hectoring as he was to complaints about Noel's preaching and had little problem with Enid's going off to America on a suffragette tour or to Barnard Castle, where she campaigned for Henderson despite her misgivings about his views on women.

By 1903 Enid had established a substantial reputation: she was well known among all the Labour leaders in Britain and the United States. She was still young, but after a lengthy tour of the USA she had to take a week's rest on developing a thrombosis, which was at first incorrectly diagnosed. When she got up the following Monday morning the thrombosis became an aneurism and Enid died swiftly. Widdrington was devastated but within months had moved on to a new parish at Halton, where another of the founding members of the League, Harold Hastings, had taken on his family's living. It was from Halton that both Widdrington and Hastings travelled to the Morecambe meeting in 1906.

Although all his theological formation had been at the feet of the leading lights of the League, Widdrington was never quite happy with it. At the first meeting he moved an amendment to its 'Basis', which was rejected, and his dissatisfaction with its aims remained unaltered until well into the 1920s. 'I had a feeling,' he wrote, 'the most important purpose of a Church Socialist League was to elaborate a Christian approach to the problems of the new era. So I ventured to plead for the inclusion in the Basis of "the adumbration of a Christian sociology".'[28] Furthermore, from the outset Widdrington was concerned about the effortless superiority of Donaldson's complete identification of Christianity with socialism, at a time when socialism was still a term of 'considerable vagueness'.

By the time of the war Widdrington was rector of St Peter's, Coventry, and worried that the League was 'perilously near to becoming a political society'. Indeed, in 1916 he proposed a resolution at the September special conference of the League establishing it as a 'religious' rather than a 'political' society. Fr Bedale, of the Society of the Sacred Mission at Kelham, was keen to go further in focusing the League's efforts on the ecclesiastical rather than the political arena, and it was the subsequent row with Noel that led in part to his departure from the League. Widdrington himself, however, attributed the eventual transformation of the CSL into a religious movement to its discussion of Guild Socialism.

144

In 1912 the Roman Catholic Liberal MP Hilaire Belloc published *The Servile State*, in which he criticised what he saw as the increasing move within socialism towards collectivist solutions, 'putting the means of production into the hands of the *politicians* to hold in trust for the community'. Instead he sought a 'Distributive State', which would be more equitable in its allocation of resources but would still retain the concept of private property. In 1907 he had entered into a lengthy correspondence with G. K. Chesterton, H. G. Wells and Bernard Shaw on the virtues of socialism, when Chesterton had supported him in his concern that 'socialism will be imposed on [the working classes] by a handful of decorative artists and Oxford dons and journalists and countesses on the spree'. Shaw and Wells had challenged Belloc to come up with something better than the 'Utopias' they so much criticised, and distributivism was Belloc's somewhat delayed answer.

Similar worries were expressed by Widdrington, writing in November 1912 in the new *Church Socialist*. 'What I see coming, unless the working class rouse themselves, is State Capitalism and the Servile State, not Democracy, which has been defined as "that form of social organisation which tends to develop to the maximum the conscience and responsibility of the individual".'[29]

Some time earlier Arthur Penty, a Christian member of the ILP, the Fabians and the CSL and one of the prime movers and designers of the Garden City Movement, had published *The Restoration of the Gild System* in 1906 in support of a highly medievalist return to handicraft industry. Clearly owing something to the whole Arts and Crafts movement and, in particular, the aesthetic aspect of William Morris's work, Penty lay somewhat ignored until this growing concern within the League about economic collectivism came to the fore. S. G. Hobson, a one-time Quaker, alighted on Penty's ideas and, through the pages of *New Age*, introduced his concept of Guild Socialism in October 1912.

In February 1913 the editor of the *Church Socialist*, a young wealthy member of the League and close ally of Widdrington, Maurice B. Reckitt, picked up these concerns in an article in the magazine entitled 'The Future of the Socialist Ideal', thereby introducing the CSL to Guild Socialism. Widdrington later wrote, 'I date the movement within the League away from party politics towards an endeavour to rediscover a Christian Sociology to the time when Guild Socialism began to be discussed in the CSL and in our branches.'[30]

The major proponent of Guild Socialism, however, and its most original thinker, was another member of the CR at Mirfield, J. Neville Figgis. Figgis's father had been a prominent Nonconformist minister, and after studying mathematics and history at St Catherine's College, Cambridge, he had trained for ordination at Wells Theological College. Ordained in 1894, he returned to Cambridge and then spent five years as vicar of Marnhull in Dorset. In 1907 he saw one of Shaw's plays and came out determined to go to Mirfield. He wrote, 'I am going to Mirfield because I have more and more come to see that if we want people to think we are sincere in Christianity, it is desirable to live so that you ... appear to *mean* it i.e. a life of poverty.'[31] Figgis's politics were far from party-aligned. He believed that neither socialism nor individualism found warrant in the Gospel, and was never a member of the CSL, yet he was an avowed trade-union supporter, believing the movement expressed the essential Christian ideal of brotherhood. Certainly the Church must take an interest in politics, and in some sense side with the poor, because she 'ought to do the deepest penance for her share in producing the existing relations between the fortunate classes and the disinherited; and also for the widespread opinion, which must have some foundation, that she represents the cause rather of the rich than of the poor'.[32]

Yet Figgis was more a philosopher with a keen interest in the concept of community than a politician. The State was significant only in so far as it enabled community, for 'the real question of freedom in our day is the freedom of smaller unions to live within the whole'.[33] The ideal for society was a series of groups 'all having some of the qualities of public law, and most of them showing clear signs of a life of their own, inherent and not derived from the concessions of the State'.[34] In his *Churches in the Modern*

*State* he argued: 'The State did not create the family, nor did it create the churches, nor even in any real sense can it be said to have created the club or the trades unions, not, in the Middle Ages, the guild or the religious order, hardly even the universities; they have all arisen out of the natural associative instinct of mankind.'[35]

Figgis's work chimed perfectly with that of the secular Guild Socialists, who in 1915 set up the National Guilds League, arguing not for State ownership but for national guilds, which, based on trades unions, would take control of every industry. Many of the CSL joined and played an influential role, including Reckitt and Widdrington, thereby reinforcing the ideological rift between those who saw socialism as extending the role of the State and those who feared State socialism as potentially despotic or overly bureaucratic.

Figgis's contribution was rightly recognised as significant by many in the Labour movement, including R. H. Tawney. In some ways it provided a vital antidote to the over-identification of socialism with a centralising collectivism and an apparent disregard for personal responsibility. Figgis himself, however, was not a fortunate man. His manuscript for *Civilisation at the Crossroads* went down with the *Titanic*, and in 1919, after many prolonged bouts of depression, he was admitted to a psychiatric hospital, where he died. Few Church histories of the twentieth century even mention him, yet much of his work on community prefigures the work of MacMurray and Tawney and is of particular interest in an era when the role of the State is being questioned as much by socialists as by Conservatives.

Guild Socialism did not last long. Much of its influence had been played out by the time of the 1924 Labour Government, and it is difficult to assess whether it exemplified a simple lack of nerve about 'true socialism' or a valuable attempt to define an ethical socialism without a State that demanded servility of its citizens. Undoubtedly many of its core ideas relied on an exaggerated respect for the Middle Ages, and the national guilds would have been little different from nationalised industries in the hands of trades unions, but the core concepts of associative communities building together, under an enabling State, into the co-operative society still has much to recommend it.

In its time, however, Guild Socialism dealt a significant blow to the CSL. With Noel taking many of the most decisively Anglo-Catholic economic socialists with him at the same time as the Labour Party was adopting its new constitution and declaring itself for 'the common ownership of the means of production, distribution and exchange', and Widdrington, Bull and Reckitt moving in the direction of Guild Socialism, there was little common ground for Church Socialism.

Widdrington's work in the League had not been limited to Guild Socialism, however. With the end of the war he had moved parish again, to Great Easton where Lady Warwick had offered him the neighbouring living to Noel's, and where he was to remain as vicar for thirty-seven years. Though he expressed concern at the overtly political nature of the League, he was little concerned about supporting Labour candidates himself, running the 1919 campaign for William Lash from the rectory. Yet through the 1920s Widdrington steadily withdrew from the Labour Party, no longer convinced by its leaders, who, he felt, 'still live on the catch words of a rather sentimental Socialism'.[36]

In 1919 Widdrington returned to the core aim he had argued for at the first meeting of the CSL, to establish a 'Christian sociology'. Just as the CSU was becoming the Industrial Christian Fellowship, Widdrington, together with Reckitt and Harold Buxton, organised a series of summer schools at the same Paycocke's House in Essex where Noel had stayed in 1910. Noel attended, as did several of the League's members, including Lionel Thornton of the CR, who wrote the school up for the September *Church Socialist*. Clearly a hard core of League members felt that 'a new venture is needed'[37] and Thornton promised a book of essays to address their concerns. The book did not, in fact, arrive until 1922, when *The Return of Christendom* was published with a rather non-commital introduction by Gore and an epilogue by

G. K. Chesterton after two further summer schools had been held at Paycocke's. The contributors, including Penty, Bull, Thornton and Henry Slesser, were, in Gore's words, to be thought of as socialists only in the most general sense, in that 'they are all at one in believing that no stable or healthy industrial or social fabric can be built upon the assertion of Individualism'.[38] The deep disillusionment of the writers with the Labour movement is transparent, 'owing to its lack of dominant and guiding principles, and its consequent tendency to internal faction and division'.[39] The message of the book was at its clearest in Widdrington's chapter that contained a challenge to the Church to 'remaster its message' by making 'The Kingdom of God regulative of our theology'.[40] The Church had fallen short of her mission to proclaim the Kingdom, had lapsed into introspection, and socialists had confounded their work with the Kingdom's. A truer theology, therefore, must see the Kingdom as God's work, in which we participate, not ours. 'The Church, once delivered from ecclesiastical-mindedness and aflame with the faith of the Kingdom, will be compelled to adopt towards our industrial system the same attitude which our missionaries take towards the social order of heathendom.'[41]

*Christendom* the book was soon followed by Christendom the group. For the following year, at the annual meeting of the CSL in Birmingham, Henry Slesser, later the first Labour Solicitor-General, presided over the transformation of the Church Socialist League into the League of the Kingdom of God (LKG), rejecting the old Basis and establishing a new, far more theological, series of objects. Widdrington later described the change: 'we disentangled ourselves from political parties, and focused our minds and energies on the recovery and restatement of the idea of Christendom.'[42] Egerton Swann became the new Secretary, and Donaldson and Widdrington joined the executive, which was chaired by T. C. Gobat of Birmingham. Clearly the idea was to be less overtly 'political', and many of the executive eagerly anticipated a flood of new members who might previously have been put off by the clear avowal of socialism, which Slesser had explicitly denied as the only possible alternative to capitalism at the annual meeting. Numbers did not increase, however. In fact, though the Christendom group was to play an important part in later conferences, such as COPEC and Malvern, it was to remain small and eclectic.

Nineteen twenty-three was also the year of the second Anglo-Catholic Congress at the Royal Albert Hall, at which the socialist gauntlet was thrown down by Bishop Frank Weston, who had recently returned from Africa. In a sparkling address he followed up the Christendom challenge to conventional Anglo-Catholic theology:

> You cannot claim to worship Jesus in the Tabernacle, if you do not pity Jesus in the slum . . . It is folly . . . to suppose that you can worship Jesus in the Sacrament and Jesus on the throne of glory, when you are sweating him in the souls and bodies of his children . . . Look for Jesus in the ragged . . . and when you see him, gird yourselves with his towel and try to wash his feet.[43]

A set of Anglo-Catholic leaders followed up Weston's challenge by approaching the LKG to organise summer schools of sociology, the first of which was held at Keble in 1925 and which ran through to 1955, when Michael Ramsey addressed the group. In 1931 the Christendom group started a new quarterly magazine, having used the *Commonwealth* for their newsletter for several years. The new *Christendom* fed off the work of V. A. Demant's Research Committee of the Christian Social Council, which had also run Easter conferences since 1929, and from 1932 Widdrington himself organised and chaired Christendom conferences at the CR house at St Leonard's-on-Sea. It was these conferences which finally gave its name to the Christendom Group, although the key figures of Slesser, Reckitt and Widdrington had been referred to by the sobriquet since the publication of *The Return of Christendom*.

Considering his desire to emancipate the CSL from political

parties, it is ironic that by the start of the Second World War Widdrington had grown concerned about the LKG and the younger generation of Christendom who, he felt, had lost contact with organised labour. Indeed, it is a criticism reflected by many commentators on Christendom, who have argued with John Oliver in *The Church and Social Order*[44] that most of the Christendom writers had little or no concept of the desperate, crushing poverty of the majority of mankind, and that they therefore resorted far too readily to unrealistic panaceas such as Major C. H. Douglas's social-credit scheme, which Temple described in 1922 as 'still in the stage of incomprehensibility to all except a few'.[45] Moreover, even their espousal of Guild Socialism seemed to lack the sophistication of other socialist writers. G. D. H. Cole's argument[46] was based on the need to challenge the assumption that it was poverty rather than slavery that was the fundamental social evil to be addressed, but the Christendom writers were more concerned with 'capitalist pluto-cracy' and a return to Catholic dogma. None the less, when Temple was organising the Malvern conference in 1940 he deliberately chose many Christendom figures to prepare the written contributions, and though Widdrington resigned his chair-manship of the Oxford summer schools in 1945, he contributed to the group's final publication that same summer, *The Prospect for Christendom*, and other members of the Group, most notably Reckitt, were active well into the 1960s.

In essence, the distinctive work of the CSL had ceased long before it metamorphosed into the LKG and the seeds of its eventual demise had been around ever since its first meeting.

Because so many of the CSL's members belonged at varying stages to both the GSM and the CSU, it is hard to assess its independent significance. Yet at its core there was an indubitably secure link, for the first time, with the real Labour movement. Maurice and Kingsley may have met Chartists. Headlam may have lived on a working-class estate. Gore and Holland may have supported industrial disputes. But it was only the CSL that actually had Labour leaders like George Lansbury among its members. Noel, Moll and Bull were as well known in the ILP as any union leader, and though it fought shy of direct affiliation, yet the CSL was the first to align itself with Labour candidates at elections, thereby at least in part overcoming the long-held assumption that party politics must be an arena in which the Gospel should not shed its light. Indeed, the demise of the CSL, though it may lie ideologically with the political challenge of Guild Socialism and the theological reversal of Christendom, lay emotionally with a falling out of love of many church people with the processes of politics. It may be that social divisions between the rather polite and financially cushioned clergy of the League and the rather rawer political nerves of the Labour leaders led to this, or it may simply be that the euphoria of 1906 could never have lasted. Either way, between those who felt that Labour was not socialist enough, those who felt that it was theologically inaccurate to equate the Kingdom of God with the socialist agenda and those who believed socialism did not just or necessarily mean the newly adopted Clause Four of the Labour Party's constitution, the League rapidly lost most of its supporters. Certainly its life continued, in the work of Noel, Widdrington and Reckitt, well into the 1940s and 1950s, but the primary concerns that soon developed, with a 'Christian sociology' and with the purity of the socialist message, at a time when socialism was being defined in history more by the Russian soviets than by the ethical prophets of a new social order, became increasingly recondite and irrelevant to the emerging Labour movement.

The important theological task of asserting the Kingdom of God as the dominating political concern for Christian Socialists in many ways prefigured some of the work of later theologians. First, it corrected the tendency of many political activists to assume that their work in some way was issuing in God's work. Second, the theological method of attempting to create first principles from theological truths, that might then form the basis of a Christian intervention in politics, was essentially that pursued by both Temple and Tawney. Third, aspects of Guild Socialism, especially in its pluralist forms, have much to recommend themselves at a time when the task of socialism seems far more clearly to be the strengthening of 'community' rather than the State.

Yet the League's birth in the heady days of Labour's early successes in 1906 meant that almost too much was expected of Labour. It was as if a new dawn had broken and the mists of the old dispensation were about to disperse. Disillusionment was almost inevitable, but the constant schisms in the period up to 1923, when the League folded, might have been more readily avoided if from the very outset its enthusiasm had been more measured and its theology more acute.

# 6

## *Faith of Our Fathers*

Tie in a living tether
The prince and priest and thrall,
Bind all our lives together,
Smite us and save us all;
In ire and exultation
Aflame with faith, and free,
Lift up a living nation,
A single sword to thee.

G. K. Chesterton, 'O God of earth and altar'

The God of the Bible is a God who not only governs history, but who orientates it in the direction of the establishment of justice and right. He is more than a provident God. He takes sides with the poor and liberates them from slavery and oppression.

Gustavo Gutierrez, *The Power of the Poor in History*

On Monday, 1 July 1912, there was a small gathering of the local ILP at the town cross in Shettleston, to the east of Glasgow. More had been expected, as the meeting was meant to defend one of their members from a virulent attack from the pulpit by the local Roman Catholic priest, Fr Andrew O'Brien, eight days earlier. In the event, far more of the assembled crowd were there to attack than support the man whom Fr O'Brien had singled out for his supposedly anti-Catholic politics, a rotund, bespectacled local businessman called John Wheatley. A fight ensued, and protesters marched on Wheatley's house, where they burnt an effigy of him to the accompaniment of 'Faith of our Fathers'. Wheatley, who

154

was at home with his family and some friends, watched the proceedings for some time before coolly walking out between the crowds without so much as a look over his shoulder or a harsh word. His reply came a few days later in *Forward*, a left-wing Glasgow paper:

On Monday night, you gathered in your hundreds and in thousands to demonstrate that you hate me [he began]. If I am your enemy, am I your only enemy? Don't you know that God who gave you life has created for you green fields and sunny skies, that he has given you the material and the power to have in abundance beautiful homes, healthy food, education, leisure, travel and all that aids in the development of cultured men and women? These gifts of God have been stolen from you.[1]

The following Sunday he and his family were back at Mass, and his calm courage had won him new friends.

Thus Wheatley faced down the obloquy of his own parish priest in a community that overwhelmingly owed its allegiance to Catholicism. For the area to which Wheatley's parents had moved from Co. Waterford in Ireland in 1876, when he was seven, was predominantly Roman Catholic, with a large first-generation Irish community. Baillieston, where the family of eight children first lived, was a pit village in which both father and son worked down the narrow, seamed mines and families living in a single room shared one ashpit for sanitation between twelve households. The immigrant Catholic Irish were frequently used by the mine-owners as a source of cheap labour, and political divisions focused sharply between native Scottish and Irish Protestants in the Orange Lodges on the one hand and, on the other, Roman Catholics committed to Irish Home Rule. This was the political environment from which Wheatley escaped of an evening to make the ten-mile round-trip to the Athenaeum in Glasgow, where he attended evening classes as the sole miner.

Wheatley's brush with the Church, however, started with his

formation of the Catholic Socialist Society (CSS). He had left the pits in 1893 to work with his brother Patrick in a grocery business which lasted until 1901, when he became an advertising canvasser for the *Glasgow Observer*. His father had been a member of the Irish National League, and his own early politics were defined more by his Irishness than by any specifically socialist programme, so it was natural that he should become the Chair of the local branch of the United Irish League in Shettleston, where he had moved with his wife Mary. The novelist Compton MacKenzie said of the Irish in Scotland that they 'settled in a country which seemed to them to have surrendered what they had never surrendered – nationhood',[2] and Wheatley appears to have taken some time to lose this narrowly nationalist perspective to his politics, but by 1906 he was the LRC election agent in North West Lanark, and within a couple of years he had joined the ILP.

Meanwhile Wheatley had followed up a speech that had been given by a C. S. Devas at the Athenaeum. Devas had drawn a keen distinction between the socialism of Labour's new MPs and the atheist socialism that Robert Blatchford was proclaiming. Signing himself as a 'Catholic Socialist', he argued, 'The Catholic Church has always leaned more to socialism or collectivism and equality than to individualism and inequality. It has always been the Church of the poor and all the historical attacks on it have emanated from the rich.'[3] Later that same year the Archbishop of Glasgow, Charles Maguire, welcomed the advent of the working classes to political life without explicitly commending Labour or socialism, thereby treading the fine line many Catholic hierarchs had to walk following papal condemnation of socialism in the *Syllabus of Errors* in 1864.

That autumn Wheatley, his brother Patrick, William Regan from Rutherglen and Stephen Pullman of St Rollox met regularly as a group of Roman Catholics committed to socialism, gradually growing in numbers until there were fifteen of them meeting in Wheatley's home. A first open meeting was then called, through an advertisement in the *Glasgow Observer*, on 28 October, at which Catholicism and socialism was to be discussed. In fact, the barely disguised aim of the meeting was to form a Catholic socialist society, and speakers such as the miners' leader James Donaldson of Renfrew were planted in the audience to move the formation of a committee to draft rules and organise further meetings. The next meeting was called for a fortnight later, with Keir Hardie's brother George as the main speaker, and thus the first Catholic Socialist Society was formed with the explicit aim of 'the propagation of Socialism among Catholics by means of meetings, lectures and distribution of literature'.[4]

While at this distance it seems inevitable that at least some Roman Catholics should adopt socialism, for the Scottish Roman Catholic Church of the time it did seem exceptional. Indeed, Wheatley's campaign over the following years to open Catholicism to the claims of socialism made him many enemies, and it was not only his own parish priest who condemned him. Most notably the Jesuit Leo Puissant of Muirkirk attacked the CSS and socialism itself, trying thereby to force the Archbishop into a public condemnation of Scottish socialism. In fact, an Archdiocesan Committee on Socialism was set up and in 1908 described Wheatley as a 'malcontent Catholic' but generally urged greater study of the matter, mindful of the fact that while the Liberal Party had been the natural home of most immigrant Catholics when it unambiguously supported Home Rule for Ireland, many Catholics were already transferring their loyalties to Labour. For the hierarchy to condemn Labour in the same terms as the Pope had anathematised Italian socialism would already have been to risk alienating many of the faithful. Wisely Maguire decided to leave the question unanswered.

Wheatley was not the first British Roman Catholic to urge the claims of socialism. Indeed, he was entering a tradition that stemmed from Leo XIII's papal encyclical of 1891, *Rerum Novarum*, and much of his writing makes sense only as a reaction to that tradition. When in 1909 he published *The Catholic Workingman* he cited none other than Cardinal Manning, the Archbishop of Westminster who had died eighteen years earlier and had played a key role in forming the ideas behind *Rerum Novarum*.

Manning's part in the 1889 London Dock Strike we have already recorded, but his significance for the development of a rapprochement between British Roman Catholicism and socialism is vital.

Henry Edward Manning was born into the English mercantile establishment in 1808, the youngest son of William Manning, MP for Evesham, ex-Lord Mayor of the City of London and Governor of the Bank of England. Educated at Harrow and Balliol, where he met his lifetime friend W. E. Gladstone, he toyed with a parliamentary career just as Gladstone was preparing for ordination. In 1831, however, his father's sugar business collapsed, and Manning had to forget parliamentary ambitions. For a while he worked as a clerk in the Colonial Office. Fairly soon afterwards he had something of an evangelical conversion experience and decided to put himself forward for ordination. In 1832 he was elected to an Oxford fellowship at Merton and was then ordained. The following year he was made curate of Upwalden in the parish of Lavington, where he married Caroline, the youngest daughter of his rector, John Sargent. Sargent died very soon afterwards, and Manning was promoted to rector by his own grandmother-in-law, who was the patron of the parish. Caroline also died, only four years later, of tuberculosis, and Manning was left to plough his solitary furrow in his rural parish. During this time he developed a friendship with Maurice and Kingsley and started to take a very specific interest in the working conditions of rural labourers, condemning the local Duke of Richmond for pressing his workmen too hard and chastising the 'sin of exacting the largest rent while doing the least repairs'.[5]

In 1841, at the ambitious age of thirty-three, he was made Archdeacon of Chichester. By now his early evangelical theology, which he had inherited in part from his father, a theological and political supporter of Wilberforce, had changed to a pronounced Anglo-Catholicism. Newman had influenced him profoundly at Oxford, and when Newman left the Church of England for Rome in 1845, Manning replaced him as one of the remaining key Anglican Tractarian figures. As archdeacon he also began to acquire a reputation for championing the agricultural poor. In 1845 he argued, 'We have a people straitened by poverty, worn down by toil; they labour from the rising to the setting of the sun; and the human spirit will faint and break at last.'[6] His radicalism, however, did not seem to harm his career prospects, and there remained a strong expectation that he would rise to one of the two archiepiscopal sees.

In 1847, however, the Bishop of Exeter refused to institute the Revd G. C. Gorham as vicar of Brampford Speke on the grounds that he believed his theology was not orthodox. Gorham appealed to the recently created Judicial Committee of the Privy Council, which decided against the bishop, and when the bishop still refused to institute him, the Archbishop of Canterbury had to conduct the service himself. The final straw for many Tractarians came in 1851, when the High Court finally decided against the bishop. Keble's 1833 sermon on 'National Apostasy' had been prompted by Parliament's suppression of ten Irish bishoprics, but now Parliament was not only deciding the shape and size of dioceses but also determining what was and what was not orthodox Church of England doctrine, against the advice of the bishops. That the Archbishop of Canterbury had backed Parliament rather than his fellow bishop was yet further proof that the Church of England had lost its independence and its pride. Manning wrote extensively on the matter and felt compelled to resign from the Church of England. On Passion Sunday 1851 he was received into the Roman Catholic Church at Farm Street in Mayfair.

Manning's decision was scarcely spontaneous. Newman's move in 1845 had affected him deeply, and he had visited Pope Pius IX in Rome. Furthermore, Rome had decided in 1850 to restore the Catholic episcopacy in England, and there were twelve new bishops. The Catholic Emancipation Act of 1829 and the repeal of the 1819 Tests and Corporations Act meant that the Roman Catholic Church could no longer be thought of simply as a foreign power supported by a few old Catholic families and a large number of Irish immigrants. So within months Manning was (re)ordained by the Archbishop of Westminster. He studied for a couple of years in Rome and worked in the slum parish of Bayswater, and in 1857 the Pope made him Provost of the Westminster metropolitan chapter, much against the will of many hereditary Catholics who saw him as theologically *arriviste*. None the less, when Cardinal Wiseman died in 1864 the Pope again turned to Manning, overlooking both the majority of bishops' preference for Bishop Errington and Manning's own suggestion, Bishop Ullathorne. Manning was appointed Archbishop of Westminster and Metropolitan of the English Province and in 1875 gained a cardinal's hat to boot.

Manning's politics, though heavily conditioned by his personal friendship with Gladstone, lay very close to those of Maurice and were influenced by his experience of his new Church, which was very much the Church of the poor. As Wiseman had commented, 'Close under the Abbey of Westminster there lie concealed labyrinths of lanes and courts, alleys and slums, nests of ignorance and vice, depravity and crime, as well as squalor, wretchedness and disease: whose atmosphere is typhus, whose ventilation is cholera in which swarms a huge countless population, in great measure Catholic.'[7] Manning found himself politicised by his new allegiance, deeply critical of the old Catholic families who seemed to care little for the poverty of many of their Catholic brethren: 'What are our people doing? Oh, I forgot; they have no time. They are examining their consciences or praying for success in finding a really satisfactory maid.'[8]

His theology, of course, was different from that of any of his former Anglican colleagues and, indeed, set him at odds yet again with many old Catholics who had survived religious repression by keeping quiet and toning down the Roman aspect of their Catholicism. Manning, by contrast, fought ferociously at the first Vatican Council for the Infallibility of the Pope. He was as fervent a teetotaller as any Methodist and set up the League of the Cross as a Catholic temperance movement.

More radically, he also took a leading role in supporting Joseph Arch's National Agricultural Labourers' Union in 1872, speaking at an inaugural meeting and arguing for legislation to regulate child agricultural labour and the conditions of rural housing as well as trying to abolish the system whereby most labourers were paid in kind instead of cash. Manning felt equally keenly the demands of industrial labour. 'I claim for Labour,' he stated in 1874, 'and the skill which is acquired by Labour, the rights of Capital. Labour is the origin of our greatness and the true Capital of our country.'[9]

Naturally, not all Manning's promptings were purely ideological. He, like Maurice, was fearful that if the Church did not respond to the growing emancipation of labour, then it would be left behind, and Christianity would become no more than an irrelevance. For Manning this fear had a peculiar piquancy, as he saw a clear opportunity for Roman Catholicism to break out of its enforced ghetto and to play a significant part in the affairs of the State, to become a religion for the nation, and he was quick to take advantage of any weakness in the Church of England, as in the London dock strike of 1889. As the *Tablet* put it in a tribute to Manning on his Silver Jubilee as Archbishop, 'To Cardinal Manning more than to any man it is due that English Catholics have at last outgrown the narrow cramped life of their past persecution and stand in all things on a footing of equality with their fellow-countrymen'.[10] Manning's motives were, then, clearly mixed: 'he feared revolution and felt that the Church could enable real improvements in the lives of the poor and thereby avoid violent upheaval, and he wanted the Roman Catholic Church in England to be able to hold its head up high.

Manning's involvement in the dock strike we have already discussed, but his final, and much more important, contribution to the life of the Church lay in his campaign, in which he was joined by Cardinal Gibbons of Baltimore, for Pope Leo XIII to make a clear statement on social justice. In 1891 this bore fruit in *Rerum Novarum*, the papal encyclical on the condition of the working classes which, more than any other document, shaped the future of Catholic social teaching.

It reads as if Manning had written it, steering a careful middle way between *laissez-faire* economics and Marxism but giving as a starting point the fact that 'the great majority of [the poor] live undeservedly in miserable and wretched conditions.'[11] It is not only poverty that is at issue but 'abounding wealth among a very small number and destitution among the masses' and 'increased self-reliance on the part of workers as well as a closer bond of union one with another'.[12] In language that Kingsley would have been proud of, 'devouring usury' and 'avaricious and grasping men'[13] are condemned. Human dignity, moreover, means that 'it is shameful and inhuman . . . to use men as things for gain and to put no more value on them than what they are worth in muscle and energy.'[14] Indeed, the encyclical goes on to argue for 'that justice which is called *distributive*',[15] for a limit to working hours, for the value of trades unions and for wages based on an element of 'natural justice' and not simply on what the market determines.

All of this sounds remarkably similar to much late-nineteenth-century British Christian Socialism. The encyclical, however, places all these comments in the context of a ferocious attack on what it terms socialism. As in the earlier *Syllabus of Errors* of 1864, socialism is seen as a denial of two fundamental elements of human existence, which are regarded as derived from natural law. Because socialists 'seek to transfer the goods of private persons to the community at large',[16] they deny man's right, conferred on him by 'nature', to private property. Furthermore their insistence that all are equal belies the fact that 'in civil society the lowest cannot be made equal with the highest.'[17] The role of the State must be narrowly circumspect, and while it may seek to 'improve in particular the condition of the workers',[18] it cannot legislate for what offends natural law.

Manning condemned such a simplistic understanding of God's will and subordinated the 'right to property' aspect of natural law to the right to life in a much criticised comment that owes as much to Victor Hugo as to the Vatican: 'a starving man commits no theft if he saves his life by eating of his neighbour's bread so much as is necessary for the support of his existence.'[19] Clearly there is an argument that without a concept of natural law it is impossible to posit that human rights are 'self-evident and true', and it is in this arena that Christian Socialist theology still has much work to do. For the concept of God's immutable will is antithetical to that of a compassionate Father, and the idea that, in the words of the hymn, 'God is working his purpose out as year succeeds to year' is far more in tune with an incarnate divinity. With God's will constantly responding to the new problems of creation, it is more possible to hold up what seems 'natural' today against the ethical demands of the constantly evolving Gospel while still holding to some moral absolutes. Thus the right to own private property is part of human nature, and the Vatican was right to uphold it, but later experience has shown both that capitalism can deny the rights of those on the margins to own property and that the right to hold property in common is also consonant with the way God designed us. Indeed, different aspects of our 'natural' humanity can often conflict, as we have already seen Manning point out.

There are other problems with *Rerum Novarum*. Although its interpretation of socialism would have rung true to Italian social-ists, whose party was launched in the year of its publication, in Britain it would really have been acknowledged only by some of Hyndman's supporters and bears little resemblance to much British Christian Socialism except in its emphasis on equality. A more informed encyclical, however, might have done far more harm, for by condemning only a particular brand of socialism it left the field open for Catholics to define a different form of socialism. In Wheatley's terms this was vitally important, for if he could prove that his Catholic socialism was markedly different from that condemned by Leo, he could claim the encyclical in his support. Thus *Rerum Novarum* formed an essential part of the vindication of Christian Socialism in Britain, not least in asserting that 'the favour of God Himself seems to incline more toward the unfortunate as a class.'[20]

Manning did not live long after the publication of *Rerum Novarum*, for which he provided much of the English translation, but he was delighted with it. He had broken the back of

Catholicism's opposition to all things socialist and had simultaneously established the Roman Catholic Church in England as a vital force in the life of the nation. He did so with considerable intelligence and with all the establishment *savoir faire* of an ex-Anglican but also with a sure eye for the internal politics of his adopted Church.

When Wheatley wrote of Catholic socialism at the turn of the century he was already, as we have noted, writing in a tradition. In all his most substantial workings of the Catholic socialist theme he cites both Manning and his own Archbishop Maguire at some length. He also, as we have seen, had to make explicit the difference between his own socialism and that denounced by *Rerum Novarum*. Thus in *Mines, Miners and Misery* he argued, 'Our Socialism is not a confiscation nor robbery nor the destruction of family life, nor anything like what you have heard our opponents describe it. It differs from the Socialism condemned by the Pope in that it retains the right to own private property. It is simply a scheme to abolish poverty.'[21]

Wheatley was not the only Roman Catholic working at a realignment of Catholicism in favour of a non-Marxist socialism at the turn of the century. A young Jesuit novice by the name of Charles Dominic Plater, born in London in 1875, who was studying at Pope's Hall in Oxford, had started a series of retreats for working men which he recounted in a striking article in 1908 in the *Hibbert Journal* arguing that personal sanctity and social emancipation must go hand in hand. A year later this led to the formation of the Catholic Social Guild under Plater's leadership, which ran retreats and study clubs and embraced a wide range of mainly ordained Roman Catholics, including Monsignor Henry Parkinson, Frs Martindale and McNabb, Leslie Toke and Henry Somerville. Plater, writing after his ordination in *The Priest and Social Action*, which appeared in 1914 with the Vicar General's imprimatur, put the case for a complete change of gear in Catholicism's response to poverty: 'Charitable action, in the narrower sense of the term, seeks to *relieve* poverty, misery and sickness. Social action tries to *prevent* them as far as possible by removing their causes.'[22] As in *Rerum Novarum*, the linchpin of Plater's argument is that the economic relations of men cannot be studied in isolation from ethical considerations, and he quotes Pope Leo XIII in *Graves de Communi*: 'It is the opinion of some, which is caught up by the masses that "the social question" as they call it, is merely "economic". The opposite is the truth, that it is first of all moral and *religious*.'[23]

Plater then goes on to establish, as others had within their own denominations, that though it was the duty of the Church to save men's souls, the relief and prevention of poverty were two of the prime ways in which the Church could fulfil that very aim, and that therefore the political endeavour, engaging in the economic, political and industrial life of the nation, was a fundamental duty of both Catholic priest and lay people. In fact, 'every encouragement should be given by the clergy to Catholic laymen engaged in public life.'[24]

It is important to note what a significant statement this was in 1914, as it demonstrates a new-found confidence in a Church that only fifty years earlier had been excluded from nearly every arena of public activity. And it is equally significant that while Plater does not directly argue for socialism or for Labour candidates, none the less the drift of his argument is clear, and the majority of new Catholics in Parliament came in with Labour.

Wheatley was one of the first of these. Elected a councillor for Shettleston in the same year as the riots outside his house, he became, by fortune of the amalgamation of Shettleston with Glasgow, a Glasgow City councillor, rapidly gaining expertise in the most pressing problem in Glasgow, its housing. For though Glasgow had initiated some slum clearance, and under the Liberals had come to be known as an exponent of 'municipal socialism', in fact little had been done to provide badly needed new homes. The war also led to attempts by private landlords to institute dramatic rent rises, all of which pressed down on an already poor community. In 1913 Wheatley published a plan for using the Glasgow Tramway Department's surplus for building new homes for rent. Entitled *Eight Pound Cottages for Glasgow Citizens*, it contained a detailed argument for replacing the tenement slums, which were the 'slaughter-houses of the poor', with decent housing that would dramatically alter tuberculosis rates and prevent overcrowding. His plans were never implemented, but when in 1915 he supported and led the Glasgow rent strikes, he was much more successful, and the rent rises were stopped.

In 1922, (after an unsuccessful attempt in 1918) Wheatley was elected MP for Shettleston, and, along with a gaggle of new Scottish Labour MPs, set off for London from St Enoch's Station in Glasgow. The gathered crowds were rapturous, and the MPs arrived in London convinced that they could really achieve something. It is therefore perhaps hardly surprising that within a year two of the Glasgow group, Wheatley and Jimmy Maxton, had been suspended from the Commons for calling the Government ministers murderers for withdrawing finances from the Scottish Health Department budget.

When the 1924 election came and Labour formed its first minority Government Wheatley, after refusing a junior post, was appointed to the Ministry of Health. The Ministry had recently been founded to accommodate the Liberal Christopher Addison, who eventually resigned over the Treasury's refusal to take health issues seriously. The job seemed designed for Wheatley, who immediately set about working on the housing element of his portfolio. Wheatley hardly had a free hand, however. Labour was not even the largest party in the House, and Snowden, as Chancellor, was keen to maintain a steady financial course. MacDonald's aim, moreover, was to prove Labour's ability to govern, and no minister had much room for either controversial or costly policies.

None the less Wheatley has often been described as one of the few successes of the brief 1924 administration. Involving representatives from the building employers and the trades unions, he put together a Housing Act that guaranteed a fifteen-year plan to build 2.5 million houses, with a National House Building Committee to oversee the work. Amendments in the committee stage nearly laid the Bill to rest, but Wheatley craftily brought the Liberal Charles Masterman on board to get the Bill through, while he always sought to allay opposition fears by arguing that this was not the 'socialist measure' he would prefer to be putting before the House. Masterman's tribute to him, when the Bill finally came on to the Statute Book, was glowing: 'He has been the conspicuous success in the new parliament. A short, squat, middle-aged man with a chubby face beaming behind large spectacles, he trots about like a benign Pickwick.'[25]

In the meantime, the complementary Building Materials Bill, which would have seen Wheatley's Housing (Financial Provisions) Act extend its benefits from suburbia to the inner cities, disappeared in the quicksands of parliamentary procedure, and by the time of the general election Wheatley had to content himself with the one impressive Act.

In fact, by this time Wheatley had become increasingly isolated on the Labour front bench, and actually saw Labour as being 'freed from a difficult position'[26] by losing the election. Indeed, for the rest of his career he argued that Labour should not govern as a minority and agitated for a more clearly left-wing Labour agenda.

Many left-wing socialists have identified Wheatley as a hero, mostly because of his uncompromisingly critical attitude towards the Labour leadership in his later years. Others have rightly pointed to the fact that he alone of the 1924 Labour Cabinet managed to achieve a lasting memorial in the shape of a consensual Housing Act that lasted for nine years and produced about 500,000 new homes. Others, more importantly, have pointed out that his courageous campaign to get the Roman Catholic Church to adopt a more sophisticated attitude towards socialism was essential in the process of wooing lay Roman Catholics for Labour when Liberal support for Irish Home Rule had already weakened. Yet there was much about Wheatley that was less than saintly. It seems likely that his business dealings were not exactly a model of labour practice, and much criticism was levelled at him during his time as Minister of Health for his inability to see beyond the housing issue to questions of education and birth control. He could, like Snowden, be vituperative, and though he was an excellent political manoeuvrer within Catholic Glasgow politics and showed great skill in gathering Liberal support for his Housing Act, he had next to no patience for the business of *Realpolitik* on the wider national scale and at times was a mischievous and unhelpful member of the parliamentary party. None the less he established, for the first time, the significant contribution that Roman Catholic MPs could make to the life of both the Labour Party and the nation.

If *Rerum Novarum* seemed radical in its day, its successor encyclical, *Quadrogesimo Anno*, which appeared the year after Wheatley's death, was even more assertive in its reinterpretation of the Christian response to social issues.

Of course, *Quadrogesimo Anno* is not exactly a ringing endorsement of socialism either. Indeed, it explicitly states that though, 'like all errors, Socialism contains a certain element of truth', yet ' "Religious Socialism" and "Christian Socialism" are expressions implying a contradiction in terms. No one can be at the same time a sincere Catholic and a true Socialist.'[27] The argument used is that since socialism is 'entirely ignorant of . . . [the] sublime end both of individuals and of society',[28] it must be antithetical to Christianity, which holds that 'man, endowed with a social nature, is placed here on earth in order that . . . by fulfilling faithfully the duties of his station he may attain to temporal and eternal happiness.'[29] Yet again the concept of 'his station' is used without comment, and socialists are presumed to have no metaphysical concern beyond their desire to improve the material conditions of the poor – in fact, to improve people's 'station' or to do away with the false concepts of people's worth that the word 'station' implies.

That said, however, *Quadrogesimo Anno* is a remarkable document. It dismisses the 'tottering tenets of Liberalism which had long hampered effective interference by the government'[30] and asserts an enhanced role for the State. It urges legislation for a minimum or just wage as a means of overcoming the operation of the market in lowering prices and wages. It again seeks a just distribution so that the common good of all is promoted. It also moderates Leo XIII's interpretation of the inviolability of the right to property by asserting that ownership has two aspects, individual and social, and that ownership therefore entails not only providing for one's own needs, but also enabling the 'goods which the Creator has destined for the human race' truly to serve this purpose. Punitive rates of taxation are condemned, but 'superfluous income' is seen not simply as a matter for personal discretion but as a resource for the whole community.

Pius XI also went on to define the primary duty of the State as being 'to abolish conflict between the classes with divergent interests'[31] and outlined the principle of subsidiarity, which still stands as a vital Christian principle for government:

> Just as it is wrong to withdraw from the individual and commit to the community at large what private enterprise and industry can accomplish, so too it is an injustice, a grave evil and a disturbance of right order, for a larger and higher association to arrogate to itself functions which can be performed efficiently by smaller and lower bodies. This is a fundamental principle of social philosophy ... and it retains its full truth today. Of its very nature the true aim of all social activity should be to help members of the social body, but never to destroy or absorb them.[32]

Nowadays this sounds like an impressive argument for devolution to local government or a Europe of the Regions, and *Quadrogesimo Anno* has often been cited as a key element in the development of Jacques Delors' and others' Catholic socialist vision for the European Union, but in its time it was intended far more as a vital corollary to the centralising dangers of both capitalism and collectivist socialism. When seen in its proper context, it comes across as more akin to the pluralism of Figgis and the Guild Socialists. A sceptic, of course, might reply to this call for subsidiarity from the Pope, 'Physician, heal thyself,' but the authoritative condemnation of capitalism is clear throughout the encyclical: 'Free competition has destroyed itself; economic domination has taken the place of the open market.'[33]

Finally, it should be pointed out that *Quadrogesimo Anno* first introduced into Catholic teaching the term 'social justice', to be set alongside the more traditional, and equally fuzzy, 'natural justice'. Donal Dorr, in his otherwise rather optimistic analysis of Catholic social teaching *Option for the Poor*, acknowledges that the encyclical offers less an 'alternative socio-economic system' than some 'fundamental principles of social morality',[34] but while the assumption prior to 1931 had always been that Roman Catholicism was broadly conservative in its politics and opposed the Welfare State, some of the suspicion of an increased role for the State is eroded in *Quadrogesimo Anno*, and its publication was undoubtedly a significant moment for many British Roman Catholic socialists.

The course of Catholic social teaching through to today has not run quite as smoothly as many have suggested. Indeed, only six years after *Quadrogesimo Anno*, Pius XI produced another encyclical, *Ingravescentibus Malis*, which was yet more virulent in its attack on socialism, urging the recitation of the rosary as a weapon against Communism to 'rout these subverters of Christian and human culture'. Furthermore, as Ken Leech has pointed out:

> this was the period when, dominated by the fears of Communism, the Latin Catholic *bloc* took sides in the class war against the workers, and allied with Fascism and reaction. So we have Pius XI's concordat with Mussolini, the long alliance between the Roman Church and the Christian Democrats in Italy, the support of Franco and his followers ('dearest sons of Catholic Spain') and the silence on Nazism on the grounds that the Pope is the Father of all near and remote, culprits and victims.[35]

Furthermore successive papal blessings seem to have fallen as often on the unjust as on the just. So the Salazar regime in Portugal received the explicit support not only of the arch-traditionalist Archbishop Lefebvre (who also preached in favour of the military junta in Argentina) but of John XXIII, and Liberation theologians in the 1970s and 1980s were given a rough ride by the hierarchy. Furthermore, the number of individual Roman Catholics in Britain who put their head above the parapet to argue for Catholic socialism between the 1920s and the 1960s was tiny. In Spain and France there was an organised Catholic-left resistance to Nazism, and in the USA Dorothy Day and the Catholic Worker collective developed a coherent left-wing Catholic critique of modern capitalism, but in Britain it was not until the 1960s that Catholic socialism was to appear in any clear form again.

Later papal encyclicals dramatically altered the Vatican's position regarding many aspects of socialist teaching. In particular the two 1960s encyclicals, *Mater et Magistra* and *Pacem in Terris*, broke new ground in what Donal Dorr has called 'the process of breaking the long alliance between Roman Catholicism and socially conservative forces'.[36] Thus *Mater et Magistra*, acknowledging the interdependence of humans, allowed for significant levels of State intervention, even arguing that 'the remuneration of work is not something that can be left to the laws of the marketplace.'[37] *Pacem in Terris* allowed for the use of the just-war doctrine in considering the legitimacy of violent insurgence against an oppressive regime, and *Gaudium et Spes*, the statement of the second Vatican Council in 1965, proposed that it is a central duty for all Christians to make provision for the poor, 'and to do so not merely out of their superfluous goods'.[38] Paul VI's *Populorum Progressio* attacked 'the baseless theory . . . which considers material gain the key motive for economic progress, competition as the supreme law of economics, and private ownership of the means of production as an absolute right that has no limits',[39] and *Octagesima Adveniens* in 1971, which was an indirect response to the 1968 decision of the Latin American bishops at Medellin to make a 'preferential but not exclusive option for the poor', toned down the critique of socialism as just not a 'complete and self-sufficient picture of man'.[40]

But this is to step far beyond our remit and to race ahead of ourselves. At the time of Wheatley's formation of the Catholic Socialist Society the official position of the Roman Catholic Church was clear – socialism was inconsistent with Christian faith because it posited an end to private property. By the time of his death in 1930 some advances had been made. Labour's Christian and ethical rather than Marxist roots, and the predominance of the immigrant working classes among the Roman Catholic faithful, made it difficult for the hierarchy to attack British socialism in quite the same terms as in other countries. By the time of *Quadrogesimo Anno* many Roman Catholics, if not most, were already voting Labour and had no intention of changing their allegiance. But overall the influence of Roman Catholic social teaching on British politics was not to be felt until the 1960s and 1970s, when the work of the Slant Group and Liberation theology gained a wide audience.

# 7

## *Two Boys from Rugby*

'Good-morning; good-morning!' the General said
When we met him last week on our way to the line.
Now the soldiers he smiled at are most of 'em dead,
And we're cursing his staff for incompetent swine.
'He's a cheery old card,' grunted Harry to Jack
As they slogged up to Arras with rifle and pack.

But he did for them both by his plan of attack.

Siegfried Sassoon, 'The General'

If you could hear, at every jolt, the blood
Come gargling from the froth-corrupted lungs,
Obscene as cancer, bitter as the cud
Of vile, incurable sores on innocent tongues, –
My friend, you would not tell with such high zest
To children ardent for some desperate glory,
The old lie: Dulce et decorum est
Pro patria mori.

Wilfred Owen, 'Dulce et decorum est'

Today's images of the First World War are sanitised versions of a horror that descended upon Britain for four unremitting years. Through the harsh but measured words of Wilfred Owen, Siegfried Sassoon and Robert Graves we have a picture of dug-outs and gas, trenches and shellshock. But the images have become comfortable to us, well worn and incapable of conveying the tragedy and devastation that the war produced. Yet the First World War was in every sense awful. The sheer number of

173

casualties, the protracted horror of futile expeditions 'over the top', the permanent psychological scars of shellshock, the terrors of unexploded mines and the experience of a debilitating war of attrition all challenged not only those at the Front but the whole nation to think again about the nature of society.

At the start few doubted the class-bound structures of the military high command, yet by the end the evidence of their incompetence questioned the very class system upon which their authority was based. In the mud of the trenches class distinctions seemed to lose their meaning, and what mattered more than upbringing was loyalty, courage and ability.

Even the Church was not insensible to the social transformation that the Great War engendered. Many Churches experienced something of a boom at the start of the war, and though clergy, as members of a protected profession, were not required to sign up, many did. Their experiences at the Front, meeting working men for the first time on an equal footing, informed their politics as much as the horror of war challenged their theology.

Among these was the vicar of St Paul's, Worcester, Geoffrey Antekel Studdert Kennedy, who joined up soon after the start of the war and, apart from a brief period back in Britain, served most of it as an army padre in France. His accounts of the Front are no more perceptive than others, yet he came to symbolise for many clergy the Church's sudden realisation that the chasm between it and ordinary working men was just as vast as the more radical bishops of the nineteenth century had always said it was. Kennedy's determination to muck in with the rest and not to shrink from the toughest battle earned him the Military Cross, and his habit of giving out cigarettes to the troops equally earned him the nickname 'Woodbine Willie'. Yet his Christian message was undiluted, and his experiences affected his work with the Industrial Christian Fellowship after the war. As he put it, 'When the war broke out there was a regular run upon the bank of God, and our churches were thronged with distracted people waving cheques for protection duly endorsed "through Jesus Christ our Lord". They soon got sick of it, of course, and fell away. In a dim way they realised it was useless.' And he added, 'A chaplain said to me the other day, "Don't discourage last-resort religion: it is better than none at all." I don't agree. It's worse than no religion. It's a base form of idolatry.'[1] For Kennedy there was a clear task ahead of the Church, to preach a Gospel that was not just for the wealthy but *for* all and intelligible *to* all. The war convinced him that violence was futile and, by extension, that the violence of the present economic system must therefore be wrong. What was needed was a social philosophy that was solely 'God-determined'. That would involve significant redistribution and social reform, but social change must always ride on the back of personal transformation, not vice versa. Thus Kennedy, though he always refused to align himself with Labour or with socialism, came to represent a national perception that the old order, of which the Church of England had been an integral part, had gasped its last on the fields of Passchendaele, the Somme and Ypres.

It was not only individual padres who interpreted the spiritual significance of the war, however. In 1916 Archbishop Davidson initiated a National Mission of Repentance and Hope, which took the form of vast numbers of revivalist meetings around the country, supplemented by a series of papers. The third of these expressed most clearly the underlying assumption upon which the Mission was based: 'A limitless desire for riches, for power, for pleasure, has run like a flame through the nations. An Ethic has taken possession of our Politics and of our Public Life which is in direct defiance of the meekness and gentleness of Christ: and the result is that all Europe is at war.'[2] The Mission was to address the inherent social problems of society as well as to tackle unbelief. In its own terms it was largely unsuccessful, yet the perception that the Church must be involved in the task of the reconstruction of a new social order after the war did take root. The Bishop of Peterborough, F. T. Woods, called in the Canterbury Convocation in 1918 for 'a spirit of adventure which would prefer bold schemes of real construction to the patchy palliatives which have often done duty in the great cause of social reform,'[3] and J. A.

Kempthorne, Bishop of Lichfield, was joined by several of the Bench of Bishops in his demand for a minimum wage and protection against unemployment. Cyril Garbett, then vicar of Portsea and later Bishop of Southwark (1919–32), Winchester (1932–42) and Archbishop of York (1942–55), went on to assert that these demands, as well as the recognition of the 'status of workers in the industries in which they are engaged are in accordance with the principles of Christianity'.[4] Thus by the end of the war there was an obvious intent, shared widely if not universally among Church leaders, that the Church's role in the process of post-war reconstruction must be one that addressed the whole social order and, in particular, the issue of labour.

In time-honoured ecclesiastical manner, the National Mission set up a series of committees to consider specific aspects of post-war society. One of these was devoted to Christianity and industrial problems and produced, in what was later termed the 'Fifth Report', perhaps the most significant outcome of the National Mission. The membership of the committee was remarkable. With Talbot as Chair and Gore, Woods and Kempthorne from the House of Bishops were Lansbury, Albert Mansbridge of the Workers' Educational Association (WEA) and R. H. Tawney. Inevitably enough, the report, which was published only days before the end of the war, came to radical conclusions. It recognised the same problems as Holland and others had seen before – the use of workers as tools rather than as people, the sharp political differences between capital and labour, the emphasis in industry on competition to the exclusion of public service – and it asserted the right of Christianity to comment on every aspect of industry. The report also called for 'a wage adequate to maintain the worker, his wife and family in health and honour, and to enable him to dispense with the subsidiary earnings of his children up to the age of sixteen'; it supported unemployment insurance; and it argued for an end to casual labour. More contentiously it stated, 'The system itself makes it exceedingly difficult to carry into practice the principles of Christianity. Its faults are not the accidental or occasional maladjustments of a social order the general spirit and tendency of which can be accepted as satisfactory by Christians. They are the expressions of certain deficiencies deeply rooted in the nature of that order itself.'[5]

The CSL was delighted with the report and proceeded to campaign vociferously for it, pointing out the part its own members had played in putting the report together. Unfortunately, the 1918 general election was less interested in such matters than in celebrating victory in the war. Lloyd George went to the country on a jingoistic platform, urging almost punitive retribution against the Germans, much to the distaste of Studdert Kennedy, who described the election as 'one of the most shameful episodes in our history'.[6] None the less Lloyd George won a resounding victory. Furthermore the report came out at a turning point in the history of Christian Socialism. The first flushes of enthusiasm at the election of Labour MPs in 1906 had worn off, and, as we have already seen, many Church Socialists were concerned about the collectivist direction the Labour Party was taking. The CSU folded into the ICF in 1919, with Studdert Kennedy as its chief missioner, steering a heavily personalist agenda and remaining very noncommital in its political conclusions; while the CSL was increasingly obsessed with Guild Socialism and the development of a Christian Sociology.

In the meantime a new generation of Christians were beginning to come to socialism, people like William Temple and R. H. Tawney, whose perceptions were framed not by the nineteenth century but by the twentieth.

Born in 1881, William Temple was the second son of Frederick Temple whom, as Bishop of London, Holland had been so keen on involving in the 1889 miners' strike and who, from 1896, was Archbishop of Canterbury. Brought up in a succession of episcopal palaces, he went to Rugby, where his father had also been headmaster, and then to his father's old college, Balliol, in 1900. After Oxford, where he had joined the CSU, he had been made a Fellow at Queen's and sought ordination from the Bishop of

Oxford in 1904. Paget had refused him on the grounds that his theology was too liberal, and so it was not until 1909 that his father's successor at Canterbury, Randall Davidson, was prevailed upon to ordain him. Temple's character of mind, if not his views, had been clearly stamped by then, for he retained his father's strength of purpose in the face of obloquy (Frederick's consecration as Bishop of Exeter had been fiercely opposed) and his intense desire to accommodate the views of others.

In the meantime he had been heavily influenced by the Master of Balliol, Edward Caird, who had introduced him to the ideas of T. H. Green. He had organised an exhibition at Oxford in 1907 on the evils of sweated industries and in 1908 declared that there was before the Church a stark choice between 'Socialism or heresy'.[7] In 1909 he chaired a significant conference for the Student Christian Movement at Matlock on 'Christianity and Social Problems' and went on to attend the Edinburgh conference on World Mission, before touring Australian universities. Following the Matlock conference he initiated, with the Quaker Lucy Gardner, the Collegium, a small, informal group of Christian Socialists dedicated to a common life of prayer and thought about social problems, and helped put together their impressive book *Competition*, which came down firmly in favour of radical economic change. In 1910 he also went to Repton as its headmaster, although his tenure as a public-school head seems to fit ill with his later condemnation of the two-tier British educational system. By the start of the war he had taken up a parochial post as vicar of the 'society' church St James's, Piccadilly in the heart of fashionable St James's.

During the war he married into a wealthy West Country family, whom his parents knew from Frederick's days as Bishop of Exeter, and acted as one of the twelve secretaries to the National Mission. He also published, in 1914, the first of many books that espoused a change in the social order. In *The Kingdom of God* he argued forcibly that no one in Britain was content with its present social conditions and that what was needed was a 'socialistic' society. He also rounded on competition as the underlying principle of industry: 'Competition is not a thing limited to business; it is a thing that pervades our whole life. It is simply organised selfishness ... It is sometimes said that if you want to get the best out of a man you must appeal to his own interest. That brings us to the crucial point. For if that is true Christ was wrong.'[8] In 1918 he joined the Labour Party and boldly announced as much in the Lower House of the Convocation of Canterbury just as Kempthorne was arguing for the minimum wage in the Upper House.

Temple's major concerns at this point, however, were as much ecclesiastical as economic. He campaigned for democratic change in the Church of England, for stronger ecumenical ties with other Churches and, above all, for the Church's independence, if not its disestablishment. To that end in 1917 he resigned his post at St James's to work full-time for the Life and Liberty Movement which he had recently inaugurated, prompted by his clerical neighbour Dick Sheppard, who was at St Martin's-in-the-Fields. By 1919 much of what he had been fighting for in Church reform was accomplished by the Enabling Act, which instituted the National Assembly of the Church of England, more commonly known as the Church Assembly, and he returned to a clerical post as canon of Westminster.

In fact, he lasted only two years at Westminster and in 1921 was made Bishop of Manchester, immediately resigning from the Labour Party, much to Tawney's annoyance, on the grounds that membership was incompatible with his episcopacy. By then he had already been instrumental, however, in setting up the Conference on Politics, Economics and Citizenship (COPEC) Council, which was to prepare for a special conference under Temple's chairmanship in Birmingham in 1924.

The Council consisted of 350 members with twelve commissions, each of which was to report on a specific area of social concern, such as education, the home, the treatment of crime. The conference was also ecumenical, with representatives from many of the Churches, including, right up until the last moment, the Roman Catholics. Several of those involved in the preparation for the conference, most notably Lucy Gardner, had also been involved in the Collegium, so it was clear that the broad thrust of the conference's deliberations would be socialist. Yet Gardner and her Co-Secretary, Charles Raven, were keen to gain official approval for the conference and its decisions from Davidson, so a deliberately broad-church approach was taken, with no avowed political affiliation. Thousands of questionnaires were sent out, research was undertaken and the whole of 1923 was spent in drawing up and agreeing the reports. Temple, still hoping to get Davidson's backing, wrote that his hope was to provide 'some principles . . . which would be more explicit than the great platitudes and less particular than a political programme'.[9] In the event Davidson refused to attend and merely sent a lukewarm greeting.

The conference ran from 5 April to the 12th and the reports were reviewed and amended by the 1,400 delegates. It is difficult to perceive a clear and consistent political agenda or even a philosophy in all the COPEC reports, and indeed Temple probably had not sought one. Certainly, there is a general presumption in favour of a new social order, but several of the reports are remarkably conservative and a mere reflection of their time, especially when it comes to issues like the role of the family, alcohol and sex. On economic matters, furthermore, COPEC seemed to speak with two minds. On the one hand, the 'Politics and Citizenship' report, which had been prepared by Reckitt, Ruth Kenyon, Lord Eustace Percy, Hugh Martin of the SCM and Lady Parmoor, the stepmother of Stafford Cripps, took a largely personalist line, urging Christians to become involved on an individual basis in social and charitable services, a position Tawney decried as 'Octavia Hill'. The report also argued that the Church and Christians should remain non-aligned in politics, although Ruth Kenyon held that the Church should 'throw its weight on the side of that party which challenges the existing social and industrial system'.[10] In contrast, the 'Industry and Property' report, to which Gore contributed and which he summed up, adopted his far more radical agenda, stipulating that the first claim on industry should be a decent living wage; that property should be for use and not for power; and that 'extremes of wealth and poverty are likewise intolerable. A Christian order involves a juster distribution.'[11] In addition, the right of property was not inviolable, for 'No inherited wealth or position can dispense any member of the Christian society from establishing by service his claim to maintenance'[12] – a view that effectively cocked a snook at the hereditary principle. During the conference one important element of the report was amended, however, when the Christian aim of 'the substitution of the motive of service for the motive of gain' was replaced with 'the predominance of the motive of service'.

The significance of COPEC for Temple himself was enormous. It drew him into sustained contact with a vast range of thinkers, politicians and church people at a time when there was a general perception that the war had brought society to its clearest view of its problems. By the end of the week Temple also seemed far clearer in his own mind about the need for Christians to involve themselves in finding answers to the problems of unemployment, in launching housing schemes and in extending educational facilities. He was even prepared to argue for specific policies such as the diminution of class sizes and the raising of the school-leaving age, thus developing a pattern for social critique which he would formalise in 1942 in *Christianity and the Social Order*.

For Christian Socialism, however, COPEC's effect was mixed. The reports were far from an undiluted statement of Christian radicalism. Indeed, its acronym was waggishly interpreted as Conventional Official Platitudes Expressing Caution, and while many delegates seemed happy to vote for the reports, John Kent is probably correct in asserting that they merely 'supported the COPEC resolutions as a moral gesture'.[13] Certainly the direct follow-up to the conference was weak (the group lasted only to 1929), and though several of those already prominent in Christian Socialist circles, including Reckitt and Kenyon, continued to work at a Christian expression of socialism, the main thrust of the 1920s and 1930s lay with those who worked more directly through the growing Labour Party than the Church reformers.

The fact that COPEC barely seemed aware that Labour was about to form a Government for the first time clearly weakened its prophetic veracity.

Furthermore, within two years both the Church and the Labour movement had to face a far more complicated political issue than the mere determining of ethical principles. For in 1926 the long-standing issue of the coal industry came to a head. In 1919 a Royal Commission under Mr Justice Sankey, on which R. H. Tawney had served with Sidney Webb, had recommended nation-alisation, a view which had been opposed by the mine-owners and overturned by the Samuel Royal Commission of 1926, which none the less backed the miners in resisting the extension of the working day. The mine-owners, however, resolved to hold out not only for longer hours but also for lower wages and on 1 May started a lock-out. Two days later the TUC came out in support of the miners, fearing general pressure on wages, and called a general strike.

Davidson, who was still at Lambeth, was stung into action and immediately called in the House of Lords for the Government to end the strike. On 7 May he applied to the BBC to broadcast an appeal for all three parties to come to the negotiating table without preconditions and was turned down, as it later transpired, on Government advice, a point which made him extremely wary of further intervention. In the meantime the TUC gave in at the first intimation of military strength by the Government and disapproval from the middle classes, ending the general strike only nine days after it had started.

This, of course, left the miners on their own, and though many Christians, including Cardinal Bourne, had been profoundly con-cerned by the challenge to a properly constituted democratic Government that the general strike represented, the support of the radical clergy for the miners' cause was strong. Temple and Kempthorne, together with the secretary of the ICF, Kirk, set up a Standing Conference of the Christian Churches on the Coal Dispute. Consistent with Temple's pronounced ecumenical concerns, the group included senior representatives of most of the Churches: M. E. Aubrey and S. M. Berry, Secretaries of the Baptist and Congregationalist Unions, W. F. Lofthouse and Henry Carter of the Methodists and the Quaker W. S. Nicholson. Clearly taking their cue from Westcott's and Gore's successful interventions in earlier strikes, the Standing Conference sought to persuade Davidson to put himself forward to chair new negotiations, and in July met with representatives of the mine-owners. A week later they met with the miners and then, on 19 July, with the Prime Minister, Stanley Baldwin, who had already published and rejected their recommendations. Temple, as one of those who attended the meeting with Baldwin, was depressed by the Government's apparent 'war attitude' but continued to argue that the role of the Church must be an impartial one. Kirk, however, prepared a 'manifesto' for the Standing Conference which very clearly supported the miners on the grounds of the Government's intransigence and the miners' privation. Davidson was incensed and rebuked Kempthorne as Chairman of the Standing Conference, and though he had earlier bowed to Temple's suggestion that the Ecclesiastical Commissioners should not use their coal shares to block nationalisation, he forced the Standing Conference to withdraw from the fray.

Assessments of the Standing Conference and Temple's role in the strike have tended to be harsh, pointing to the bishops' apparent naïveté in acting so publicly, thereby drastically 'upping the ante'. Indeed, even Temple acknowledged that there had been a 'tendency to try to make Capital for the Church out of it by publicity when the thing ought, if done at all, to have been kept entirely private'.[14] Edward Norman has been yet more scathing: 'Church social radicalism had developed in isolation from realities – in episcopal palaces, in study groups and conferences, in theological colleges and university common rooms. In 1926 the door had been opened and a very cold blast had withered the hothouse growths.'[15]

Yet this is an overstatement that buys Baldwin's line that the bishops had no more business interfering in politics than the

Federation of British Industry had in seeking a revision of the Athanasian Creed. Undoubtedly Baldwin won and came across as the more worldly-wise. Furthermore B. S. Rowntree's claim that his own endeavours, which had nearly brought the two sides together, were scuppered as soon as the miners felt 'that they had the whole of the Christian Churches behind them' because they then refused to make further concessions, is probably true. Yet the working conditions of the miners were appalling, and a cut in salaries would have meant genuine hardship. To assert, therefore, that the owners and the Government had a moral duty was no more than to pursue the argument of COPEC and the 'Fifth Report', that the first call on industry was the living wage, and it was entirely consistent with Cyril Garbett's support for the miners in the 1921 strike. Certainly Temple's suggestion that the Archbishop would hold a 'champagne lunch' for all the parties concerned smacks of idealism, but Davidson, now in his seventies, lacked the genuine courage of his early convictions, and was too concerned about impugning the honour due to his office. Temple's own evaluation, that the particular steps they took might have been ill-judged, but that their attempt to bring the two parties to reason was only what was required of them by their religion and their office, is probably fair.

Most interestingly, of course, the general strike and the Standing Conference confound a customary impression of Temple as a man who worked alone. Because of his eventual elevation to the see of Canterbury as the first avowedly socialist Archbishop, and because of his chairing of the two key conferences in Birmingham and Malvern, there has been a tendency to interpret him in isolation. Yet the truth is that when the strike was first called Temple was out of the country; it was Kempthorne who chaired the Standing Conference, not Temple; and Davidson was seeking advice from Gore. Temple's contribution was indeed unique. His ecumenical work led to the formation of the World Council of Churches. His *Readings in St John* is a classic text of biblical exegesis, and his attempt to reform the Church of England, developing the role of deaconesses, transforming the patronage system and introducing synodical government, were all part of his unique vision. Yet his politics make little sense unless they are considered in the light of the work of others of his time.

The most significant of these was his friend Richard Henry Tawney, whom Temple called Harry. Born in 1880 in Calcutta, where his father, a Sanskrit scholar, was Principal of the Presidency College, Tawney came to England in time to go to Rugby, which is where he first met Billy Temple at the railway station on his first day, starting a relationship that continued throughout their time at Balliol and through to Temple's death in 1944. Like Temple, Tawney joined the CSU at Oxford and came under the same radical influences, although they drew him towards not theology and ordination but an educational career. After graduating from Oxford with what his father termed a 'disgraceful' second in 1903, Tawney went on holiday in Germany with Temple before settling in the East End of London for three years, staying at Toynbee Hall and working as Secretary to the Children's County Holiday Fund. William Beveridge was also at Toynbee Hall at this time, and between them they started to take issue with Barnett's overly philanthropic attitude, which they felt did little to address the real social problems of unemployment and poor education.

In 1906, the year he joined the Fabians, he was offered his first academic post as an assistant in economics at Glasgow University, a job he felt curiously ill at ease with. In a much later address to the LSE Student Union he paraphrased Miss Prism, the governess in Oscar Wilde's *The Importance of Being Earnest*, 'Do not read Mill's chapter on the fall of the rupee, my dear, it is far too exciting for a young girl,' and went on, 'I found that my attitude to economics was much the same and that these austere heights were not my spiritual home.'[16] He also started a minor journalistic career, writing leaders for the *Glasgow Herald*.

Meanwhile in 1905 Tawney had become involved with Mansbridge's Workers' Educational Association and had subsequently brought Temple along to be President of its executive. In 1908 he took a major role in running the WEA Oxford conference on 'Working-class Education', which was chaired by another friend, Charles Gore. The conference's report, which argued for educational programmes around the country, led to Tawney's being asked to work full-time lecturing men and women in Langton and Rochdale, sponsored by the Oxford University Tutorial Classes Committee. Tawney was instantly popular and recognised in himself what was his vocation, to teach, to elicit ideas and frame minds, to instil a respect for learning. One of his first students at Rochdale referred to him as not a teacher but 'a man with a soul',[17] and it is undoubtedly true that Tawney brought to his work something of the passion and fervour of a moralist. His relationship with the WEA, however, was not uncritical, and frequent complaining letters winged their way to Mansbridge. Indeed, at one point there was a sharp division between them over whether Richard Acland, a prominent Liberal MP, should be appointed to the WEA executive. Ironically enough, in view of Acland's later political transformation, Tawney opposed his appointment because of his overtly Liberal politics. If he were appointed, then the WEA should also appoint a Labour and a Conservative MP. Tawney's commitment to education was not simply that of a politician *manqué*, however. Indeed, he often seemed the complete stereotype of a committed academic, with his lumbering frame, his sartorial clumsiness and the total chaos of the Tawney house in Mecklenburgh Square in London belying the eloquent precision of thought that imbues his writing. Most importantly, of course, he believed in education as the engine of social change and saw the political endeavour itself as educational. He was clear-sighted in his determination to challenge 'the beautiful English arrangement by which wealth protects learning and learning in turn admits wealth as a kind of honorary member of its placid groves'.[18] All Tawney's most significant political work lay in the field of education, for his *Secondary Education for All* of 1922 and *Education: The Socialist Policy* of 1924 not only established Labour's educational policy but eventually formed the core of the 1944 Education Act. His role in the history of British education might also have been more direct if it had not been for MacDonald's dislike of him, for in 1924 MacDonald refused to put him in the Lords and make him a Labour spokesman on education. In fact, it is probably just as well MacDonald did not ask him, for when he was later offered a peerage his reply was curt in the extreme, and he notably lambasted the Labour leaders over accepting political honours in 1935, saying that they 'sit up, like poodles in a drawing-room, wag their tails when patted and lick their lips at the social sugarplums tossed them by their masters'.[19]

Still with the WEA in 1909, Tawney was married, by Temple, to Jeanette Beveridge, the sister of their mutual friend William, and the new couple moved to Manchester, where he started work on the first of his social histories, *The Agrarian Problem in the Sixteenth Century*. Already a member of the Fabians, Tawney joined the ILP in 1909, and three years later, under the aegis of the Webbs' London School of Economics (LSE), he was appointed Director of the Ratan Tata Foundation. Named after a wealthy Indian benefactor, the Foundation aimed 'to promote the study and further the knowledge of methods of preventing and relieving poverty and destitution', and Tawney was keen to address social solutions, although in his characteristically ironic inaugural speech he commended those who sought to 'improve the character of individuals by all means – if you feel competent to do so, especially of those whose excessive incomes expose them to peculiar temptations'.[20]

After less than two years the war came, and though Hardie and MacDonald urged neutrality in the Commons, Tawney took much the same line as Arthur Henderson, who was elected to replace MacDonald as Leader of the Party, for, as Ross Terrill has put it, Tawney was not a pacifist, as 'no perfectionist ethic ever won him'.[21] Tawney enlisted in the Manchester Regiment, refusing a commission, just as, years later, he was to refuse a peerage, and determining to play a full fighting role. Tawney's accounts of the war reveal a somewhat naïve socialist coming to terms with what he perceived to be the philosophy of the working men in the trenches, namely 'get as much and give as little as you can'.[22] Tawney was based at Fricourt, where, on the first day of the Battle of the Somme in July 1916, 820 British soldiers went into battle and 450 died. Tawney himself was hit by a shell and spent twenty-four hours stranded in no-man's-land. A message was relayed to Jeanette, who in turn persuaded Beveridge, who was working in a government office in London, to use his position to get further details. Tawney was sent back to England, and to hospital in Oxford, where he insisted on an ordinary bed and where his nurse was consequently amazed that the bishop, Gore, came to visit someone she had not even realised was a 'gentleman'.

After convalescing at the Bishop's palace in Peterborough with Woods, Tawney was discharged in 1917 and went back to Balliol as a Fellow. From Oxford he was involved in both the 'Fifth Report' and the Sankey Commission; he started writing *The Sickness of an Acquisitive Society* for the *Hibbert Journal*, which was later published simply as *Acquisitive Society*; and he began to take a greater interest in Labour Party politics. In 1919 he also became a Reader at the LSE, where from 1931 to 1949 he was Professor of Economic History and where he was soon joined by Major Clement Attlee.

Tawney was rarely one of the protagonists in British politics, even in the Labour movement. As Ross Terrill has said, his 'life is notable as much for attitudes as activities',[23] and indeed the biographical material on his life is minimal. Yet his influence was immense. His publications, in particular *Religion and the Rise of Capitalism* (the Scott Holland Memorial lectures of 1922, published 1926) and *Equality* (1931), form a consistent body of work that few in the history of the Labour Movement can match, and though he was never either ordained or elected to the House of Commons, yet he became a ready mentor to a movement in which he never played a leading public part.

Certainly Tawney played a role in the party. He stood for Parliament four times, and was briefly on the Fabians' executive. He also helped Henderson prepare a new constitution for the Labour Party immediately after the war, and wrote much of the

Party's influential statement *Labour and the Nation* in 1928, but for the most part he contented himself with a backroom function, writing and teaching.

He also played a crucial part in framing the socialism of the century, unique because of his synthesis of economic and historical considerations within a Christian moral framework. Furthermore his relationship with Temple infected the bishop's understanding of what it was to talk of a Christian or a good society. His friendship with Beveridge further impregnated his famous report with a genuine sense of moral outrage, and his continuing critical devotion to the Labour Party and its leaders provided the ethical base for a brand of socialism that always took account of the full frailty of human nature. All of this was to make the eventual implementation of the Welfare State after the Second World War not only possible but morally imperative.

Yet Tawney's political tools were ideas and moral principles. Tony Wright, in his biography of Tawney, sees him as a physician, diagnosing society's maladies and proposing remedies focused on the key moral principles. But the cornerstone of Tawney's work was a secure Christian faith. He rarely wore his religion on his sleeve, and Beatrice Webb often referred to the fact that his Christianity was a mystery to her. For many years his church attendance was intermittent, and he remained supremely uninterested in theological niceties. Yet his foundational arguments are always unchallenged statements of Christian doctrine, and the edifice of his social theory essentially stands or falls by its Christian basis. In his commonplace book he wrote, 'The essence of all morality is this: to believe that every human being is of infinite importance, and therefore that no consideration of expediency can justify the oppression of one by another. But to believe that it is necessary to believe in God.'[24]

If Christianity provided the cornerstone and foundation of Tawney's social theory, its structural strength lay in four moral principles that acted as its central pillars. The first of these was his insistence that the economic order could not be left as a value-free zone. Arguing from history that 'the abdication by the Christian

Churches of one whole department of life, that of social and political conduct'[25] was a dereliction of its duty, he believed that the whole economic and industrial arena had become a purely 'acquisitive society' in which property was divorced from either work or its proper function and had been granted absolute sanctity. This new belief that 'Trade is one thing, religion is another'[26] in turn had made society preoccupied solely with the acquisition of wealth, and the individual the centre of his own universe, thereby dissolving moral principles into a choice of expediencies. The task was therefore to 'moralise economic life'[27] by 'making the acquisition of wealth contingent upon the discharge of social obligations'. A truly functional society would then be one 'which sought to proportion remuneration to service and denied it to those by whom no service was performed'.[28] Clearly this might involve a wide variety of common- or public-ownership initiatives, but it is interesting that in Tawney, somewhat uniquely for his time, the view that 'private property . . . is necessarily mischievous' is described as 'a piece of scholastic pedantry'[29] and nationalisation, a 'singularly colourless word', is 'merely one species of a considerable *genus* . . . a means to an end, not an end to itself'.[30]

Tawney's second principle is the equal worth of all, yet even here it is not simply a question of sloganising, for though his basic assumption is that all are equal because they are equal in the eyes of their creating Father, he is keen to articulate a desire to get beyond mere equalising opportunity, which he sees as 'the impertinent courtesy of an invitation offered to unwelcome guests, in the certainty that circumstances will prevent them from accepting it'.[31] It is vital to avoid a simple mathematical equality of financial remuneration, for 'what is repulsive is not that one man should earn more than others . . . it is that some classes should be excluded from the heritage of civilisation which others enjoy, and that the fact of human fellowship . . . should be obscured by economic contrasts'.[32] Tawney's moral gullet rises at the offence of inequality, and his mind is affronted by what he terms 'the religion of inequality' which the acquisitive society has espoused, which makes it more difficult for people to live moral lives -- exactly the argument of the 'Fifth Report'.

Tawney's third principle relates to freedom and provides a strategic reason why he felt little at home with the support that many socialists, including the Webbs and Conrad Noel, were providing for Soviet Communism. For Tawney Russia had adopted 'Police collectivism' and was in danger of ignoring the fact that arbitrary power was quite as problematic, morally, as functionless property. Freedom had therefore to be seen not only as an escape from tyranny but as a capacity to act independently or in association. Tawney's brief membership of the National Guilds League was related to his concern to foster such 'minor associations', and to argue against any supposed economic panacea.

Tawney's final moral principle – and it is important to note the frequent sarcasm, irony and rhetorical invective he uses, all the tools of a fierce moralist – is that of democracy. For not only did he believe that equality should lead to greater enfranchisement, he also believed that socialists would have to frame their socialism in terms that went with the grain of the psychology of the age. Thus, in a chapter added to *Equality* in the 1938 edition, he was highly critical of the Labour Party's apparent descent into 'private socialisms' that barely spoke to the people. After the 1931 parliamentary débâcle he was clearly in favour of Labour's adopting a secure commitment to socialism because he felt it had in office had no common conception of the end of political action, but he recognised that 'if the public and particularly the working-class public, is confronted with the choice between capitalist democracy ... and undemocratic socialism, it will choose the former every time.'[33] And in 1960 he supported Gaitskell in his Campaign for Democratic Socialism to resist the left-ward trend in the party, although he was always keen to argue that politicians should not necessarily avoid extreme positions, but 'they should show extreme sense in reaching them, extreme self-restraint in keeping their mouths shut till the opinions are worth stating, and extreme resolution in acting upon them, when stated'.[34]

Tawney's socialism was, then, essentially a moral endeavour with practical consequences. His language was the idiom of ethics and, in a biblical reference in the tradition of Matthew Arnold he posed the essential choice that he felt was before the British nation, between equality and inequality. He saw British socialism as 'obstinately and unashamedly ethical'[35] and derived his own ethical position almost exclusively from his religious faith. The historical corruption of Christianity was of passionate concern to him. He attacked 'the doctrine that private and public interests are coincident, and that man's self-love is God's Providence, which was the excuse of the last century for its worship of economic egotism'.[36] He urged the ideal of an equal distribution of wealth, not 'because such wealth is the most important of man's treasures, but to prove that it is not'.[37] And he held that 'the chief enemy of the life of the spirit, whether in art, culture and religion, or in the simple human associations which are the common vehicle of its revelation to ordinary men, is itself a religion. It is, as everyone knows, the idolatry of wealth.'[38]

Throughout Tawney's life he sustained this moral crusade, and it is difficult to imagine that his deep friendship with Temple did not inform his work. Certainly they kept in regular contact, and worked closely not only on the Life and Liberty movement, on the WEA executive (Tawney succeeded Temple as President) and on COPEC, but also in trying to build what he termed 'a common body of social ethics' founded on moral principles. Furthermore they both identified the key issue for society as its social reconstruction after the two world wars. Indeed, Tawney's theoretical method is almost identical to that which Temple adopted when it came to his most significant work of reconstruction, after the Malvern Conference.

Iremonger, in his biography of Temple, cites his wry, self-conscious comment in the *Spectator* that 'the first half of the twentieth century is likely to be regarded by those who have lived through it and survive to a later period as the Age of Conferences.'[39] So it is appropriate that Temple's most enduring political contribution stemmed from his chairmanship of the Malvern Conference in 1941.

The idea for the conference had come from Kirk and was in essence very similar to that of COPEC. For Malvern was to 'consider . . . what are the fundamental facts which are directly relevant to the ordering of the new society, and how Christian thought can be shaped to play a leading part in the reconstruction after the war is over'.[40] A major difference, however, was that this conference was to be solely Anglican and would have a much shorter lead-in time. Instead of commissions considering reports, this time there would be individual speakers addressing the 200 or so participants, and a set of formal 'conclusions'.

As we have already seen, many of the participants, at Temple's own instigation, were Christendom members. Yet after the conference, which appears to have been poorly prepared by Kirk and the ICF, Christendom was particularly dismissive. 'We have been told,' an editorial in the magazine read, 'that the one really depressing feature of Malvern was not merely that a number of people arose to proclaim, almost as it were with pride, that they did not understand what the speakers were talking about, but that they were loudly applauded when they did.'[41] Certainly the aims that Christendom were pursuing during the week were strongly at variance with those of Temple himself. Temple was convinced that the Church and society had missed the boat after the First World War, refusing to learn the lessons they badly needed to take on board, and that this time society would be ready for change. His close friendship with Beveridge and with Tawney made him convinced too that the parameters of a Christian society needed to be drawn before the war was over, and not after, if the Church's social teaching was to have any enduring relevance. The task was to 'think out afresh the implications of our Faith in relation to the new order already emerging'.[42]

The speakers were far from uniform in their approach. The poet T. S. Eliot, who was a right-wing member of the Christendom group, spoke on 'The Christian Conception of Education', supporting the five points that the two archbishops, the Cardinal-

Archbishop and the Moderator of the Church of Scotland had agreed, urging 'equal opportunities of education'. Dorothy L. Sayers argued for a disinterested Church, for 'the Church can only order the affairs of the world when, and so long as, she is not involved in or identified with them',[43] in direct contradiction to both Sir Richard Acland, MP, and Kenneth Ingram, who took an almost Marxist line. Reckitt's talk, which had to be read by Temple as Reckitt was ill, and V. A. Demant's were very general in their tone and concerned more with theological than practical matters. Though Demant stated that 'the channels of the national soul need cutting in new directions,'[44] he was more concerned to discern 'God's handwriting' in history and to see 'the dethronement of Trader Man' than to offer practical proposals or even core political principles that could be translated into an agenda for the 'new order' that Temple was so keen to delineate. Acland and Ingram, however, had a clear position and proposed a resolution which stated, 'we believe that the maintenance of that part of the structure of our society by which the ownership of the principal industrial resources of the community can be vested in the hands of private owners is such a stumbling block contrary to divine justice, making it harder for men to live Christian lives.' This, of course, was further than Temple wanted to go, and George Bell, the noted wartime Bishop of Chichester, moved an amendment which was narrowly carried; eventually he and Bell agreed a new form which inserted the word 'ultimate' before ownership and changed 'is' to 'may be'. Temple later expressed his reluctance to see such a watering down of the resolution, despite his concern that as Archbishop of York he could not be seen to condemn private property *per se*. Most of the Christendom Group, however, abstained on the final resolution because they felt it was simply not within the competence of Christian dogma to make such statements. Temple's subsequent letters to Kirk suggest he felt more in sympathy with Christendom than with Acland and Ingram, yet his major concern seems to have been to carry what he termed 'the movement' forward without leaving the impetus to either the Anglo-Catholics or the hard left.

Either way, Temple knew exactly what he wanted from the conference, and he got it, for within a few weeks he had published its proceedings and his 'conclusions', which by the end of the year had sold 200,000 copies, despite the fact that Demant had tried to prevent his address from being included with Ingram's. Temple's determination that the Church should help to frame the new order was pursued ruthlessly with a series of two-day meetings around the country and a reissue in 1942 of Temple's most significant work, *Christianity and the Social Order*.

Much has been written about *Christianity and the Social Order*, but its basic message is simple. Temple's foremost concern is to argue that the Church has a role to play in framing the moral contours of society, but not in determining policies. Thus 'the Church must announce Christian principles and point out where the existing social order at any time is in conflict with them'[45] and must then leave the task of reordering society to Christian citizens. Temple then goes on to enunciate some of those principles, drawing a distinction between 'primary principles', which reflect deep theological verities about the nature of God and humanity, and 'derivative principles', such as freedom, social fellowship and service, all of which must form the basis of the good society. Temple's politics are far from naïve, however. He acknowledges that 'the art of government in fact is that art of so ordering life that self-interest prompts what justice demands'[46] and is keen to explore the apparent conflicts between the principles of freedom and social fellowship. Certainly 'man is incurably social'[47] and discovers his full potential through social relationships, but this cannot deny the importance of the personal.

All of this is significant in terms of theological method, and indeed Temple's analysis of natural law is similarly interesting, but the most dramatic element of Temple's work was its reaffirmation of six core objectives that he had previously outlined in the Malvern 'conclusions', which came as close as possible to a political manifesto. Because of their centrality to the history of both Christian Socialism and the formation of the Welfare State they are worth quoting here in full:

1. Every child should find itself a member of a family housed with decency and dignity, so that it may grow up as a member of that basic community in a happy fellowship unspoilt by underfeeding or overcrowding, by dirty or drab surroundings or by mechanical monotony of environment. 2. Every child should have the opportunity of an education till years of maturity, so planned as to allow for his peculiar aptitudes and make possible their full development. This education should throughout be inspired by faith in God and find its focus in worship. 3. Every citizen should be secure in possession of such income as will enable him to maintain a home and bring up children in such conditions as are described in paragraph 1 above. 4. Every citizen should have a voice in the conduct of the business or industry which is carried on by means of his labour and the satisfaction of knowing that his labour is directed to the well-being of the community. 5. Every citizen should have sufficient daily leisure, with two days of rest in seven, and, if an employee, an annual holiday with pay, to enable him to enjoy a full personal life with such interests and activities as his tasks and talents may direct. 6. Every citizen should have assured liberty in the forms of freedom of worship, of speech, of assembly and of association for special purposes.[48]

The book, which Temple had sent to Tawney and J. M. Keynes for comments and revision, was published as a Penguin Special and sold more than 150,000, helped by the fact that though Temple was still at York when he wrote it, he had been translated by Winston Churchill to Canterbury by the time it came out.

Perhaps one of the most sterile debates in the history of Christian Socialism has focused on how socialist Temple really was, with Ronald Preston, Atherton and Iremonger all arguing that his social radicalism wilted with the years. Yet I suspect that this is to miss the point of Temple, and to read him in separation from his closest colleagues. For Temple believed that his role lay within the

Church. He was not a politician, held no mandate from the people and had no role to play in determining social policy. The Church's role was to point to the things of God, to enunciate core principles, to educate Christian citizens, and to indicate where the existing system fell short of the ideal. No political programme could be identified as 'ideal', just as no state could ever be 'ideal'. None the less the Christian faith was not simply about eternal verities. It had something to say to society because God had dwelt among us. Yet to build a political programme, this was not the task of a bishop or an archbishop. This was the task of his friends and colleagues, of Harry Tawney or William Beveridge.

We said earlier that the theoretical methods of Tawney and Temple were almost identical, and this is certainly reflected in *Christianity and the Social Order.* Tawney, we know, advised Temple to add his final attempts at a political programme on the grounds that it would make his work seem more substantial, but the shared heritage of the two schoolboy friends is far more significant. For both of them argued, from their very different spheres, that society as it stood was wrong, that it did not work, that its social mechanism was jarring, and that after the catastrophe of war there was no choice but a social reconstruction based on equality. Neither Tawney nor Temple had children, yet their inheritance was a social ethic that stated that property was correctly seen as the reward for work, held in trust; that it had social obligations; that inequality of itself implied a dysfunctional and inefficient society; and that humanity's essential social nature was destroyed by a purely acquisitive society. The answer must be to return to a social philosophy based ultimately on religion which would prevent 'the collapse of public morality in a welter of disorderly appetites'.[49] For Temple the theology of the Incarnation necessarily entailed a belief in the sanctity of human history, and for Tawney the doctrine of Creation meant that society must be based on the equal worth of all. Jointly they bequeathed a social ethic that informed the Welfare State and formed the basis of the social consensus from the end of the Second World War through to the new politics of Thatcherism.

# 8

# *Parliamentary Lives*

But just remember this. One Eva Smith has gone – but there are millions and millions of Eva Smiths ... still left with us, with their lives, their hopes and fears, their suffering, and chance of happiness, all intertwined with our lives, with what we think and say and do. We don't live alone. We are members of one body. We are responsible for each other. And I tell you that the time will soon come when, if men will not learn that lesson, then they will be taught it in fire and blood and anguish.

J. B. Priestley, *An Inspector Calls*

If the 1906 general election dramatically altered the fortunes of the Labour Party, it also transformed the style, the pattern and the focus of Christian Socialism. For although there were continuing clerical efforts through the following decades, and the role of turbulent and even seditious priests and pastors has scarcely diminished to this day, yet Christian Socialism steadily acquired a parliamentary element which brought new perceptions, new concerns and, to some degree, an altered political agenda to the tradition of Maurice and Gore. What had started as an ethical critique of the social and economic systems of the day, by clergy who were banned from standing for Parliament, slowly developed into a more coherent political strategy able to come to terms with power and, indeed, to seek it. All this started with the breakthrough of 1906, although it was not truly until Labour was in power that the parliamentary tradition of Christian Socialism could come to the fore.

Inevitably, then, the history of Christian Socialism through to

1950 becomes identified increasingly with prominent Christian Socialist MPs. Though rarely cited in conventional histories of the movement, the lives of Arthur Henderson, George Lansbury, Stafford Cripps and Richard Acland, through their entirely secular parliamentary careers, are as vital in passing on the flame as their more clearly theological counterparts in the Church.

To form an impression of the interweaving of religious, personal and political life that constituted much of the Labour Party through to 1950, it is worth looking at the party in one of its crisis years. For in 1931 Labour had three Leaders, two of whom, at least, claimed that the taproot of their socialism was their Christian faith.

That year also marked one of the most extraordinary moments in the twentieth-century constitutional history of Britain. For on 5 September 1931 the 615 members of the House of Commons gathered to witness what would have seemed unimaginable only weeks before. Face to face across the Dispatch Box were two leaders of the Labour Party, one as Prime Minister, the other as the new Leader of Her Majesty's Loyal Opposition. On Monday, 24 August, Ramsay MacDonald had resigned as Labour Prime Minister and instantly formed a National Government together with the Liberals and the Tories. MacDonald's new Cabinet included only two of his party comrades, Philip Snowden and J. H. Thomas. The rest consisted of his old Tory enemies, including Stanley Baldwin and Austen Chamberlain, and a sprinkling of Liberals. In opposition sat the man who had only recently been Foreign Secretary, Arthur Henderson, newly and reluctantly elected Leader of the Party, alongside George Lansbury, Arthur Greenwood and Herbert Morrison.

In truth it is difficult to imagine the full depth of Henderson's feelings at this point. His relationship with MacDonald had always been stormy, and though between them they had occupied the most important offices in the Labour movement for thirty-one years, working together as Secretary and Leader almost since the party was started, yet each harboured personal animosities which it was hard, in such a strained moment, to put aside. MacDonald had tried to exclude Henderson from his first Cabinet in 1924 and in 1929 had attempted to avoid giving him the post of Foreign Secretary. Even once he had appointed him, he spent fruitless hours briefing civil servants and the press against him, and frequently interfered in Foreign Office matters without reference to him. Yet Henderson had consistently remained loyal to Mac-Donald, believing him to be Labour's best proponent, hopelessly arrogant, vain and personally obsessive, but none the less its most talented and capable leader.

Henderson's personal sense of betrayal at MacDonald's desertion of the party over the issue of cuts in unemployment benefits and insurance, which Henderson and others refused to sanction in the cause of balancing the budget, was acute. At the same time he felt deeply the hurt to the Labour Party which he had fought to build up. Despite his strong Christian faith he found it difficult to forgive what Attlee later called 'the greatest betrayal in the political history of this country'.[1]

In many ways Henderson was the stereotype of a Labour MP of his time. A Methodist, a northern trade-union official, an ex-mayor and an expert at fixing committees, he came to personify the Labour Party, and though many today will not even have heard of him, his role in the development of the party was immense. For years the name of 'Uncle Arthur' was almost synonymous with that of Labour.

Like MacDonald a Scot, Henderson was born in a Glasgow slum in 1863, though he was brought up in Newcastle after his father died when he was nine. His working life began at twelve, when he was apprenticed as an iron-moulder before eventually qualifying as a journeyman in 1883, when he joined the moderate Friendly Society of Iron Founders.

By then Henderson's faith had already been stirred by a Salvation Army evangelist called Rodney 'Gypsy' Smith, and he had taken the pledge as a Wesleyan Methodist. At his local church on Elswick Road, just round the corner from St Philip's, where Moll was vicar, he taught in the Sunday school, met his wife Eleanor and became a lay preacher.

Because Henderson was never a great writer, little has survived of his religious thoughts, yet we do know that his faith continued a vital part of his life's work until his death. In 1903 he was involved in the setting up of the Methodist Union for Social Service, and was for some time President of the Brotherhood Movement, which through its 'Pleasant Sunday Afternoons' sought to bring to church meetings working men who were put off by conventional Nonconformist worship. These normally ended up as discussions about social concerns, with a couple of hymns for good measure. The movement ran a special book scheme for attendants, and many local groups, such as the one in Ashton-under-Lyne, took a leading role in political campaigns, most particularly for old-age pensions. Though Henderson himself was more directly associated with the Methodists, many of the 1906 Labour MPs who were cited as lay preachers spoke at Brotherhood meetings rather than in more conventional pulpits. Henderson's faith was inspired more by the Bible than by any modern theologies, and he would regularly appear at Methodist meetings arguing that Christianity should be shown in its real nature, 'as an aggressive force, destroying the evil of the individual life, transforming the character of the workers' environment, taking cognizance of social defects, seeking to right industrial wrongs and removing the injustices under which the workers suffer', for 'then it cannot fail to command the sympathies of the common people'.[2]

Like Hardie, Henderson's political formation came in the Liberal Party, for which he was first elected to Newcastle City Council in 1892, and in the union, for which he worked as a salaried District Organiser for eleven years. Unlike Hardie, he was still in the Liberal Party in 1895 when he went to work as election agent for Sir Joseph Pease, the Quaker Liberal MP for Barnard Castle. He moved to Darlington and in 1897 was elected to Durham County Council. By 1903 he was also a JP and Mayor of Darlington, regularly called on for Nonconformist and Liberal temperance meetings.

In the meantime he had been a union delegate at the inaugural meeting of the LRC, and it was not until 1902 that he saw a contradiction between the LRC and being a Liberal. The following year Pease died, and Henderson stood as an LRC candidate, hoping for Liberal backing. The local Liberals put up a candidate, but Henderson scraped in with the unofficial backing of the national Liberal Party. In the event Henderson's election, by forty-seven votes, was the first time Labour had defeated both Conservatives and Liberals in a single-member constituency.

Henderson arrived in Parliament as a true working-class Labour representative who had worked for nearly twenty years in an iron foundry, yet his politics were essentially still Liberal. Moreover, his immediate concerns were those of an election agent. He set about building the party, creating ward committees and women's sections, publishing a guide on electoral registration and taking on the role of party Treasurer. He more or less ran the general election campaign in 1906, determined to see the party election machine steadily grow in effectiveness.

The 1906 election, as we have already seen, brought in many Labour MPs who shared Henderson's Nonconformist and union background, but it would be false to suggest that the 1906 parliamentary party lived in easy Christian unity and harmony. Keir Hardie only scraped through the election as Chairman of the PLP over David Shackleton and almost immediately proceeded to irritate his closest colleagues, especially Henderson, who was Chief Whip, by his poor attendance and whimsical attitude to the rest of the party. When Hardie's two years as Chairman were up Henderson replaced him in 1908, just as disputes over parliamentary arrangements with the Liberal Government also led to the first violent outburst between MacDonald and Henderson, when MacDonald called him a 'bloody liar' at a public meeting. In 1910, however, Henderson relinquished the chairmanship, preferring the post of party Secretary, which MacDonald had held since the start of the LRC. As MacDonald had also perceived that the true leadership role, if not necessarily the power, would always lie at the head of the PLP, he agreed to Henderson's suggestion that he should stand as Chairman and was elected in 1912.

In 1914, however, MacDonald, like Hardie and Lansbury and most of the ILP, was at odds with the rest of the parliamentary party over the First World War, and when it approved war credits in August he resigned, and Henderson again assumed the chairmanship, although he saw himself only as a caretaker leader for the course of the war. In fact, one of the most profound ironies of history is that Henderson's personal desire to defeat Prussian militarism, which overrode his pacifist inclinations, meant that he co-operated with Asquith's war effort, becoming chairman of the Central Munitions Labour Supply Committee, and later joining the Cabinet as President of the Board of Education and Paymaster General. When the issue of conscription came up in 1916, however, the party was keen that Labour should voice its opposition and withdraw from the Government. Henderson refused to resign from the Cabinet and went on to join Lloyd George's five-man war cabinet, though his determination to attend a Stockholm meeting of the International, at which German socialists would be present, meant that he was forced to resign from the Cabinet in 1917. He simultaneously resigned as Chair of the PLP, deciding to resume his organisational work within the party. After consultation with Tawney and Cole, he put together a memorandum to the National Executive Committee proposing major reform of the party with a new constitution and statement of aims which was eventually drawn up by Sidney Webb and, when agreed at the second attempt in February 1918, came to be known as Clause 4. For many this was the moment when the Labour Party nailed its colours to the socialist mast, although in truth it was also when individual membership of the party was introduced and the trade-union domination of the party executive and conference commenced. Inevitably enough, the Methodist Secretary of the party selected Methodist Central Hall for the occasion.

The following years were something of an electoral see-saw for Henderson. He and MacDonald both lost their seats in 1918. Henderson returned in the Widnes by-election in August 1919, only to lose again in 1922, when MacDonald got back in. He was returned in January 1923, but in December he lost his seat again and was not able to take a role in the first Labour minority Government until he had won a further by-election in Burnley, very soon after the general election, when he became Home Secretary. The hasty election in 1924, in the midst of a 'Red Scare' about Labour–Soviet involvements, fortunately kept him in Parliament, and he devoted the subsequent five years in opposition to developing Labour's programme and its electoral machine from his position as party Secretary.

In 1928 he was instrumental in getting *Labour and the Nation* written by Tawney and accepted by the party; it was a document he always saw as expressing his core political and Christian beliefs, with its emphasis on the moral case for socialism. 'Socialism', it argued 'is neither a sentimental aspiration for an impossible Utopia, nor a blind movement of revolt against poverty and oppression. It is a practical recognition of the familiar commonplace that "morality is the nature of things", and that men are all, in very truth, members one of another.'[3]

Henderson's role in history, however, relates more directly to his second period in office, when, as Foreign Secretary (1929–31), he was at the forefront of change in Britain's international policy, establishing diplomatic ties with Soviet Russia, pushing for an enhanced role for the League of Nations and renegotiating Britain's exit from Egypt. In 1924 he had negotiated the Geneva Protocol with Stafford Cripps's father, Lord Parmoor, and together with Hugh Dalton, Lord Robert Cecil and Philip Noel-Baker he campaigned for the League's World Disarmament Conference, which he saw as key to averting the impending catastrophe in the 1930s. Much to MacDonald's irritation, he was appointed President of the Conference while still Foreign Secretary and continued in post even after the formation of the National Government and the loss of his seat, yet again, in the late 1931 election. Soon after re-election, in 1934, he was awarded the Nobel Peace Prize, as in later years were two of his Foreign Office team.

Henderson's career was purely secular. He was never a great academic or an intellectual theologian. He was a Christian and a socialist, and understood his political work as an attempt to put social flesh on biblical principles, yet it would be inappropriate to attempt to dissect the uniqueness of his Christian Socialism. Certainly he held firmly to his Methodist faith and often had to defend his appearances on Nonconformist platforms which were still associated with the Liberals. But in essence he was a party man who knew how to build an organisation that might be capable of winning votes, and MacDonald's underestimation of him was a mistake.

It was the 1931 general election, which unseated Henderson and most of Labour's front bench, that sealed the future of the party and brought back into prominence the old warrior of the East End, George Lansbury.

Identified by the *Daily Herald* as 'not only the most loved figure in the Labour movement, but perhaps in the whole of politics',[4] George Lansbury's primary fame by this time was founded on his local-government career. For in 1919, together with the other thirty-nine Labour Poplar Borough councillors, he had refused, as mayor, to pay the Poplar precept to the London County Council on the grounds that boroughs such as Westminster, which were much less deprived, had far greater resources. Campaigning for an equalisation of the rates, so that poorer boroughs would not be permanently disadvantaged, Poplar set an illegal budget, and Lansbury and others were imprisoned for contempt of court. Other Labour local-government leaders, especially Herbert Morrison from Hackney, refused to back Poplar, though Clement Attlee in Stepney did vote to follow his lead. None the less, the Government gave in eventually, creating a common fund across London under the London Authorities (Financial Provision) Act of 1921 and effectively granting local government a redistributive function. The Poplar councillors argued their case in a short pamphlet entitled *Guilty and Proud of It*, which started with a quotation from the New Testament book of James (AV, 1:26), 'Pure religion and undefiled before God and the Father is this: to visit the fatherless and widows in their affliction', thereby highlighting what they saw as the ethical and religious basis of their campaign.

Lansbury had resigned his seat in 1912, and it was not until the 1922 general election, when Attlee and the 'Red Clydesiders' took seats for the first time, that he returned. Re-elected at the end of 1923, when Labour secured 191 seats to the Conservatives' 258 and the Liberals' 159, Lansbury was the most significant omission from Ramsay MacDonald's minority Government Cabinet, largely due to his left-wing credentials, which MacDonald distrusted as potentially revolutionary. By 1929 Lansbury had hardly toned down his socialism, having unconditionally supported the general strike of 1926 in opposition to the Labour Party's official line. None the less MacDonald did reluctantly include him in the Cabinet in 1929, in the minor post of Minister of Works. Lansbury's experience in local government, where he was used to running the show and making things happen, stood him in excellent stead and he made much of his responsibility, transforming a moribund department, used to looking after dusty buildings, into one with a vision of leisure amenities for everyone. Many of the parks of London were revolutionised, with new swimming pools, concerts and open access for all.

His politics remained as fiery as ever; he took an uncompromising attitude over women's suffrage, unemployment, foreign policy and pacifism, all of which seemed designed to irritate MacDonald. It was inevitable, therefore, that he would condemn MacDonald's actions in 1931, and when Henderson lost his seat, it was equally certain that he would be elected the new Labour Leader, despite being seventy-two years old.

It has been fashionable to underestimate Lansbury's contribution as Leader of the Labour Party largely because of his undiluted pacifism, which increasingly put him in an untenable position as Hitler came to power in Germany and the Second World War approached. The party's concerns were to oppose Fascism at home and abroad, to preserve peace if possible, but not at the cost of appeasement, and to ensure that the aims of any war Britain might be engaged in were just. None of these concerns could readily accommodate the non-violent position that Lansbury felt compelled by his faith to adopt, and history has judged him largely on this basis as a hopeless idealist. Yet his real task in 1931 was to rebuild the morale of a party which had lost its most dominant and astute figure to the opposition, to give it reassurance, to provide continuity with the great campaigning spirits of the founding members.

In many ways Lansbury was an archetype of the CSL member. A Christian first, he discovered socialism as a result of his faith, as he recognised in his autobiography: 'My reading and my prayers have all united to confirm my faith that Socialism, which means love, co-operation and brotherhood in every department of human affairs, is the only outward expression of a Christian faith.'[5] A hard-working prophet, he would have agreed with Hardie that 'the need of the hour is for a fresh crusade to restore religion to something like its pristine purity,' yet his work was not that of the purist who refused to muddy his ideology in the slow waters of parliamentary politics. He realised that change could come only through legislative reform and that only coherent concerted party work could deliver that reform. At times he felt the need to hold out for an unpopular view or, as in the case of the Poplar revolt, to flout the law in order to change it. Yet he was not a rebel by nature and did not succumb to the vanity of the easy radical. He bound the party together at a time when its spirit was bruised, and he enabled it to rediscover its soul, to reinvent its politics. His heart-felt pacifism made it difficult for him to lead Labour into the fight against Fascism in Europe, but the personal qualities he brought to the task of rebuilding the party – honesty, openness, availability and a complete lack of abrogating vanity – all make him one of the most likeable of all Labour luminaries and Christian Socialists.

Few have argued the same for Stafford Cripps. Indeed, history has tended to see him as one of the mose austere of Labour politicians. Cripps was one of Labour's most recent acquisitions, having been elected for Bristol East in a by-election only in January 1931. In fact, he had been urged to stand by MacDonald quite soon after Herbert Morrison had persuaded him to join the party, and he had been brought in specifically for his legal skills, having become the youngest King's Counsel in 1926. MacDonald had appointed him Solicitor-General following a series of outstanding legal cases in which he had acted for trades unions, acquiring a name as an effective and radical senior lawyer.

Cripps's early childhood had been about as different from Lansbury's as can be imagined. Born in 1889, his family had been of old English stock, numbering several Conservative parliamentarians and clergy in its past. The family estates at Parmoor were extensive. He went to Winchester and, unusually, chose to forgo a New College place at Oxford for a chemistry degree at University College, London. None the less he inherited a radical streak, for his mother's sister was Beatrice Potter, who later married Sidney Webb, and his father's conservatism soon ran out after he lost his own parliamentary seat in 1908 and he was ennobled by Asquith as Lord Parmoor in 1914. In fact, by the end of the First World War Parmoor's respect for his second wife's Quaker beliefs had turned him into a convinced pacifist who campaigned with bishops Temple, Gore and Burge in favour of the League of Nations. This move to the left was finally completed in 1924 when MacDonald made him Lord President of the Council, and he, together with his brother-in-law Webb, joined the Cabinet.

Meanwhile Cripps himself had been called to the Bar and had started the war as a Red Cross lorry driver in Boulogne. When he was badly injured he returned to England to use his chemistry degree as an explosives expert in the Munitions Ministry. Returning to the Bar after the war, he was elected to the National Assembly of the Church of England for the diocese of Oxford in 1920, just as his father became the first chairman of its House of Laity. In 1929 Parmoor was again appointed Lord President of the Council and took an active interest in trying to involve his son in the party, which eventually paid off when Morrison approached him and asked him to join.

So it was that in 1931 both Parmoor and Cripps held within

the Labour Party influential positions that they had effectively been handed by MacDonald without having to climb the Labour hierarchy the slow way. In fact, when MacDonald formed the National Government Cripps was recuperating from a recurring intestinal problem that he had contracted in the war and had rendered his digestive system so weak that he only ever ate raw fruit or vegetables, brown bread and butter and soured milk and that required him to take cold baths every morning at four. MacDonald asked him by telegraph to remain in post in the new Government, but after careful consideration he declined.

If Lansbury was to be the reassuring figure that would remind the party of its roots and inspire it with confidence, Cripps was to be the new boy with radical ideas of how the party could forge a distinct identity, more clearly wedded to socialism and less prepared to adopt the 'gradualist approach'.

Thus in April 1932 the Countess of Warwick, who had already been so helpful to Conrad Noel, together with G. D. H. Cole, played host at Easton Lodge to Lansbury, Cripps, Hugh Dalton, Manny Shinwell and Attlee to discuss why Labour had done so poorly at the general election and to frame the socialism of the new post-MacDonald party. Later that year six of the ILP MPs left Labour, and those that remained joined the Easton Lodge set to form the Socialist League, which brought together a wide range of Christian Socialists and secular radicals. Its executive included Cripps, Tawney, Attlee, Sir Charles Trevelyan and Aneurin Bevan. One of the League's most notable successes was the establishment of the left-wing newspaper *Tribune*. The League was not, however, universally popular. It saw itself as a ginger group for new ideas within the party. Others saw it as either an intellectual huddle or a party within the party, devised to further Cripps's own career. Moreover, many on the trade-union right of the party came to object to his politics, to resent his apparent ambition and to envy his effortless rise to prominence. When, therefore, in the run-up to the war he supported the call for a Popular Front of Socialists and Communists to defeat the National Government and fight Fascism he found himself in the wilderness. Many interpreted both the League and the Front as ill-considered and ill-disciplined attempts to circumvent the party, and when he also made a couple of *faux pas* regarding the Royal Family he came to be cast as an irresponsible revolutionary.

Cripps was undoubtedly ambitious, as several of his father's letters show. Yet to interpret him in terms of his ambitions alone would be a mistake. For a vital element of his political make-up was his faith, and much of his work in the 1930s reflected the common concerns of other Christian Socialists. He was indeed close to many of the leading Christian figures on the left and acted as something of a recruiting agent for Christian Socialism, converting to socialism the young Mervyn Stockwood, whose parish was in his constituency and was later Bishop of Southwark and a founding member of the Christian Socialist Movement. John Collins, who later founded CND with J. B. Priestley and others, also came to know Cripps through Stockwood and after the war persuaded him to become one of the founding members of Christian Action.

More significantly, however, throughout the 1930s a lively debate raged in the Church press and among many intellectual Christians about the morality of Communism and the possibility of constructive dialogue between Christianity and Marxism. Marx himself, of course, had pointed to the ideological role Christianity could play, and had played, in capitalist society, and defined religion as 'the opiate of the people', in a phrase remarkably similar to Kingsley's independent 'opium dose for keeping beasts of burden patient'. In the *Communist Manifesto* Marx had also reserved especial condemnation for Christian Socialism as 'the holy water with which the priest consecrates the heart burnings of the aristocrat.' Clearly, for Christians who felt sympathetic to the moral purpose of Communism there was work to be done in rectifying Soviet atheism and in explaining the ethical foundation of the revolution to the Church and society at large. Inevitably sympathy with the USSR became for many a badge of socialist commitment, as much within the Churches as within the Communist Party, from which Labour kept a safe distance.

Many Christians had addressed this ideological aspect of Marx's work earlier than 1930, but it was only then that Christian leaders had an opportunity to see the supposed working out of Marx's theories at first hand in Communist Russia. Of course, the Russian Revolution itself had prompted much discussion about the rights and wrongs of both revolutionary activity and the soviet system. Lansbury had addressed more than a thousand people at the Royal Albert Hall in 1917 to celebrate the Revolution, and the Catholic Crusade had welcomed Lenin's victory with great jubilation in 1918. Alec Vidler was also engaged in what he described as taking a leaf out of the Communists' book by forming small Christian cells under the title *'koinonia'*, which would develop a Christian understanding of society. But in national politics the Soviet issue was brought into sharp focus by the 1924 'Red Scare' election and, in 1929, by the question of whether Britain should re-open diplomatic relations with Russia, thereby making all pro-Russian sympathisers and, by association, all Communists seem unpatriotic. In Christian circles it was a series of visits to Russia by a set of senior clerics that prompted a wide-ranging debate about the theological relevance of the revolution and the possibility of Christian–Marxist dialogue. Cripps's own visits to Soviet Russia, and his attempt to co-operate with the British Communist Party, might have seemed outrageous to the Labour Party and to the press, but in Christian Socialist circles they seemed only natural, not least because the way Russia turned in the fight against Fascism would be a determining factor in any eventual war with Germany.

Two extra-parliamentary figures stand out in this attempt to come to terms with Communism during the 1930s: the 'Red Dean' Hewlett Johnson and Professor John MacMurray.

Johnson was born in 1874 into a wealthy Manchester family of nine, and retained sterling characteristics from both his parents. From his mother, a resolute Presbyterian and convinced sabbatarian, he inherited a clear perception of what he believed to be right, and the ability to shrug off unpopularity. From his father, who was an industrialist, he acquired both a training in engineering and a determination to face real industrial issues. After studying at Owens College (later Manchester University) he started work for the Ashbury Railway Carriage Iron Company as an engineer, where he first came into contact with Trades Unionists and socialists. His faith had already taken shape, and in 1900, as an avowed evangelical, he did a year's training at Wycliffe Hall in Oxford, before starting a theology MA at Wadham. In 1904 he was ordained to a curacy in the affluent parish of Dunham Massey at Altrincham, where in 1908 he became the vicar.

Johnson's politics were already radical, although he had little in common, theologically, with many of the leading Church Socialist Leaguers of the day. He was a low-church clergyman interested more in biblical exegesis and injunctions than in Anglo-Catholic ritual. None the less he started and edited the *Interpreter*, and several of the CSL's leading lights wrote for it on social issues, most notably Lewis Donaldson, who became a close lifetime friend, and Conrad Noel. In 1917 he took part in Temple's Life and Liberty campaign, and was briefly on its executive, thus cementing a relationship which, in 1924, became a close partnership, when Johnson was appointed Dean of Manchester at Temple's suggestion. It was a Labour Prime Minister who put his name forward to the King in 1924, and it was under Labour again, in 1931, that he was moved to the senior cathedral of the Church of England, as Dean of Canterbury, a post he held through to 1963, again overlapping with Temple as dean and bishop for Temple's brief wartime period at Canterbury.

If Temple was the epitome of theological seriousness and socialist moderation, Johnson was the embodiment of radical rebellion. For all his wealth and privileged upbringing – he retained several houses in London and in Wales – he rapidly became in the 1930s the most convinced advocate of Communism in the Church of England.

What distinguished him from most Christian Socialists, though, was his friendship with Victor Gollancz of the Left Book Club, which was founded in 1936, in the midst of national ferment about the role of Russia and, therefore, of Communism itself. Many of the authors were Communists, although Gollancz himself never joined the Party, and the Club did attempt to widen its sphere of influence by trying to rename itself the Anti-Fascist Alliance. Gollancz invited Johnson to speak at a packed Left Book Club rally in 1937 at the Queen's Hall, just prior to the Dean's first visit to Russia, and commissioned him to write up his experiences for publication, which he did under the title *The Socialist Sixth of the World*. He returned to Russia at the end of the war, when he met Stalin, and he was later awarded the Stalin Peace Prize for his stout defence of the Soviet system, which he restated in his *Christians and Communism*.

John MacMurray could scarcely have been a more different figure from the quixotic Johnson. MacMurray was yet another Scot, born in Kirkcudbrightshire in 1891 and brought up in Aberdeen on the north-east coast of Scotland. His parents were resolutely middle-class – his father was a civil servant – and Calvinist with something of an evangelical twist. After studying classics at Glasgow University from 1909 to 1913, during which time he became closely involved in the Student Christian Movement and attended the same Edinburgh conference on Mission as Temple and Gore, he went to Tawney's Balliol College, where he started more specific studies in philosophy.

He served in the First World War, first in the Medical Corps, and then, from 1916, as an officer in the Cameron Highlanders, with whom he fought in the Somme and was wounded at Arras. MacMurray ascribed much of his later commitment to reshaping society to his wartime experiences: 'We went into war in a blaze of idealism, to save little Belgium and to put an end to war. We discovered stage by stage, what childish nonsense all this idealism was. We learned that war was simply stupidity, destruction, waste and futility . . . By the end of the war we soldiers had largely lost faith in the society we had been fighting for.'[6] Like Tawney, his life after the war was spent in education, although he took the rather more formal route of a professorship in Johannesburg, a fellowship at Balliol and from 1928 the Grote Chair of the

Philosophy of Mind and Logic at London University. From there in 1944 he moved to Edinburgh as Professor of Moral Philosophy, from which he retired in 1958 to live in the Quaker community at Jordans in Buckinghamshire.

In the 1930s MacMurray's primary concern was to come to a philosophical understanding of Communism. He believed that the traditional Platonic philosophical belief in the primacy of ideas over things needed to be inverted by a Christian Marxist emphasis on action as the fruit of theory. All theories, including Christianity itself, must then be judged in practice, and right action rather than right doctrine must become the determining factor of Christian life.

MacMurray was thus reasserting in philosophical terms the theological challenge that Maurice and Gore had insisted on, that a division between mind and matter, between theory and action, between secular and sacred, must be false. He went further though:

If social development is to be planned and controlled, the struggle for power must cease and social relations must, therefore, cease to be determined through the control and ownership of the means of production. In particular, the division of society into a class which owns the means of production and a class which does not must disappear. The primary condition of a planned social development and, therefore, of the disappearance of economic determinism in the development of society is the realisation of a society without social classes. And a classless society is a communist society. Communism is, therefore, the necessary basis of real freedom.[7]

In this conclusion MacMurray sounds remarkably similar to Johnson. Yet MacMurray's argument is far more intellectually robust than the Dean's, and he goes on in his other works to analyse the very nature of humanity in terms of the 'personal', returning to a theme of Scott Holland and Gore's. Here Mac-

Murray's work is at its most dense, but the core ideas are straightforward. Believing that classical philosophy has been wrong to assert the primacy of the individual on the premise that 'I think therefore I am', MacMurray prefers to state 'I *do* therefore I am', and that it is therefore only in relating to other individuals through actions that the individual becomes 'personal'. 'Thus human experience is, in principle, shared experience; human life even in its most individual elements is a common life.'[8] MacMurray's tight philosophical argument is then used to put the case for a social order that recognises community as its central aim:

> The model of the family is to be realised in society at large. A community . . . is a unity of persons as persons. It cannot be defined in functional terms, by relation to a common purpose. It is not organic in structure, and cannot be constituted or maintained by organisation, but only by the motives which sustain the personal relations of its members. It is constituted and maintained by a mutual affection. This can only mean that each member of the group is in positive personal relation to each of the others taken severally. The structure of a community is the nexus or network of the active relations of friendship between all possible pairs of its members.[9]

In essence, of course, this is very close to John Donne's 'No man is an island', but the refinement of thought that MacMurray brought to his analysis of the nature of humanity as communitarian marks him out from nearly every other socialist thinker.

In 1937 the Christian left was concerned with one issue, war. For some, the question was whether war could be justified in any event at all. Dick Sheppard, who had been Johnson's predecessor at Canterbury and had resigned to become a canon of St Paul's in 1931, initiated the 'War We Say No' campaign, bringing together a wide selection of Christian Socialists, including Lansbury, the writers A. A. Milne and Laurence Housman, Vera Brittain and

# Possible Dreams

the young Donald Soper. For other Christian Socialists the issue was whether it would be possible to get Russia to support the war against German Fascism. For yet others it was the attempt to get the aims of any potential war limited to non-retribution. It is against this background that Cripps's solicitations for a combined assault on the National Government make sense.

For early in 1937 the Socialist League, together with the ILP and the Communist Party, launched independent campaigns for a 'People's Front' to replace the National Government. Over the next two years Cripps and others argued that Labour had to work with the Communists to secure power for an anti-Fascist Government that would fight if necessary, but would uphold a 'positive policy of peace by collective action'.[10] In January 1939 Cripps moved a special resolution at the NEC, urging Labour to come out as the leader of such a combined opposition. The NEC voted overwhelmingly against him, but rather than save his fight for another day, Cripps issued his resolution in the form of a memorandum to the press and resolved to fight the issue at the party's conference that year. At the next meeting of the NEC he was condemned for bringing the party into disrepute and was asked to withdraw his memorandum. He refused and was promptly expelled from the party. Immediately he launched a more public campaign with a national petition and support from Ellen Wilkinson, J. M. Keynes and Nye Bevan. Bevan was also expelled, along with all those who supported Cripps in his constituency, including Mervyn Stockwood. At Conference in Southport standing orders were suspended for twenty minutes to allow Cripps to speak, but the expulsions were ratified by 2,100,000 votes to 402,000, and Cripps had to spend the whole of the Second World War as an Independent MP, although he still enjoyed the support of his constituency party in Bristol.

Cripps's flirtation with the Communist Party was short-lived. That of Hewlett Johnson and John MacMurray was in the end insubstantial: Johnson's amounted to no more than a fascination with Russia; MacMurray's was far more profound yet lacked political fibre. The only person who really sought to build a

216

political programme on the basis of a Christian form of Common Ownership was Richard Acland, 'a crusading Liberal with a keen Christian conscience,'[11] who founded the Common Wealth Party expressly for that purpose.

Richard Acland was born in 1906 to a titled family whose hereditary baronetcy went back to the Civil War. Richard's father Francis became the fourteenth baronet in 1926, and, like most of his ancestors, took a Liberal line in politics, representing four constituencies and serving as a junior minister in Asquith's government. Richard, like Tawney and Temple, went to both Rugby and Balliol and graduated in 1926, to be called to the Bar in 1927. In 1929 and 1931 he stood unsuccessfully for Parliament and finally managed to get elected for Barnstaple in 1935, with his father one of only twenty-one Liberal MPs.

By this stage Acland's politics were largely unformed. He had come into contact with Victor Gollancz and had taken a very similar stance to Cripps over the Soviet Union and appeasement, but it was not until he read Keynes that he came to the clear belief that society had to be rearranged on the basis of common ownership. This new emphasis was first expressed soon after his father's death in 1939, when he became the fifteenth baronet and published a brief pamphlet *What Now?* in which he argued that the aim of the war must be not only the defeat of Fascism but the creation of a social order based on common ownership. The following year Acland followed this up with a Penguin Special *Unser Kampf: Our Struggle*, which sold 130,000 copies and asked interested people to get in touch with him at the House of Commons. In March he formed the Our Struggle Committee from those who had responded, including Kenneth Ingram, an Anglo-Catholic barrister and journalist who had been convinced of socialism by John MacMurray, and who held that 'Socialism was not merely a political cause, it had arisen as the paramount religious demand of our time, and therefore to meet its claims involved a widening and disturbance of one's spiritual perspective.'[12]

Temple, who was related to Acland by marriage, invited him to speak at Malvern, as we have seen, and indeed his and Ingram's contributions largely dominated the meeting. In the meantime Acland had been writing another book, *The Forward March*, the title of which was a reference to a speech of Churchill's, which articulated a cogent case for Christian common ownership as the basis of a renewed social order. The Our Struggle group was soon renamed Forward March, around the time that the writer J. B. Priestley, who had made a name for himself with a series of epilogues after the nine o'clock news, founded the very similar 1941 Committee, which numbered MacMurray and Alfred Blunt, the Bishop of Bradford, among its members. In May 1942 the two bodies virtually joined together with the signing of a nine-point declaration by Acland, Priestley, MacMurray and others, and on 25 July the two groups merged to become Common Wealth, with Acland as Vice-President and Priestley as President. Both organisations had grown rapidly in the hothouse atmosphere of the war, and it took time to merge the two offices and 195 local branches that had already developed, which led to considerable friction between Acland and Priestley, who resigned in September, leaving Acland in charge of his own political party at the age of thirty-five. At last Acland resigned the Liberal whip.

Acland had inherited considerable wealth on the death of his father, including the 12,000 acre Holnicote estate in North Devon and the 6,000 acre Killerton estate near Exeter, both of which his disabled wife had run for several years. In 1943, just prior to the Eddisbury by-election, he decided to give both his estates to the National Trust, with the Trust meeting an assortment of financial liabilities, thereby solving at one blow two quandaries: his own financial problems, which had been compounded by death duties and the increasing costs of Common Wealth, and the apparent inconsistency, if not hypocrisy, of a wealthy landowner preaching common ownership. In fact, the move which made him one of the National Trust's greatest-ever donors proved a publicity coup, as had Sir Charles Tevelyan's donation of his Wallington estate in 1941. Trevelyan had stated that 'As a socialist, I am not hampered

218

by any sentiment of ownership,'[13] and clearly Acland saw his bequest in the same political light. Certainly the electorate at Eddisbury did, for though Common Wealth had failed in six by-elections, the Common Wealth candidate, a Methodist by the name of J. Loverseed, was elected. In fact, this was not Acland's first electoral success, as Tom Driberg had successfully stood for Maldon the previous year on an Independent ticket but with Acland's capable support. Common Wealth itself had nearly 10,500 members by now and a small group of MPs who would vote with them in Parliament, sometimes including Bevan, whose later wife Jennie Lee was backed as an Independent by Acland in a Bristol Central by-election. Common Wealth soon started to adopt candidates for the next general election. Cripps, although privately supportive of the new party, knew he could never back it publicly. He still had every intention of seeking readmission to the Labour Party, and besides, he was a member of the National Government and could hardly support candidates against it.

At the start of 1944 a further by-election was won at Skipton by Hugh Lawson, although by the end of the year the tide was beginning to turn against the party. Indeed, in November Loverseed defected to Labour, and though a third by-election was won in Chelmsford in April 1945, this was the only seat the party held in the subsequent general election, which saw Labour sweep to power. Acland and the senior figures in the party decided to leave Common Wealth almost immediately, although a special conference in September decided to carry on, and the surviving MP, Millington, joined Labour, as did Acland, who was elected MP for Gravesend in a 1947 by-election, and Driberg, who rather more prudently joined the party immediately before the general election. Acland's later career included writing for the 1950 Group of Christian Socialists, which met at the House of Commons, and founding War on Want in 1952. Acland remained in Parliament until 1955, when he resigned his seat over Labour's support for the hydrogen bomb, although he fought and lost the seat in the general election as an Independent. From 1955 on he worked in education, teaching religious education in Wandsworth and at St Luke's Teacher Training College in Exeter. He died in 1990.

Common Wealth's lifespan was brief, and it rarely merits more than a mention in a footnote in many twentieth-century British histories, most of which attribute its success to the political uncertainties of war and the consequent respectability of political independence. Historians of Christian Socialism have never mentioned it at all. Yet Common Wealth represented in its time the most radical attempt to create a new social order the British electorate has been prepared to vote for. And for many of its members its core principle, common ownership, was the very quintessence of the politics of the early Christians who 'held everything in common'. Acland himself wrote extensively about his Christian faith, relating politics solely to moral questions, and many of the other leading lights in the movement derived their political beliefs from their faith as active Christians.

Thus the history of Christian Socialism through to 1950 lay as much outside the Labour Party itself as within it, a fact no better illustrated than by the brief success of Common Wealth. Undoubtedly some of its success can be attributed to the personality of Acland himself, who managed to harness an incredible energy to the task of politics. Like Cripps, an ascetic by nature, he also had monumental organisational capacities, and Tom Driberg, who was elected as an Independent in 1942, largely ascribed his victory to Acland's role in the campaign. Similarly Jennie Lee, another Independent by-election candidate in the seat next door to Cripps's, was delighted to be assisted not only by Acland but also by the local vicar, Mervyn Stockwood. Yet the success of Common Wealth must also lie with the clarity of its message at a time when Labour was so immersed in the National Government that it could not speak freely. Acland preached with the confidence of a convert and berated Labour Party socialism for its faith in public control rather than ownership of private industry. At Malvern he pushed for his central argument, that though the Church could not espouse a positive political agenda, yet it 'could and should courageously point to those things which are wrong in our lay society, which are simultaneously a stumbling block preventing our leading Christian lives, and a proof that we have not yet achieved a living Christianity.'[14] And even in 1969 he was still concerned, with Tom Driberg, who approached him about the possibility of founding a new Common Wealth Party, that the public control of private ownership was not enough, that common ownership, in a variety of forms, was the only way in which all the stumbling blocks to the Kingdom of God could be removed.

Needless to say the demise of Common Wealth was as understandable as its birth. With the reassertion of Labour's independence it was difficult to see the difference between Labour and Common Wealth, except that Labour seemed less extreme and more likely to win. What is more it was inevitable that Acland's brand of Christian Socialism should be subsumed in the Bevanite left wing of the Labour Party, for figures with very similar views to his own were at its helm.

Cripps's expulsion from the party was treated in the press as a monumental act of folly by Labour, yet he remained a whipless MP until late 1944 when, last of all the expulsions, he was readmitted to the party in time to join Attlee's first Cabinet as President of the Board of Trade. In the meantime his independent status had enabled Churchill to make use of him during the war. After a brief period without a job, in which he visited Russia in a private capacity, he was deputed by Churchill to negotiate the Russian entry into the Alliance and was then appointed Leader of the House and Lord Privy Seal. By then Labour had joined the wartime Government and Cripps thus became one of a War Cabinet of six which included his colleagues Attlee and Bevin as well as Anthony Eden, John Anderson and Churchill. After rumours that he was seeking to replace Churchill as Prime Minister he was demoted to Minister of Aircraft Production halfway through the war and came out of the Cabinet. Cripps's hard work and dedication throughout the war were matched only by his relentless preaching schedule, and it is during this time that his sense of a clear role for a post-war politics developed. As he preached to students at Glasgow University in 1945, 'If we can become more alive and active in their leadership, we can instil a moral purpose into the world, without which it will drift from war to war and decline into chaos.'[15] None the less he was keen throughout the war years, though party-less, not to act as an Independent because he still had every intention of returning to the fold.

At the end of 1944 Attlee was delighted to be able to welcome him back into the party and, soon after, to offer him the post of President of the Board of Trade. Cripps's reputation as a man of stern moral fibre was immediately enhanced by his resolute campaign for the increased productivity which Britain needed to rescue its economy. It was as if the Protestant work ethic had become government policy. With his grasp of parliamentary process Cripps also became a vital part of the effort to get through the vast legislative framework of the Attlee Government, with the Family Allowance, the National Insurance and National Health Service Acts all following on in swift succession. Cripps's role in the Labour Government was vital, but he was not exactly immune to plotting and in 1947 was at the centre of a campaign to oust Attlee and replace him with Bevin. Bevin himself was still loyal to Attlee, and Bevan was not keen on replacing him with Bevin, so Cripps was left to confront Attlee alone. In fact Attlee managed a dramatic coup by giving Cripps responsibility for economic affairs, bridging the gap between the Treasury and Industry there and then.

At the same time Cripps's campaign for greater productivity took on a clearly moral tone, with his emphasis on the need to make sacrifices now to ensure prosperity later, and his austerity measures were couched in ethical terms: 'there are greater values in our lives than the mere material things of which we may now have to go short.'[16] In November Dalton, on his way to the Commons, accidentally revealed a key element of his budget and resigned as Chancellor, and Cripps moved to No. 11 Downing Street. In Attlee's biography Kenneth Harris says of the decision to appoint Cripps, 'It could only be Cripps . . . Cripps symbolised spiritual faith and physical self-discipline. If austerity could be made charismatic he was the man to do it.'[17]

Many have argued that Chancellor Cripps was very different from Socialist League Cripps. His austerity measures were soon accompanied by a move towards indirect taxation which told more heavily on the poor, and his 1950 budget seemed to eschew much of the semi-Marxist ideas he had held in the 1930s. Yet Cripps's time as Chancellor saw a growing conviction that self-sacrifice and personal discipline were to be a key part of the social change he had always campaigned for. Cripps and his wife Isobel formed, with John Collins and his wife Diana, Acland, Stockwood and Bishop Bell of Chichester, the core of the Church Reform League which had adopted, under the usual pressure from Acland, as a rule of membership, 'that it must be known of each member of the group that he regards the system of Big Business and Monopoly Capitalism . . . as evil',[18] but the group foundered fairly soon after its inception. In 1948 Cripps put his office and a secretary at the disposal of Collins, who had been asked to organise a rally at the Royal Albert Hall for Christians committed to the development of a Western European Union, which rapidly became a call to social responsibility. He also became a founding member of Christian Action, and in the midst of the general election in 1950 preached at St Paul's, reasserting his ethical challenge to the nation.

Thus Cripps's association with Christian Socialism throughout this time remained strong. Mervyn Stockwood, who was elected to Bristol City Council in 1946, became a close friend and would regularly stay with the Crippses at No. 11. He recounted later a comment Cripps had made during a late-night walk: 'A totalitarian dictatorship is a pathetic sort cut to Utopia. It cannot give men the full life. Only a democracy based on an inner spiritual disicpline can do that. I wonder whether we have a sufficient faith in God in this country for that spiritual discipline.'[19] Indeed, it was from Stockwood's rectory that Cripps finally resigned after his health started to give way in 1950. He had retained his seat and his post in the Cabinet in the general election, when Labour was returned with a tiny majority of five, but much of his work was already being done by Hugh Gaitskell as Minister for Economic Affairs, and he was content to pass on his constituency to Tony Benn, whom Roy Jenkins and Tony Crosland had recommended to him. Stockwood also visited Cripps in Switzerland, and when he died in Zurich in April 1952 buried his ashes in the Cotswolds.

What is most interesting about all the senior parliamentary figures in this chapter is that none of them seems to have worried about being seen to be Christian. Admittedly, Britain could, arguably, still have thought of itself as a Christian nation through to the 1950s, and the electorate would not have been troubled by a politician speaking of his or her own religious creed. None the less it has been rare for modern Labour politicians to speak publicly of their faith, either because they fear a savage attack from the press for self-righteousness or because they genuinely believe that faith is a private matter for the individual conscience. What Cripps, Acland, Lansbury and Henderson would all have argued, though, is that the reducing of faith to a private world of individual moral choices is the most dangerous of first steps. It leads to a faith that has nothing to say to the modern world, to the financial and economic institutions of today or to society itself. It also tends towards a narrow faith that refuses to learn new insights because it does not like to make itself known and enter into debate. What all these parliamentarians showed was that it is possible as a politician to bear witness to one's faith without either claiming to be morally superior to others or co-opting God to one's side. Furthermore, the very fact of a party politician affirming faith symbolises that all of Creation, even the confrontational party-political system, is the proper sphere of God, and Christians' involvement.

# 9

# United in Diversity

Judge Eternal, throned in splendour,
Lord of lords and King of kings,
With thy living fire of judgment
Purge this realm of bitter things:
Solace all its wide dominion
With the healing of thy wings.

Henry Scott Holland, hymn in *Commonwealth*

Christ's great work was to teach the oneness of the human race to
remove the causes which divided man from man, to make it
impossible for the strong to oppress the weak or the rich to rob the
poor.

J. Keir Hardie, 'Manifesto by Christian Ministers'

When Stanley Evans wrote his account of the history of Christian
Socialism in 1965 he left out one of the most significant, and long-
standing, of all the organisations that formed part of the British
Christian Socialist movement, most probably because he had
never belonged to it himself. Indeed, his account, which first
appeared in outline in a pamphlet for the Christian Socialist
Movement, seems to suggest that between the collapse of the
Church Socialist League and the formation of the CSM in 1960
there was no more than a random collection of groupings that
never amounted to a real movement. Few other histories or
biographies have made mention of it, and Mervyn Stockwood
could not recall it, yet from 1924 to 1960 the longest-living of all
the Christian Socialist organisations held sway.

225

For the atomisation of the Church Socialist League into its several parts in the 1920s led not only to the Catholic Crusade, the League of the Kingdom of God and the Christendom Group. Indeed, those originally attracted to Church Socialism had always included more than just semi-Marxist Anglo-Catholics and those who were more concerned with a 'Christian sociology'. As we have seen, there was a keen pacifist strand in the Church Socialist League, as well as a large section of people whose main political aim was parliamentary Labour representation. For them the advance of the ILP and the Labour Party was synonymous with working for the Kingdom of God. Furthermore, the League had been exclusively Anglican, but both pacifists and parliamentary Labour supporters had many allies from other denominations, some of whom had briefly organised in small denominational groups like the Socialist Quaker Society (1898–1924), Charles Marson's Christian Socialist Society (1886–92), John Clifford's Christian Socialist League (1894–8) and the Free Church Socialist League (1909–12). The Catholic Crusade and the League of the Kingdom of God were not for the likes of these. The COPEC conference in April 1924 had sought to embrace all the Churches, and it was only the Roman Catholic Church that had ended up excluding itself. Yet even this had not led to any long-term follow-up.

Nature, and politics, abhors a vacuum, and so on the demise of the Church Socialist League in 1923 Claude Stuart Smith, the previous Secretary of the League, met with Charles Record and the Anglican priest John Corner Spokes and persuaded the trade-union organiser Fred Hughes to 'join in an effort to reconstruct the old League as a Socialist organisation'.[1]

One of the central tenets of the Society of Socialist Christians (SSC), and the key to its longevity, was its genuine diversity. For here was to be no holy huddle of like-minded Anglo-Catholic clerics, nor an ivory tower of socialist academics. From the outset the society enjoyed the support of most of the Christian denominations. Of course, there were some of the established Anglo-Catholic socialists, like Lewis Donaldson and others, but Fred

Hughes managed to bring in with him a whole new set of important figures from the Free Churches, key Methodists like Samuel Keeble, Congregationalists like A. D. Belden of Whitefield's Tabernacle and, most significantly, the Quakers.

The Society was characterised, however, by more than denominational diversity. For it brought together socialist Christians who had never before entertained conjecture of working together and consequently managed to avoid being identified too firmly with the fortunes of one person or clique. There was no Headlam figure, no dominant ideology and no predominant theological position. The very diversity of the SSC has meant that its history has never really been told, and even today it is difficult to string together a coherent story without drawing out the individual strands, the Quakers, the Methodists, the Labour Church followers and the Anglo-Catholics.

One of the first overtures to be made when Hughes was looking around for possible members was to the tiny Socialist Quaker Society (SQS), which had been founded in 1898.

There have been radical Quakers, of course, ever since their foundation. Indeed the *raison d'être* and structure of the Society of Friends, with its emphasis on freedom of thought and religion, and on consensus rather than confrontation, has always acted as a social critique, a pointer to a different social order. As we have already seen, many of its central figures shared an iconoclastic vision of a new social order. Yet by the end of the nineteenth century many senior Quakers had achieved a degree of respectability and success within Victorian England that had dulled the edge of their political involvement. In the 1890s this spurred a younger generation of Quakers to look afresh at the political responsibilities of Quakers in the light of both the new exigencies of slum poverty and the work of pioneering socialists. Thus in 1898 the small Socialist Quaker Society was formed, with the deliberately circumscribed aim of revitalising the Friends' witness on social issues.

Appropriately enough, the SQS was fashioned in the Friends'

own particular style. Aspiring members were interviewed for their suitability and commitment by two established members before admittance, and the Society was run with only one fixed office, the 'clerk'. Inevitably and deliberately the SQS remained tiny: in its first year there were only seven members. But a series of tracts was soon started by Mary O'Brien, a Fabian executive member who married the Society's clerk, J. Theodore Harris, who in turn had been closely involved in John Trevor's Labour Church Movement and Bruce Wallace's Brotherhood Trust. Other key early figures, all in their thirties when the SQS was founded, included the Congregationalist-turned-Friend, Percy Alden, another Fabian, who was elected to Parliament in 1906 and had sat on Clifford's Christian Socialist League executive in 1898; Edward Pease, who was later Secretary of the Fabians; and the Guild Socialist and Fabian who was Keir Hardie's secretary, Samuel Hobson.

Several of the SQS tracts ploughed a fairly common furrow. Competition was seen as the source of most of society's ills, so a new social order must be built on co-operation. Ruskin's 'There is no wealth but life' was regularly repeated as a central Christian maxim, and socialism was seen not only as a political aim but also as 'a means of translating into action our highest aspirations and our deepest convictions'.[2] A formal SQS Basis was drawn up in 1900, stating that since society was founded on 'land monopoly' and industry on the profit motive, universal brotherhood was impossible and employment would always remain uncertain. The only answer was production for use, not for profit, and the collective ownership of the means of production. All of which was staple Christian Socialist fare, with the added zest of the Friends' commitment to personal conscience and consensual democracy.

The Society did not really take off, however, until 1910, when two close friends of Hobson started to take a more prominent part in its proceedings. Alfred and Mary Thorne had met Hobson when training at Sidcot School in Somerset, and when Mary became clerk of the Society in 1910 she set about challenging the wider Society of Friends with an attack on the limitations of the individualistic philanthropy to which many prominent Quakers, such as Seebohm Rowntree and George Cadbury, had committed themselves. Meanwhile she had met another Friend in Derby, the pioneering photographer Loftus Hare, who joined the Society and helped her draw up a letter which was sent in January 1912 to 9,000 Friends, arguing the case for socialism and against modern 'capitalist' war. This instantly garnered in many new members, and a new journal was started with Hare as editor. Entitled the *Ploughshare*, it ran from 1912 to 1919 and rehearsed many of the topics that were simultaneously being covered in the *Church Socialist*. Concerns about war and capitalism were intermingled with a particularly keen sense of the vital political role of personal conscience and freedom. As Hare wrote in his final editorial 'What political freedom gave with one hand, industrial freedom took away with the other . . . for the very liberty of property, of trade and of contract brought about a bondage – hence come wars.'[3]

In the meantime the yearly meeting of the whole Society of Friends had agreed in 1918 to the incorporation of eight 'Foundations of a True Social Order', which had largely come from the SQS, though they had been shorn of any explicit socialist terminology, thus effectively committing all British Quakers to a Christian Socialist diagnosis of society's ills, if not to its prescription for a cure.

By 1924, therefore, the SQS had pretty much achieved its aim of revitalising the Quaker social conscience, and its few remaining members were keen to join the new SSC. Indeed, Theodore Harris became an early and influential member of the SSC executive, and one of the keenest members of the new Society was another Quaker, the recently elected MP Dr Alfred Salter. Salter had been born in Greenwich in 1873 and while studying at Guy's Hospital gained the nickname 'Citizen Salter' for his political views, though he became the star student of his year. Instead of taking up a wealthy suburban or Harley Street practice, he resolved to work in the predominantly slum area of Bermondsey in south London, where he helped to found both the local ILP branch and the Co-op Bakery. First elected to Bermondsey Borough Council in 1903,

he became an alderman in 1919 and was elected MP for Bermondsey in 1922, a seat he held until he died in 1945. A prominent
pacifist and, unusually, a republican, he worked closely with
Lansbury and travelled with him to the USA in 1936, soon after
Lansbury's defeat over pacifism at the Labour Party Conference.
Salter's political concerns were related mostly to health and
environment issues, but at his first election in 1922 he spoke
forcefully in favour of prohibition, and during the First World
War he was a conscientious objector. When a large crowd
gathered outside his house and started chanting and throwing
bricks, he hurled open the doors and challenged them: 'I've looked
after you when you were sick, I've served you night and day. Is
that the way you reward me? Go home, you sinners.'[4]

Quakers were not the only group to join the new interdenominational society, for the SSC managed to appeal too to a radical
strain of Wesleyan Methodism, thus finally shaking the Victorian
assumption that Nonconformist religion went hand in glove with
Liberal politics.

The Methodists themselves were not a united body at this time,
but their largest group, the Wesleyans, had already had their fair
share of socialists. Most notably Hugh Price Hughes, as leader of
the Forward Movement in the 1880s and 1890s, had brought
enormous changes to a predominantly Liberal-voting and conserv-
ative-thinking Church. Born of a Welsh doctor and a Jewish
mother in Carmarthen in 1847, Hughes served in a series of
circuits before becoming the first Superintendent Minister of the
West London Mission and, in 1898, achieving the rare honour,
for a radical, of becoming President of the Wesleyan Methodist
Conference. In 1896 he also became President of the recently
founded Free Church Council and could, therefore, quite legitimately claim to be the foremost Nonconformist leader in the
land. In the year of the London dock strike he published a series
of his sermons under the title *Social Christianity* and mounted a
very public scathing attack on the bastions of Victorian morality.
'How do you expect virtue and morality,' he asked, in the same

vein as Keir Hardie, 'from people living in one room?'[5] Hughes was keen to establish the egalitarian aspect of Christianity and to dispel the cosy, respectable niceness of much Methodism, and he deliberately set out to shock his congregation into taking note of the cutting edge of faith: 'a harlot is dying in a back slum . . . That harlot is as dear to Christ as the Queen of England herself . . . Let us once realise the sacredness of every human being, however poor, however ignorant, however degraded, and tyranny becomes impossible, lust becomes impossible, war becomes impossible.'[6]

Hughes was much criticised by later socialist Methodists for strong reactionary tendencies, but most acknowledged that within the Wesleyans he was the predominant figure to challenge the overwhelmingly middle-class and professional assumptions of his Church and mount anything like a Christian Socialist critique. There were, of course, other Wesleyans, such as the East London Mission minister and founder of the Anti-sweating League, Peter Thompson, and the Labour Lord Mayor of Leeds, D. B. Foster, who as a Methodist lay preacher was President of the Labour Church Union and started his own socialist Christian church in Bradford. But it was to Hughes that the great names of socialist Methodism have always referred.

Hughes died in 1902. By then another Wesleyan had assumed his mantle. Samuel Keeble was born only six years after Hughes, in 1853, but survived him by a full forty-four years. An orphan, he was brought up by his brothers, and after studying at Didsbury College in Manchester he served the usual itinerant ministry of a Wesleyan, in fourteen different circuits, finally retiring in 1912. An early ally of Hughes, he wrote articles for his *Methodist Times* but fell out with him over the Boer War, when Hughes adopted a heavily imperialist line. Keeble never achieved any seniority in the Methodist Church, but by the 1920s he had acquired a reputation for a thoroughgoing Christian Socialism on the back of a lengthy list of publications, each of which betrayed a remarkable degree of economic and political knowledge. The policies he advocated, of course, were not that different from those of many of his CSU and Church Socialist contemporaries, for he supported universal education, government intervention to prevent unemployment and economic and political justice for women, and he was actively involved in COPEC in 1924. Nor was he particularly committed to the Parliamentary Labour Party, despite having converted Labour's first Chancellor of the Exchequer, Philip Snowden, to socialism.

What did set Keeble apart, however, was his economic expertise. Where many Christian Socialists would cite the Bible, other theologians or, at a push, a poet or two, Keeble's written works are well larded with scholarly references to economists and philosophers, and he is reputed to be the first Methodist to have read *Das Kapital*. His *Industrial Daydreams* of 1896 argued forcefully for a socialism purged of 'all morally obnoxious features, as well as economic fallacies . . . for a purified Socialism is simply an industrially applied Christianity',[7] and he was clearly well qualified to criticise Marxist over-reliance on materialism and Hegelian philosophy. Keeble was also perhaps the readiest critic of his own Church, perceiving its evangelical pietism as corrosive of true spirituality. Despite being theologically conservative – in a debate with R. J. Campbell he argued that 'a New Theology that denies sin, grace, redeeming love, and the new birth, cannot suffice for the spiritual necessities of the Labour Movement'[8] – he was certain that Methodists were too narrow and that the theories about eternal punishment of some of his colleagues were offensive. In an attempt to reclaim the whole of society as the legitimate concern of Methodists Keeble helped to form, with Arthur Henderson, the non-partisan Wesleyan Methodist Union for Social Service in 1905 and the more radical Sigma Society in 1909. This last paralleled the Liverpool Baptist minister Herbert Dunnico's Free Church Socialist League, which was formed as a direct response to the establishment that same year of an Anti-Socialist Union at Baptist Church House. Neither group lasted long, or grew above a hundred members, but when the new SSC was being formed it was natural that both Keeble and Dunnico should be asked to join, and indeed, like Harris, they took a leading role in the new society.

By 1924 Keeble was seventy-one. A full fifty years younger than he was another Wesleyan who attended Temple's COPEC conference and subsequently joined the SSC. Donald Soper was born in 1903 of a teetotal, puritanical Wesleyan family in Wandsworth. After schooling in Hatcham and university at Cambridge, he trained for the ministry and started work at the South London Mission in 1926, from where he read for a doctorate at the London School of Economics on the rather recondite subject (for a Methodist) of 'Gallicanism and Ultramontanism'. In 1929 he moved to the Central London Mission and in 1936 became Superintendent of the West London Mission, with its base at Hugh Price Hughes's massive and now redundant Kingsway Hall. Unusually, and inexplicably, he managed to avoid the itinerant fate of all his colleagues and remained at the West London Mission for forty-two years.

It is difficult to ascertain quite when Soper joined the Society, as his first mention in its magazine does not occur until 1930, and in later years there was something of a campaign to get him to rejoin, which would suggest that he resigned or let his membership lapse at some point. In later years, of course, Soper was to play a central role in both the pacifist and the Christian Socialist movements, but at the founding of the SSC he was an earnest, radical, wealthy and rather puritanical young minister with a fairly convinced conservative theology.

The new SSC, however, was far from uniform in its theology. There were the theologically conservative like Keeble and Soper, but there was an equally significant group of liberals, such as Reginald Sorensen and F. R. Swan, who represented a whole swathe of Christian Socialists who had found a first expression of their religion and their politics in the Labour Church movement.

This had been founded in Manchester in 1891 by a Unitarian Minister called John Trevor. Trevor had been brought up a Johnsonian Baptist by relatives in Wisbech after his parents' early death, and after studying to be an architect he toured Australia and America, finally reading theology in Pennsylvania. On returning to Britain he dropped the Calvinism of his relatives and worked as an architect while seeking a Unitarian pulpit. In 1890 he finally became minister of the Upper Brook Street Free Church in Manchester, where, a year later, he inaugurated the first Labour Church. Over the next few years he also became instrumental in helping Robert Blatchford to start ILP branches in Manchester and Salford and attended the 1893 ILP inaugural meeting in Bradford.

Trevor's major concern, however, was the fact that Nonconformist Churches seemed deeply unattractive to many labouring men. His aim, quite simply, while still running the Unitarian Church of which he was minister, was to hold Sunday-afternoon meetings where the working classes would feel at home, where the religious atmosphere would be rooted in ordinary living and where what bound people together would be their class and their politics rather than their intellectual credal adherence. Trevor's argument, that the Tories had the Church of England, that the Liberals had the Free Churches and that Labour needed its own Church, was persuasive to many congregations, and Labour Churches, mostly associated with the Nonconformists, sprang up throughout the 1890s. A very few of them, especially in the Midlands, lasted into the 1930s, but because of a vitriolic split between Trevor and his close colleague Fred Brocklehurst, who was later a Conservative MP, the Labour Church movement was for the most part moribund by 1910.

The pattern of Labour Church meetings varied considerably, but they often started with a hymn, followed by a reading, which would not normally be biblical but might be. There would then be an address followed by an intense period of questions, either to the speaker or to leaders of the Church. The final hymn was then followed by a social gathering. There was a special Labour Church hymn book, from which 'Jerusalem', 'These things shall be' and 'England, arise' seem to have been the favourites, but otherwise liturgy was kept to a minimum, unlike in the socialist Sunday schools, which, through being adopted directly by the ILP, outlived the Labour Churches and produced their own humanist ten commandments. Nonetheless some Labour Churches held their own rites of passage, and one Leeds Labour Church was registered for marriages.

Part of the impetus for the Labour Church movement came from a perception that the mainstream Churches, as Trevor put it, had 'a desire to save individual souls for another world, but the idea of getting rid, once and for all, of our cesspools of misery on earth was not dreamed of. They worshipped devoutly on Sunday, and on Monday went on with their work and accepted the social order'.[9] Through the *Labour Prophet* and his two books, *Theology and the Slums* and *My Quest for God*, Trevor propagated a highly idiosyncratic Gospel, reminiscent of that of Maurice and Gore but shot through with an iconoclastic disregard for the niceties of doctrine. In fact, his own history was almost as sad as that of the movement he founded, for when his wife died and he rather hastily remarried he was forced to resign his ministry, gave up editing the *Labour Prophet* and had a serious nervous breakdown. His quirky theology, which was matched by an equally bizarre dress sense (his favourite leggings were speckled breeches), left him at odds with the mainstream Churches, yet his attempt to synthesise a Christian social ethic with a predominantly class-focused socialism steered him remarkably close to some of the work of the Liberation theologians sixty years later.

His tradition did not entirely die with him, for the first two decades of the century saw the flourishing of what was loosely termed 'New Theology'. Centred on the pioneering work of R. J. Campbell at the Congregational City Temple on Holborn Viaduct in London, this again sought to challenge the incipient and corrosive individualism of the Church and, in particular, of the Nonconformist Churches. Campbell had been brought up in Ulster and read theology at Christ Church, Oxford, as an Anglican. By 1895, however, he had joined the Congregational Church, and he went on to serve two Congregational ministries, in Brighton for eight years, and at the City Temple for twelve years, before returning to the Anglican fold in 1915. In 1907 he formed the League of Progressive Thought and Social Service, which was 'to work for a social reconstruction which will give economic emancipation to all workers . . . and establish a new social order based on co-operation for life instead of competition for existence'.[10]

Although not overtly Christian, the Progressive League had as its basis Campbell's New Theology. This attempted to combine three ideas: Adolf Harnak's recently published view of the Kingdom of God as far more central to Jesus's teaching than his own person; a strong social conscience; and support for Labour parliamentary representation. By many Churches this theological approach was seen as heretical. After all, if the New Theology asserted that Christianity was the religion *of* Jesus, not *about* Jesus, this was perilously close to denying the significance, if not the reality, of the divinity of Christ. In fact, Campbell ended up denying his New Theology in 1915, but in the first decade of the century his ideas were extremely potent, and he acquired many disciples. Indeed, two of those most closely connected with the Society of Socialist Christians were associates of Campbell: Reginald Sorensen and F. R. Swan.

Reginald Sorensen was one of the young men he recruited and trained as 'Pioneer Preachers' to broadcast the ideas of the New Theology. Sorensen became the minister of the Free Christian Church at Walthamstow and then Chair of the SSC in 1931. At first a Labour member of Essex County Council, he later became MP successively for Leyton West and Walthamstow, only leaving the Commons for the Lords in 1965, so as, in theory, to allow Patrick Gordon-Walker, a Cabinet minister who had lost his seat at the general election, to re-enter Parliament. The ploy did not work, as Labour rather ignominiously lost the by-election. None the less Reg Sorensen was to be one of the few linchpin members of the SSC who saw it right the way through from 1924 to its end in 1960.

The second associate of Campbell to figure prominently in the SSC, F. R. Swan, was another Congregational minister who had been born in 1868 and brought up in Nottingham. For seven years he was minister at Marsden, but following the Labour successes in 1906 he worked full-time for the ILP in Colne Valley. In 1910 he moved to Bruce Wallace's Brotherhood Church off the Southgate Road in Hackney, a post he remained in until his death in 1938. He was the founding Secretary of the Progressive League and in his *The Immanence of Christ in Modern Life*, published in 1907, went almost as far as Campbell in advocating a thoroughly secularist Christianity. His Church, which had started off as Bruce Wallace's Congregational Church and had changed its name in 1892, hosted the 1907 Russian Social Democratic (Labour) Party conference, and affiliated *en bloc* to the SSC, but had to move premises to Brotherhood House in the late 1930s, and eventually collapsed after Swan's death.

Needless to say, it would be impossible to run a Christian Socialist group without the active involvement of the Anglo-Catholics. With Noel's formation of the Catholic Crusade in 1918 many had left the broader Church Socialist League, but from its earliest years the SSC attracted some notable figures who hankered after a less personalised, more ecumenical group than Noel could offer.

Perhaps the most attractive of all these was a young priest who had been born in the Australian outback in 1890. Beverley St John Groser had come to Britain at the turn of the century to live with two older ladies in Hertfordshire and was ordained in 1914 to the dockside All Saints church in Newcastle. Despite not being academically gifted – he had received very little classical education from his father and took six years to complete his ordination exams – Groser soon developed a style all his own. In 1918 he met Noel while briefly serving in St Winnow in Cornwall, and he joined the Catholic Crusade, whose manifesto appealed above all because of its romantic allure: 'We offer you nothing – nothing but adventure, risks, battle, perhaps ruin; with the love and loyalty of comrades and the peace of God which passeth understanding.'[11]

In 1922 Groser and his brother-in-law Jack Bucknall went to the East End of London as curates at St Michael's in Poplar. Both Bucknall and Groser were under the Noel spell, although Bucknall had been summarily dismissed as Noel's curate simply because Noel felt that two years was quite long enough to work with someone. Within a year the two curates had managed so to rankle their vicar, a less Anglo-Catholic and less socialist Fr Langdon, that they were constantly at loggerheads. Langdon's successor, Kenneth Ashcroft, was more amenable to Groser's frequent sallies into politics and his regular processions with the Red Flag and the Cross, but in 1927 Groser felt he had to resign and to seek another job. For more than a year he made do with occasional odd jobs, as a weaver and a clerk, but it was not until 1929 that the Church hierarchy decided to entrust him with a full-time job, taking care of Christ Church, Watney Street, while a commission decided whether to close it or not. Fortunately enough, the commission never reported, and Groser stayed in his charge until Christ Church was bombed in the war and he had to move to St George's-in-the-East. There he stayed until 1948, when he became Master of the newly installed Royal Foundation of St Katherine's, which had returned to the East End from Regent's Park.

In the meantime Groser had split with Noel. For in the 1931 Stepney by-election Groser decided to support the Labour candidate instead of the Communist Harry Pollitt. The Catholic Crusade itself went on to fracture in 1936 over whether to support Trotsky's incisive criticism of Stalinist Russia. Noel, with Bucknall, Jim Wilson and Harold Mason went on to form the tiny anti-Stalinist Order of the Church Militant, while Groser turned his attention to the SSC. His theology was dramatically different from that of many of his fellow socialist Christians, with a strong emphasis on the reality of sin and society's need for Christ's redemption. Furthermore, he was convinced that the Christian task in politics had to be class-based. 'Our first job,' he stated in a lecture at the Geneva Châtaigneraie Conference in 1933, 'is to reckon with the fact of sin and make our amends by identification when possible with the suffering victims of a class system; not a theoretical identification but a practical one.'[12] For all his revolutionary fervour, however, Groser was keen to maintain a distance from Marxism, which he saw as fundamentally flawed because it could not acknowledge either 'an authority beyond itself'[13] or the fact that 'sin carries with it a penalty that must be faced and cannot be shirked.'[14]

All in all the new Society of Socialist Christians, the first group to invert the noun and adjective, was also the first true hotch-potch of Christian Socialists: lay and ordained, high- and low-church, liberal and conservative in theology and, above all, successfully interdenominational. None the less the SSC's definition of itself and its aims recalled those of many of its predecessor organis-ations almost word for word:

> a body of people who, acknowledging the leadership of Jesus Christ, pledge themselves to work and to pray for the spiritual and economic emancipation of all people from the bondage of material things, and for the establishment of the Common-wealth of God on earth ... the creation of an international Socialist order based on the communal control of the means of life and co-operation in freedom for the common weal.[15]

What was dramatically new about the SSC, however, was that it embraced wholeheartedly what the Church Socialist League had battled over so ferociously and refused to accept, affiliation to the Labour Party. Indeed, its statement of aims declared that the Society 'will work as part of the Labour Movement'.[16] Clearly this was a dramatic new overture, not least because it meant that Socialist Christians were officially present at the Labour Party's annual conference and could play both a national and a local role within the party. MPs who were members of the SSC often spoke for the society on party platforms, and the Labour Party increas-ingly used the SSC in marginal constituencies to gain support in the wider community.

This meant in part that the society itself grew increasingly dependent on many of its member MPs, and it regularly published lists of its parliamentary candidates. Thus in 1929 the Labour candidates in Bristol North and South, Motherwell, Norfolk

North, Reading, Newton, Spen Valley, Islington North, Colchester, Leyton West and Dulwich were all SSC members, and eight of them were elected. Charles Record, the society's Secretary had successfully campaigned for one of its members, Charles Roden Buxton, to be the Labour candidate in Elland and had organised the dispatch of a public letter to Christians calling on them to vote Labour which was signed by most of the executive, as well as Conrad Noel, Paul Bull, Alfred Salter and Samuel Keeble. For several years Somerville Hastings represented the society at the Labour Party Conference and was nominated to the NEC, and Margaret Bondfield, a Methodist and Labour's first woman minister, was a regular speaker at SSC meetings.

From the outset the main vehicle for the SSC's ideas had been John Spokes's magazine the *Crusader*, which he had put at the disposal of the society and which Hughes had edited. In late 1928, however, the name was felt to be too militaristic for an organisation that had a large pacifist membership, and it was relaunched under the name the *Socialist Christian*.

In 1930 the Society expended a great deal of effort in trying to co-ordinate the work of the many Christian Labour MPs, and in 1931 this bore fruit in the shape of the Christian Socialist Crusade. In tone, theology and politics this was the most revivalist of all Christian Socialist endeavours, with town-hall meetings up and down the country and a series of pamphlets, articles and 'calls to the nation' organised primarily by the parliamentarians, with Lansbury as President, Hastings as Chair and twenty-four other MPs. Though the Crusade was independent of the SSC, many SSC members were involved, and it was more successful in attracting to the society those who already considered themselves Christian Socialists than in converting any stray atheist socialists or Christian conservatives. Indeed, the young Donald Soper was first drawn into the SSC through his work for the Crusade.

When it came to its end in early 1932, a merger with the SSC was mooted and finally agreed on 17 September. What had started as Fred Hughes's attempt to get more Christian MPs to be serious and open about their faith had become a parliamentary revivalist

campaign, but it ended up reforming the SSC itself. The new
body, with a set of aims very similar to the SSC's, was named the
Socialist Christian League; Lansbury became President, Belden
and Donaldson Vice-Presidents and Sorensen, for a couple of
years, its Chair, while Hughes remained editor of the *Socialist
Christian*. The SSC's original intention to work with the 'Labour
movement' was altered slightly to the 'Labour and Socialist
movement', perhaps as a result of the recent débâcle over Mac-
Donald's and Snowden's desertion of the Labour Party.

By 1933 the League had started to attract new members, most
notably from disaffected parts of the Catholic Crusade. John
Groser's small League of the Redemption affiliated, as did F. R.
Swan's Brotherhood Church. Rallies were held at Trafalgar
Square and a first fringe meeting was convened at the new
combined Methodist conference, with Jack Lawson, MP, in the
chair and Keeble and Soper both talking on Methodism and
socialism.

At the annual meeting in September, however, a resolution was
moved that the League should disaffiliate from the Labour Party
because of the recent dramatic increase in levies charged to
affiliated organisations. The vote was carried fairly easily, but the
debate revealed the tensions between a Christian Socialist organisation and a democratic socialist party that needed to win power
– a debate that still runs today.

At the same rumbustious meeting a resolution was moved that
would have committed the League to a doctrinaire pacifist
position and that Lansbury and others would have supported.
Feelings clearly ran high at the meeting, and it was decided that
the issue should not be put to the vote, on the grounds that it
would prove overly divisive on an issue where there was a
legitimate difference of opinion. Instead an International Council
was set up to produce recommendations on the issue of war. Over
the next year this drew up a complicated questionnaire, which
was sent out to all members, and in 1934 there was a series of
reports on the great diversity of League members' views. Three

broad positions seemed to emerge: an absolute rejection of war and all forms of violence; a conditional acceptance of violence to protect the weak; and a revolutionary acceptance of violence as a means to fight for, or defend, socialism. Within each of these positions there was room for even more diversity of opinion. Some supported unilateral British disarmament as an act of Christian witness. Others wanted Britain to form a defensive alliance with the Soviet Union, Sweden and Denmark. Others again wanted Britain to hold enough arms to protect the realm and no more. So again in 1934 no official position was adopted, although it seems likely that a narrow majority of the still tiny membership would have voted for a complete rejection of war.

The closely interlinked issues of how to foster peace and whether war can ever be just have exercised Christians since Jesus's arrest in the Garden of Gethsemane, when Peter is reported to have brought along a sword to defend Him. The Church's broadly accepted doctrinal stance had for centuries relied most heavily on Thomas Aquinas's three key prerequisites: that war can be waged only by a properly constituted authority; that its cause must be just; and that those engaged in the war must intend either to advance good or to assault evil. To this many added Francisco de Vitoria's sixteenth-century injunction that war must be waged by 'proper means'. For the majority of Christians in Britain, perhaps only excepting the Anabaptists and Quakers, this view had prevailed through to the end of the Victorian era, although, as we have already seen, the reaction of many Christians to the Boer and Crimean wars was one of horror and distrust.

By the 1930s, however, the lasting memory of the Great War had inspired a whole group of leading Christians to campaign against the very principle of war. The Fellowship of Reconciliation and the Methodist Peace Fellowship had a growing membership. Dick Sheppard, the vicar of St Martin-in-the-Fields and Dean of Canterbury, had initiated the 'War We Say No' campaign to ensure that war, especially war such as that experienced between 1914 and 1918, should never be repeated and had drawn to him people like Charles Raven, Vera Brittain, Laurence Housman, A.

A. Milne, Alex Wood and, most notably, Donald Soper. In June 1936, at a packed rally at Maumbury Rings near Dorchester, which Soper later remembered as the 'high-water mark of the "War We Say No" campaign'[17] and one of the most significant events in his life, Sheppard reiterated his call for the renunciation of war, and Brittain gave what she was to call 'my customary little speech in support of collective security'.[18] By the end of the year the new Peace Pledge Union (PPU) had more than 100,000 signatories. Meanwhile another group, mostly of Roman Catholics such as the sculptor and social philosopher Eric Gill, F. Stratmann, G. Vann and E. I. Watkin, was arguing that while warfare might once have been justifiable, its present operation required wholesale bombing and destruction, which could never be conceived of as 'proper means'. By no means all the pacifists in the inter-war years were socialists, or indeed Christians, but within Christian Socialist circles they played an extraordinarily powerful and emotive part. Thus, when Lansbury and Cripps, who joined the League in 1934, attended the 1935 Labour Party Conference and spoke for pacifism, they undoubtedly felt part of a strong and assertive body of Christian thought. The speech that Lansbury had given on countless platforms, with Soper, Sheppard and Raven to back him up, may have seemed mawkish to the Labour Party Conference, but in Trafalgar Square or Dorchester it had the fire of authentic prophecy; and though pacifism was not the official position of the League, when its President lost the vote at the Labour Party Conference the League leapt to his defence. As Reg Sorensen put it in the *Socialist Christian*, perhaps without recognising the essentially emotive nature of the Labour Party, 'there are few stranger incidents in political history than that of a party leader receiving an overwhelming tribute of affection and respect from those who emphatically reject his advice.'[19]

By 1937 the pacifist group within the League had grown far more vociferous, although Hughes was resolutely anti-pacifist and held firmly to the belief that Fascism must, at all costs, be defeated. Soper, who was beginning to take a more prominent role within the League, was also now Vice-Chair of the PPU, which had started its own magazine with a circulation of 20,000. So when Sheppard died that year Soper became the most renowned of all the pacifist clergy, and when war eventually came he found himself, as a conscientious objector, reviled equally by members of the public, who sent him white feathers for cowardice, and the BBC, which banned him.

Not all Christian Socialists agreed with Soper and the pacifist line. From as far away as America Reinhold Niebuhr, who was one of the great US theorists of a social critique of capitalism, condemned the purists for what he saw as their appeasement of Nazism. At home Temple also felt that the theology of pacifism was wrong because it seemed to suggest that the New Testament, with its emphasis on the law of love, had done away with the Old Testament, with its law of justice. Many, like Maude Royden, who had been a pacifist all her days and had joined the PPU, faced with the dramatic clash of two principles, peace and justice, resolved that for the Christian individual or nation to stand by while injustice flourished was an abdication of responsibility and ended up supporting the war. Cripps took a similar line, almost accusing pacifists of spiritual pride. And even the Quaker Philip Noel-Baker, who was a colleague of Henderson at the Disarmament Conference and later received the Nobel Peace Prize, agreed to be a joint parliamentary secretary to the Ministry of War.

Soper, who remained true to his non-violent beliefs, holds that the reason why many pacifists abjured the cause in the immediate run-up to the war was because their pacifism had been founded largely on an emotional reaction to the horrors of the First World War or an intellectual response that failed to recognise that 'the moral argument is supreme.' Citing Sheppard's quip about the pig who 'complained to the hen that eggs and bacon for breakfast were all very well for the chicken, who was only required to make a contribution, whereas for the pig it was a total commitment', he went on to state his ultimately sacrificial ethical position, that 'armed violence against evil, however comprehensive and dastardly that evil may be, is not the way to overthrow it . . . [It] is a process of evil.'[20]

Remarkably little energy was spent by League members, though, on trying to stop the war once it had started, for in all the major cities there was a more immediate and vital task to be done in protecting the weak, looking after the bombed and housing the homeless. Thus Groser, who had aggressively opposed the war up to 1939, spent much of it trying to make adequate provision for his parishioners in the East End of London throughout the Blitz, which left one in three homeless, and Soper's Kingsway Hall ran a breakfast canteen for those who slept overnight in the Underground for nearly four years.

Nevertheless key figures like Bishop George Bell of Chichester, who was undoubtedly Europe's foremost and most celebrated ecumenist of the day, maintained a constant pressure on the Government to wage the war through 'proper means', arguing against the blanket-bombing of Dresden and all strategies that aimed at civilian casualties. His campaign, which relied entirely on an assiduous collection of press clippings that pieced together the real, undoctored story of the war, earned him the Prime Minister's disdain, and when Temple died in 1944 Churchill made sure he was succeeded not by his friend Bell but by the tedious and more obliging Fisher. Bell's lonely crusade, in which Temple refused to support him, was all the more courageous because it struck at the heart of the moral issues of modern warfare. Arthur Harris, as Commander-in-Chief of Bomber Command, had an obvious rationale for obliteration-bombing. After all, it would take only six weeks to replace a bombed factory, but it took a whole generation to replace all of its workmen. As a weapon of war, then, the destruction of civilian populations would undoubtedly be effective. Yet many of the bombers themselves expressed their deep concern that the bombing raids made them unfit to receive communion, and Bell was the only senior cleric to speak openly of the moral offence that Harris's methods entailed.

Bell's concern with how the war was waged was matched in others by a determination to see that when it was over a new social order would be built. As Charles Record put it in the *Socialist Christian*, 'If chaos or defeat are escaped sacrifice will be due from us, both in building peace and in social reconstruction, if the sacrifices of the young are to be justified.'[21] The war would thus become a purgative catharsis, a consuming fire out of which would grow a new society, a 'Common Wealth' such as Acland expounded in an interview in the March 1942 *Socialist Christian*. Acland, by now a socialist by any other name who none the less refused to use the word because he felt it made people think of a Civil Service bureaucracy, expressed his support for a Popular Front which could unite Britain around this new vision and which he hoped cripps would lead. This matched Kenneth Ingram's call for a United Christian Socialist Front, which would follow up the Malvern Conference with real proposals for a new Britain where not only poverty was abolished but also private wealth, and where the wealthy would readily assent to this social sacrifice. This, for many Christian Socialists, was the shape of the hoped-for New Jerusalem.

The last year of the war, 1945, was a bad one for the League. First Salter died, after twenty years as MP for Bermondsey, and then the extremely frail Keeble followed him. When the general election came, perhaps out of weariness with the protracted wartime electoral pact, the *Socialist Christian* adopted a critical attitude towards the party machine and supported not just Labour candidates but, in a rather oblique reference, the 'best Socialist' candidates, which might include Common Wealth candidates, as Tom Sargent of the Common Wealth executive was clearly involved in the League at this point, writing occasionally for the magazine. All but one of the Common Wealth MPs lost their seats, and though Labour won a resounding victory and many of the issues for which Christian Socialists had fought for years were now to be political realities, the SCL seemed largely irrelevant. After all, it was tied, however loosely, to the new Government, and the oppositional politics the League was used to sat oddly beside a majority Labour Government with plenty on its plate.

By contrast, the Council of Clergy and Ministers for Common Ownership, which grew out of the Malvern Conference in May 1942, had a clear task, to make sure the Labour Government

246

adopted common ownership, so there was a degree of jealousy between the two organisations. Furthermore, the election of a whole new generation of Labour politicians shifted the emphasis of Christian Socialist activities back towards Parliament, where real battles had to be won against Tory indifference or opposition.

None the less nine League members were elected, including Jim Simmons in Birmingham West and Tom Skeffington Lodge in Reading. Simmons was a Methodist lay preacher who had been involved in the Labour Church movement near Stourbridge, had lost a leg during the First World War and had briefly held the Erdington seat from 1929 to 1931. Dennis Howell recounts that soon after the war ended Simmons was addressing a meeting in Stourbridge on the matter of the Feeding of the Five Thousand when a heckler shouted out, 'It can't be done, it can't be done.' Simmons replied, 'Are you challenging the Lord's arithmetic? I can tell you, the Lord is very good at multiplication. It's mankind that's useless at division.'[22] Though later involved in the Christian Socialist Movement, Simmons was not connected with the SCL, unlike another new MP, Tom Skeffington Lodge, who was not only a member, but soon became Chair of the League.

One of those to lose in 1945 was Acland, and it was not until 1947 that he was to return to the parliamentary fray on winning the Gravesend by-election for Labour. This instantly gave him back the platform he had had during the war years, and in 1949 he was instrumental in setting up the 1950 Group, which described itself as a 'centre for Socialist Christian research and information', produced a couple of publications and intended to organise a regular annual conference. One of Acland's long-time allies, Tom Driberg, who had entered Parliament as an Independent during the war but had joined Labour days before the general election and kept his seat, chaired the group, while Acland acted as its Honorary Secretary, and the Revd Joseph McCulloch was its Research Officer. Not a membership organisation itself, it sought to work closely with the SCL and, indeed, encouraged interested parties to join the SCL, perhaps at the instigation of Groser, who attended most of its Westminster meetings.

In the meantime a parallel attempt to revitalise Christian Socialism in Parliament was mounted in 1949 in the form of Skeffington Lodge's Parliamentary Socialist Christian Group, which he convened against the sage warnings of the SCL executive. This attracted an initial membership of eighty-one MPs, including Acland, Sorensen, Hastings, Henderson's son, (also called Arthur), Roy Jenkins, Harold Wilson, Leah Manning, Geoffrey de Freitas, Hugh Delargy and Bob Mellish. Its appeal was short-lived, despite a joint conference in June with the SCL and the publication of *Faith, Hope and 1950*, a brief pamphlet based on work by Groser, Driberg, Eric Fenn, Skeffington Lodge and, briefly, Acland. By 1952 Skeffington Lodge, who lost his own seat in 1950, was apologising to the SCL for wasting his efforts on the group, and it was clearly defunct.

The 1950s were stagnant years for the SCL. Nearly all the leading lights of the original Church Socialist League had died, and while there had been a renewed interest in Christian Socialism following the war, membership remained at about 300, and there were frequent complaints that the League was dominated by old men. Even those who had joined the League in the late 1930s and the 1940s were far from young, and Maurice Reckitt, who joined the SCL after the collapse of the Christendom Group, started to write regularly for the magazine at the age of sixty-two.

Furthermore, some of those who were closely associated with the SCL took on roles within their own Churches which made it difficult for them to devote either time or political commitment to the League. Thus in 1953 Soper became President of the Methodist Conference, and while this gave him an excellent platform for his pacifist and generally socialist views, it took him away from the League – so much so that the *Socialist Christian* commented, 'it is unbearable that he should stand aside from the SCL,'[23] suggesting that he temporarily resign his membership, although by the end of the year he had agreed to become a Vice-President of the League, along with Belden, the MP Tony Greenwood and George MacLeod.

*

MacLeod was not by nature a man to join organisations, and though he remained faithful to Christian Socialism all his life, he rarely took part in any of its organised forms. Born in 1895 of admirable Presbyterian stock – his family could boast five Moderators of the Church of Scotland, including the author of 'Courage, brother! do not stumble' – and with a Unionist MP for a father, MacLeod was sent away to school at Winchester, where he was confirmed as an Anglican, and then started to read law at Oriel College, Oxford, before enlisting in the Argyll and Sutherland Highlanders. Like many other later pacifists, MacLeod was decorated in the war, and returned to Britain looking for something to do. He decided to read theology in Edinburgh and in 1921 spent some time in New York, at Union Seminary, where he met Tubby Clayton, the founder of Toc H, whose motto, purloined from Dante, was 'Abandon rank all ye who enter here'. MacLeod then worked for Toc H as its Glasgow padre, although in 1926 he left over a dispute with the Anglicans about the genuine interdenominationalism of the movement and moved to St Cuthbert's, Edinburgh, as the assistant minister, soon acquiring a reputation as the 'Rudolf Valentino of the Edinburgh pulpit'. In 1929 he was offered the pulpit at Govan parish church, a post his grandfather had held, but he turned it down, suggesting a friend instead. When the friend died only six months later of tuberculosis, MacLeod felt obliged to accept the renewed offer, and so started an extraordinary career. For Govan, though a beautiful old churching dating back to the sixth century and St Constantine, stood in the very heart of the Clydeside docks; and the problems of 1930s Glasgow, its unemployment and its poverty, were transparent even to the most obdurate well-bred gent. None the less it was not until MacLeod went to Jerusalem in 1933 to recuperate from a nervous breakdown that he was inspired, on hearing the early-morning Russian Orthodox liturgy, to return to Govan with a new vision of building a strong Christian community that would live in the midst of Govan's inner-city problems. Soon the parish's Pearce Institute was converted and members recruited to create 'that

Christian Common Wealth which alone can satisfy our legitimate aspirations'.[24]

MacLeod was already well known in Scottish society, and when he tried to raise money for this new community it came from the least likely of sources and within two years it was set up. Meanwhile MacLeod's memories of Ypres had simmered away in the deeper corners of his mind. He had become a convinced pacifist and in 1937 ran Dick Sheppard's campaign for the rectorship of Glasgow University, in which he defeated Winston Churchill, only to die two days later. He had also come to believe that the real problems of the day were not, in the narrow sense, political but moral, for 'Before we can deal with the details of "how to share" (Politics) we feel we must capture the "will to share" (Religion).'[25] He saw the political role of Christianity as providing no blueprint for a new social order, but an experience from which fundamental principles might be adduced.

Meanwhile the small community at the Pearce Institute was growing, and MacLeod started to have designs on the tiny island off Mull where St Columba had first landed on his mission from Ireland in AD 561. Iona Abbey, the traditional burial place of the kings of Scotland, had fallen into disrepair, but in 1910 a certain amount of restoration had been done to the church itself by its trustees, and in 1935 MacLeod put forward plans for a community based at the Abbey, preparing men for Church of Scotland ministry. Having persuaded the trustees, he gave up his post at Govan and recruited some backers, a previous Moderator, John White, and Sir David Young Cameron, the Limner to the King. He also set about raising the vast sums that the community would need to restore the whole Abbey and to live on. He recounted that one of his first requests for cash was to Sir James Lithgow. 'I asked him for £5,000. He invited me to spend the night. This surprised me because we were not very close: he was building battleships and I was already a pacifist. Before I left, he asked, "If I give you £5,000, will you give up your pacifism?" "Not on your life," I replied. Then he said, "Then I will give you £5,000." '[26]

So in 1939 the Iona Community began, despite considerable

suspicion from many Church of Scotland worthies, who objected to rumoured 'Romish' practices such as keeping the Church calendar and the placing of a Cross on the table – or was it an altar? During the war Iona initiated retreats and study weeks for visitors, but the main community continued to rebuild the Abbey and act as a preparatory college for ordinands.

To most of his friends' consternation, MacLeod married in 1948 and through the 1950s took an increasingly active role in politics, joining the Co-op Party, speaking for Labour candidates and organising a Christian Socialist group at the Glasgow Community House, where Ralph and Jenny Morton led regular debates with young politicians like Bruce Millan and Gregor MacKenzie and celebrities like Cripps, Huddleston and the actress Sybil Thorndike. The Community itself had a manifest commitment to justice, peace and the integrity of Creation as part of its membership rule of life, and though not all the members would have considered themselves pacifists, the vast majority would have supported a Labour Government and a socialist agenda.

The Community was not quite the idyll it might seem, however. For many of the second generation of its members saw MacLeod as autocratic and self-centred, and grew to resent him. In the confined atmosphere of the small island insignificant matters could easily get overblown. So it was with some relief all round that in 1956 MacLeod was elected Moderator of the Church of Scotland, despite frequent complaints about his liturgical inventions, such as introducing a sculpture of the Virgin Mary to the Abbey. MacLeod's investiture was the only Moderatorial ceremony ever to be challenged, though interestingly the complaint was over his theology, not his politics.

By 1965 the Iona Community had grown away from MacLeod, even though he was still its leader, and against his wishes it agreed to change the work of the Abbey; it became a year-round centre for meetings and conferences, while the Community became a dispersed set of people committed to the same rule of life and to regular visits to the Abbey. Four years later it took a second decision that MacLeod objected to, recruiting the first woman to membership of the Community, Dr Nancy Brash, but by then, despite having refused to use the title that had passed to him on his cousin's death in 1944, he was given a peerage, and took advantage of the moment to resign as leader of the Community.

One of MacLeod's closest English colleagues, and an equally individualistic personality, was Cripps's friend Mervyn Stockwood, who both visited Iona and tried to persuade MacLeod to work with him in a joint parish in Bristol. In the late 1930s Stockwood, at Lansbury's suggestion, organised several Sunday-evening open-air meetings for the SCL on the Clifton Downs, and just after the war he was elected to Bristol City Council, where he became Chair of Health and Vice-Chair, appropriately enough for the local vicar, of Cemeteries. Never a great one for party or Church discipline, he nearly lost the whip on the Council in 1953, and despite having only just joined the party he was expelled, along with all Cripps's supporters in 1938. Stockwood's Church in Bristol, St Matthew's, Moorfields, was regularly treated to fairly exotic socialist preachers, from MacLeod to Victor Gollancz, George Thomas and Stephen Spender, but it was his own preaching that gained him the reputation of being one of the most innovative of Anglican clergy, notably infuriating the Government over his criticism of British zinc sales to Japan in 1939. In 1955 Stockwood moved to Great St Mary's, the university church in Cambridge, and within a year was elected to Cambridge City Council, although his tenure of this his last elected post was only brief, as in 1960 he was to become Bishop of Southwark. On being appointed he was reported to have said, 'I am, and shall remain, a convinced and enthusiastic member of the Labour Party,' and to have added *sotto voce*, 'until the next time they throw me out'.[27] For all his protestations, however, Stockwood's political intervention did at times seem like a dalliance with socialism. Thus though he later signed the *Papers from the Lamb*, he never joined the Christian Socialist Movement, and many distrusted his flamboyance, misreading it as lack of substance. Yet he demonstrated an astuteness that others lacked. Like MacLeod, he was far from blinded by Communism and attacked Johnson's hyperbolic glorification of the Soviet system long before the worst horrors of Stalin's reign were widely known. Nevertheless, he always wore his Labour connections lightly, and after Cripps's death his contribution to formal Christian Socialist groups was only incidental.

In 1953 Skeffington Lodge stood down as Chairman of the SCL, and there was, for the first time in many years, a contested election between Charles Record, who was then Treasurer of the League, and had been a member nearly from the beginning, and Jack Boggis. Both had been early members of the Communist Party, although Record had left in 1924 when 'the growing incompetence and signs of dishonesty in the leadership ... drove [him] out'[28] and Boggis had been converted from atheism and joined the Catholic Crusade as a result of meeting Groser in the late 1920s. Record, by occupation a lecturer in electrical engineering at Huddersfield Technology College, had been a member of the Church Socialist League and a founding member of the SCL, editor of its magazine and its General Secretary. Boggis, by contrast, was an Anglo-Catholic priest who had followed Groser as vicar of St George's-in-the-East and was also Chair of the Council of Clergy and Ministers for Common Ownership, which had renamed itself the Society of Socialist Clergy and Ministers (SSCM). By 1953 it still retained some of its fervour and published a small magazine, *Magnificat*, but, like the SCL, it was looking for a larger membership and a more significant role. Several articles in the *Socialist Christian* had already referred to the SSCM as a rival body, so it was intriguing that Boggis narrowly defeated Record, by thirty-two votes to thirty-one, to become Chair of both the leading Christian Socialist organisations simultaneously.

In fact, Boggis did not remain Chairman of the League for long, as in 1956 he moved to a new job and felt obliged to stand down, allowing Doris Pulsford to take over for two years as the first, and to this date the only, woman to chair any of the Christian Socialist organisations. None the less Boggis's joint chairmanship did raise a fundamental question that had been echoing in many members' minds for several years: what was the point of running two separate organisations when their aims were so similar, they embraced many of the same members and they were both so small?

So began, largely at Doris Pulsford's suggestion, a period of internal reflection within the League about the future of Christian Socialism. In 1957 she asked, in the *Socialist Christian*, what the quintessential role of the League was: to be a mass movement, a pressure group, or a voice? Coming down very firmly on the side of the League's value as an independent Christian voice within politics, acting as a conscience to the Labour movement and providing an alternative commentary on society, she effectively called for a combined organisation that could better perform that function.

Meanwhile similar discussions had been going on in the SSCM, where another east London Anglo-Catholic priest, Stanley Evans, had argued for a united Christian Socialist front. So later in 1957 a small committee was set up under the chairmanship of Tom Driberg, with Record, Evans and Jim Desormeaux, who was now Secretary of the SCL, to consider the common basis upon which such an organisation could be founded. This started to meet in late 1957 at Driberg's local pub in Holborn, the Lamb, where they thrashed out the vital issues – common ownership, pacifism, Christian unity and equality – in an attempt to produce a common paper which could be circulated to key figures in both organisations before publication.

As usual when a committee is drafting a report, the process took considerably longer than any of those involved had anticipated, and both organisations grew impatient, while several members suspected that the delay was related to the fact that some of the SSCM wanted to bounce the SCL into a new constitution without adequate consultation. There were also personal differences, which made it difficult to secure agreement. Stewart Purkis, by now editor of the *Socialist Christian*, had a violent objection to Stanley Evans and argued that one prerequisite for a united organisation 'may be a determination by all socialist Christians that no loyalty to party shall bind them',[29] thus getting in a dig not at political parties but at Church parties such as the Anglo-Catholics. Indeed, Evans seems to have attracted quite a degree of antagonism throughout this period from SCL members, which may well have been connected with his only recently ditched support for Stalin, for whom he had preached a ludicrously positive memorial sermon. As Stockwood recounted, 'as a member of the Communist Party he had denounced me as a Fascist because of my criticism of the Soviet Union,'[30] and it was not until the Russian invasion of Hungary and the Twentieth Congress at which Khrushchev denounced Stalin's worst atrocities in 1956 that he was to alter his views. Stockwood's own disdain for Evans's and Johnson's views on the Soviet system was fairly marked. In his *Dictionary of National Biography* obituary of Johnson he wrote, 'He went [to the Soviet Union], he saw and he was conquered . . . No matter what adverse reports reached him – of secret trials, terrorism, concentration camps, the atrocities of Stalin, the invasion of Hungary – he was unmoved.'[31] Johnson had been the preacher at the second annual meeting of the SSCM, and Evans was one of its prime movers, so it is easy to imagine the feelings that many SCL members would have had about the possibility of amalgamating with such an uncritically pro-Soviet group. Indeed, there were tensions enough within the SCL itself. The Christian response to war was as hotly debated as ever, but in 1958 the formation of the Campaign for Nuclear Disarmament (CND) raised the temperature a couple more degrees. Several of the key figures were, naturally enough, Christian Socialists, including the ubiquitous Canon John Collins, whose Christian Action had been founded with support from Cripps, although it was ostensibly non-partisan and had Conservative and Liberal sponsors. One of Christian Action's first conferences had invited Victor Gollancz to speak, and in 1950 Gollancz also published *A Year of Grace*, which was full of quotations from all sorts of religious and humanist backgrounds. With Collins Gollancz then wrote a brief pamphlet entitled *Christianity and the War Crisis*, in which they couched a plea to the world to put aside its nationalistic pride and to use the resources presently being squandered on killing people to feed the poor. So successful was the pamphlet that an appeal was launched, and an Association for World Peace was formed. Gollancz's own interest soon waned, and the project was taken over by a new chair, the young Harold Wilson, who, at Acland's suggestion, renamed it War on Want.

Collins was a well-established figure on the Christian left, although he fought shy of direct involvement in explicitly socialist organisations which he had not founded himself. Soper's estimation of him was not complimentary, as he saw him as a very imperfect leader, but in 1958 both men were keen to see an end to the H-bomb. Other Christian Socialists involved from the beginning were the playwright J. B. Priestley, Acland and Mac-Leod. CND, of course, was not the first anti-nuclear national campaign. In 1954, soon after finishing his term as Methodist President, Soper had chaired the H-Bomb National Campaign in response to the 5 April Government decision to manufacture a British H-bomb. That May he led a rally in the West End of London and addressed a 1,000-strong meeting at Friends' House, determined to get the bomb stopped. In 1955 Acland resigned his Gravesend seat to fight the by-election on the H-bomb issue, and he and Soper continued throughout the decade to campaign for Britain to give up its arms, unilaterally if necessary. When CND was formed, then, on 17 February 1957, and the meeting ended with a call to support the planned Direct Action Committee March to the Aldermaston Research Establishment, both Soper and Acland became active sponsors, and Soper agreed to lead the march.

The campaign against nuclear weapons was not waged only on the streets. Soper, together with his friends Michael Foot, Tony Benn and Tony Greenwood, fought hard to get the Labour Party to adopt an anti-nuclear stance in the face of one of Soper's closest allies, Nye Bevan, who shocked his left-wing colleagues and the whole party by announcing that unilateral disarmament would be a profound mistake and would send a Foreign Secretary naked into the conference chamber. In 1960 a resolution calling for nuclear disarmament was eventually carried at the Labour Party Conference, though, as in 1935, it was against the advice of the Labour leader, and Hugh Gaitskell pre-empted his defeat with the famous lines, 'We will fight and fight and fight again to bring back sanity and honesty and dignity, so that our party with its great past may retain its glory and its greatness.'[32] Soper is quoted as saying, with deliberate hyperbole, 'For me the Kingdom had come when the Labour Party had accepted the CND position at its conference at Scarborough in 1960.'[33] A year later the resolution had been reversed.

Christian Socialists, together with an array of artists and screen stars (Henry Moore, Benjamin Britten, Peggy Ashcroft and others) formed the backbone of CND. Yet by no means all Christians adopted a unilateralist approach, just as they failed to agree over many of the economic issues of the day. Thus a Comrade Curr wrote in the winter 1953 edition of the *Socialist Christian* that public ownership was synonymous with socialism, and that consequently anyone who did not support State ownership was not fit to be a member of the SCL. This prompted a fierce internal debate, which many of the predominantly Anglican SSCM regarded with some suspicion. Tawney, now President of the SCL, had himself argued that public ownership was a means, not an end, and Robert Woodifield, who was a member of the executive, replied to Curr:

> we have a right to claim that it is an essential Christian principle that those things to which all people must have access in order to live – the means of production – should be freely accessible to all, and therefore their ownership should not be concentrated in the hands of a few ... But Christians can legitimately differ with regard to the best way – or ways – of applying that principle.[34]

In 1959 Christian Socialism was passing through the doldrums. There were some notable characters who could, without too much difficulty, fill a fringe meeting at the Labour Party Conference – Donald Soper as ex-President of the Methodist Conference or George MacLeod as former Moderator of the General Assembly of the Church of Scotland. There were senior Labour politicians, mainly on the Bevanite left of the party – Tom Driberg and Tony Greenwood. There were nationally renowned clergy who had provided moral strength and support for disarmament, for peace, or for Eastern Bloc contacts – Stanley Evans, John Collins, Mervyn Stockwood. There were political theorists who had for several decades advocated Christian principles in political life – R. H. Tawney, Richard Acland, Philip Noel-Baker. And there were parish clergy, teachers, engineers, of every theological hue, who were keen to see a new social order and to integrate their Christian faith with their political ideals – Jack Boggis, Edward Charles, John Groser.

But what was missing was any clarity of purpose, any coherent body of opinion that had something to offer Britain on the threshold of the 1960s. Ironically, what had been the SCL's greatest strengths, its diversity, its independence from any one person or brand of theology, were now its weaknesses, and its members regularly queried the League's relevance. The SSCM could not really decide whether it was a sister organisation or a distant cousin, and its members had been engaged in some rapid rethinking after the 1956 Twentieth Congress of the Communist Party of the Soviet Union.

# 10

# A Moral Crusade

To be discontented with the divine discontent, and to be ashamed with the noble shame, is the very germ and first upgrowth of all virtue.

Charles Kingsley, *Health and Education*

As long as men are men, a poor society cannot be too poor to find a right order of life, nor a rich society too rich to have need to seek it.

R. H. Tawney, *The Acquisitive Society*

On May Day 1959 the long-awaited report from Tom Driberg's group was published. Named, with some humour, *Papers from the Lamb*, which might have suggested to a theological ear the Lamb of God rather than the Lamb public house in Holborn, they sought to test the water as to the likely success of any amalgamated Christian Socialist organisation.

In fact, the *Papers* maintain that the group had decided to form drafting subcommittees to consider statements on subjects 'on which there are known to be differences among Christian Socialists'[1] and that these subcommittees reported back to the whole group. But in the light of the fact that many of the names appended to the introduction were those of people who could not attend any of the group's meetings 'but expressed strong interest and sympathy',[2] it seems likely that this is an exaggeration. What is more probable is that the small group deputed to consider the amalgamation of the two organisations invited a few others to join in, and individual chapters were written over the course of the two years before being sent out to senior figures in either organisation for their comments. Certainly Stockwood and Soper, who signed *Papers from the Lamb*, had not attended any of the meetings, and much of the text reads like the work of Tom Driberg.

Either way, the expressed aim of the *Papers* was to answer one question: 'should an attempt be made to form a new organisation of Christian Socialists, in which existing organisations could, if they wished, unite?'[3] In theory the answer was to depend on the response to the *Papers*, although in truth the key figures in both organisations had already made their minds up and were looking for a means of amalgamation without losing control.

In the end it took Donald Soper, who was immersed in his work for CND, was a recently appointed alderman of the Greater London Council and was still preaching from his soap-box every week at Tower Hill and Speakers' Corner, to get the ball rolling. He was the ideal candidate for the job. A Methodist President with high-church leanings, a respected columnist in *Tribune*, a Vice-President of the SCL, an unremitting Clause Four socialist who had none the less criticised a too narrow interpretation of Christian Socialism, he could, to some degree, stand above the fray and command respect, and, above all, he was none of the others.

So on 22 and 23 January he called a two-day meeting at the Kingsway Hall for all those interested in forming a new Christian Socialist Movement (CSM). A draft constitution was drawn up, evoking countless predecessor organisations but retaining remarkably little of the SCL's statement of aims. CSM members formally pledged themselves to 'pray, give and work' for Christian unity, international reconciliation, redistribution of wealth and a classless society 'combining social and racial equality with personal responsibility and freedom of speech and association'. Two further commitments were to 'world peace with nuclear and general disarmament' and 'the common ownership and democratic control of the productive resources of the earth', both of which established CSM more firmly on the left of the Labour Party. Indeed, there was a debate about whether to seek party affiliation, but 'independence was preferred by most of those who attended.'[4]

The main speakers at the rather tense conference were Evans and Groser, and Driberg gave a report on the work of his subcommittee. An executive committee was also set up with a cross-section of those who had been influential in the parent organisations: from the SCL its Secretary Jim Desormeaux, Paul Derrick, Gresham Kirkby, Groser and Soper; from the SSCM its Secretary Edward Charles, Evans, Tom Sargent, Jack Putterill and Mary Barber.

The first Chairman, of course, was Soper, and there is evidence that although the Anglo-Catholics like Evans and Groser continued to take part in CSM, many felt that Soper's election was a victory for the puritans. For despite Soper's high-church credentials as President of the Methodist Sacramental Fellowship, he was an unremitting moralist. Smoking, alcohol, hunting, all came in for his unbridled condemnation, as did the Beatles and Mickey Mouse for their 'promiscuity'. So although Soper's support for the liberalisation of laws regarding male homosexuality was unambiguous, and he later welcomed the introduction of a CSM commitment to 'sexual equality', yet he had a reputation among the Anglo-Catholics for being part of the wagging-finger element of Nonconformism. The Anglo-Catholics Headlam and Noel, with their emphasis on the celebration of life in the ballet, the theatre and morris dancing, were their heroes. Soper must have seemed a respected companion but not necessarily their natural leader, and for all their political similarities it is hard to see quite how Soper got along with the main author of *Papers from the Lamb*, Tom Driberg.

Whether history or Tom Driberg himself did Driberg the worst disservice is imponderable. Certainly he is better known today for his self-confessed homosexuality and promiscuity than for his vital role in the formation of the CSM. Indeed, the Tory MP Alan

Duncan dismisses him quite simply as 'the libidinous Labour MP'.[5]

His obituary in *The Times* on 13 August 1976 was forthright and convoluted:

> Tom Driberg, who worked for some years under the name of William Hickey and died under the name of Lord Bradwell, was a journalist, an intellectual, a drinking man, a gossip, a high churchman, a liturgist, a homosexual ... a politician of the left, a Member of Parliament, a member of the Labour Party National Executive, a stylist, an unreliable man of undoubted distinction.[6]

Since then Driberg's own half-finished posthumous autobiography has appeared and a revealing biography by Francis Wheen. There have been disputed allegations by Chapman Pincher that he was a Soviet spy, and many of Driberg's own careless anecdotal descriptions of his night-time meanderings have appeared in print, all giving the impression of a man driven equally by his sexual instincts and his desire to conceal them, his political creed and his inability to live by it. For many it is now impossible to take him seriously as a political or moral figure.

Yet this is harsh. Driberg was born in an era in which it was considered immoral for a man not only to engage in sex with another man but even to be homosexual; homosexuality itself was a criminal offence for which prison was the not infrequent punishment. Little wonder that he concealed his true identity. Soper, who worked closely with Driberg for more than a decade, had no idea that he was gay until after his death, yet holds that it was Driberg's need to conceal his sexuality that made him so promiscuous and prevented him from ever becoming a real leader. Perhaps in a different era he would have been able to enjoy a more open gay life and not find his energy sapped by concealment. But this is conjecture.

What is incontrovertible is that Driberg's career started most suitably for a young gentleman. Having been born in Crowborough in Sussex, in 1905, to elderly parents who had returned from India, in 1918 he went to Lancing College, where he was fellow-sacristan with Evelyn Waugh, before going up to Christ Church, Oxford, to read classics in 1924. Having joined the Communist Party in Brighton, Driberg supported the general strike in 1926 and started writing for the party newspaper the *Sunday Worker*. Driberg's academic work, however, was not of great interest to him. He spent the night before his finals in 1927 at a ball and entered the examination room so drunk that he instantly fell asleep. He left Oxford the same day, without a degree.

Starting his working life in a bar in Soho, and getting occasional work as a film extra, he managed by Christmas to find an opening at the *Express* newspaper, where he started in the New Year as a reporter on £3 per week. His fascination with the antics of the wealthy soon gained him notoriety, and by 1932 he was writing half the *Express*'s 'Talk of London' column; by the end of the year he had taken over the whole column and had retitled it 'William Hickey' after the eighteenth-century diarist. By the time of the Second World War he was a celebrated daily columnist with decidedly left-of-centre views. He had sprung to the defence of Russia and declared forthrightly against Nazism, although he was genuinely surprised when war was declared. In 1942 he decided to stand for Parliament in the Maldon by-election for the seat where he had bought his rather grand home, Bradwell Manor, and because of the wartime electoral pact between the main parties did so as an Independent. Acland came to help run the campaign, and the Secretary of Braintree Labour Party, Jack Boggis, who was a local vicar, resigned from the party to help in the campaign, which Driberg won by nearly 6,000 votes.

When the 1945 general election came Driberg had to decide what to do. To remain an Independent would almost certainly mean losing his seat, but if he were to join the Labour Party, there was no guarantee that the local constituency party would select him. In the event the local Labour candidate was still in a Japanese prison when the campaign started, and Driberg joined the party at the very meeting at which he was offered the Labour nomination.

Driberg's parliamentary duties seem rarely to have bothered him very much, and he requested lengthy periods of absence for foreign trips, both during the 1945–50 government, and in 1950–51, when Labour's majority was wafer-thin, thus earning himself the opprobrium of his more loyal colleagues and almost losing him the whip.

None the less Driberg was well connected, both in the party and in society. Lord Mountbatten, then the gay Viceroy of India, became a close friend, and Driberg developed strong connections with the Bevanite group of Michael Foot, Barbara Castle, Harold Wilson, Richard Acland, Dick Crossman and Jennie Lee. Indeed, when Bevan, Wilson and John Freeman resigned from the Government in April 1951 over Gaitskell's imposition of charges for spectacles and false teeth, Driberg became one of the key members of this Keep Left group, which eventually delivered Wilson the leadership of the party. Meanwhile, in 1951 Driberg rather bizarrely decided to marry Mrs Ena Binfield, a Jewish divorcée who had to be baptised by Conrad Noel's successor Jack Putterill before the elaborate Anglo-Catholic wedding, which bewildered even the Roman Catholics, like the MP Hugh Delargy, who attended.

In 1959, having lost his seat in 1955 and returned to a career of journalism mixed with NEC duties, including being Party Chair in 1957–8, Driberg cemented a final connection with the Christian Socialist legacy by taking over Somerville Hastings's constituency at Barking, which he retained until 1974, when he stood down and was made Lord Bramwell.

Driberg's Christian Socialism is rather less susceptible to analysis than his more secular views, for the simple reason that many Christians have been so embarrassed by his posthumous record that he has been cast into oblivion. But in the late 1950s he was a key parliamentary figure in an attempt to bring Christianity and socialism together. He had visited Thaxted in the days of Noel, been attracted by the Catholic Crusade's offer of adventures and retained a fastidious eye for liturgical detail. Many of his allies in the Labour Party were also Christians, and Hugh Delargy, another Bevanite, was brought by Driberg into the new Christian Socialist fold, appending his name to the *Papers from the Lamb* and joining CSM. Driberg also knew Stockwood well, from having visited him in Bristol, and had worked with Acland and Tom Sargent in the Common Wealth Party. Boggis had gone out on a limb by resigning from the Labour Party to help in his campaign in 1942. Driberg was also a driving force behind the 1950 Group and helped Skeffington Lodge start the Parliamentary Christian Socialist Group. So, although Driberg rarely wrote on Christian Socialism, he was an intimate of the movement, and the *Papers from the Lamb* were almost a personal apologia.

They are an intriguing mix – biblical quotations interwoven with a bald analysis of society. Starting with Jesus's words, 'I have come that they may have life, and have it to the full,'[7] they take 'equality of opportunity for every individual' as their central theme. 'Distributive communism' was the pattern of the early Church, and 'that type and degree of common ownership which are best suited to a particular society and best secure a sharing of material goods' must then be 'an essential prerequisite of a truly Christian society', but 'the Christian concern for common ownership is a concern with abundant living for individual human persons within society. Common ownership must exist for them, not they for common ownership.'[8]

The later chapters betray Driberg's personal interests – Moral ReArmament, Soviet Russian, Christian Unity, missionary imperialism – yet follow a steady path through potentially controversial topics, opting for a broad appeal rather than narrow doctrine. The 'obligations of prayer and thought' are finally seen as the fundamentals for a community based on Christian compassion, dedicated to 'the divine purpose of so re-ordering society that the lives of countless human beings, made in the image of God, do not end in degradation and despair'.[9]

What is striking about *Papers from the Lamb* is its deliberate inclusiveness. On peace, on the economy, on theology, there is barely a hint of what has so often plagued Christian Socialism, the attempt to define, to narrow down, to stipulate a dogmatic position – what Soper has called the 'make up your mind and find a text syndrome'.[10] Yet there is very little committee-speak, and what comes across is a uniting personal credo. If it was anyone's, it was Driberg's, but, surprisingly for the brash old extrovert, it was subtle enough to harness much of the Christian Socialist spectrum.

Ironically, when CSM did a major consultation exercise with its members in the 1980s it was clear that they wanted it to act more as a forum for discussion of key themes than as a debating chamber for resolutions or a policy-making body. Yet the first few years of CSM's life saw it on a collision course with the Labour leadership over policy after policy.

In September 1965 Stanley Evans and Mary Barber, who had been close colleagues for years, Evans as vicar of Holy Trinity, Dalston, and Mary as a firebrand member of his congregation and celebrated scientist, were both killed outright in a car crash. Their deaths attracted the briefest of mentions on the radio news, but in CSM there was a much keener sense of loss. Evans had been a short-tempered man who had proved rather strong meat for many, but he had worked hard for his principles ever since the Spanish Civil War. Originally a Communist, he had been a keen member, with Boggis, of the British–Soviet Friendship Society and had studied at Mirfield before ordination in 1935. After a series of curacies, including a period with Jack Putterill at St Andrew's, Plaistow, he spent eight years, 1947–55, in the clerical wilderness, and it was not until Canon John Collins recommended him for the living of Holy Trinity, Dalston, which was in the gift of St Paul's, that he returned to work for the Church. Here his liturgical inventiveness came to the fore with, on Christmas Eve, a procession of the mistletoe as a symbol of 'love and justice and peace and freedom' and a 'Litany of Labour' for St Philip's and St James's Day. He was not at the Malvern Conference himself but soon took an active role in the CCMCO and helped steer it to the left at a time when he still believed in Stalin. After the invasion of Hungary in 1956 Evans drastically altered his views on Soviet Russian, and in 1960 Stockwood appointed him the first Principal of the Southwark Ordination Course, and he became a canon of Southwark Cathedral.

Evans was a stalwart of the ex-Communist left when CSM was founded. With Edward Charles, another Anglo-Catholic priest, he was a key figure in the SSCM, writing regularly for its periodical *Magnificat* and for his own quarterly journal *Junction* in which Edward Charles and another SSCM colleague, Kenneth Ingram, rather optimistically termed themselves 'Anglican realists'. Evans often expressed a profound distaste for the moderate world of constitutional politics which the Labour Party represented, despite being labelled a 'party hack' by some of his more recalcitrant colleagues. In his 1962 lecture on 'Equality', given in honour of Tawney soon after his death, he castigated Labour because it could not be said

> either to have achieved an equal society or to be visibly leading towards one. If you attend a Labour Party conference you are in some sense in the world of the status-seekers and you can judge the importance within the hierarchy of labour of the person you are addressing by the hotel in which he stays.[11]

Evans has attracted much criticism in his time, not least for a sometimes uncritical regard for Soviet Communism, although Alan Duncan's and Dominic Hobson's assertion in *Saturn's Children*[12] that he wrote a panegyric as an obituary of Stalin is part of a wholly inaccurate Conservative mythology. In fact, Evans preached at a memorial service for Stalin in March 1953 but dramatically amended his views, following the Twentieth Congress, in his *Russia Reviewed*. In 1962 he went further, condemning the fact that 'with that singleness of purpose which was one of the outstanding characteristics of Stalinism, the results of which some of us should have noted sooner than we did, the whole concept of equality was cast aside as a "left deviation" and a whole caste of VIPs was produced.'[13]

Meanwhile CSM was dancing a careful minuet with the Labour Party. For at the beginning of the 1960s CSM's centre of gravity was clearly on the left and the Labour Party was led by the right, in the shape of the two Hughs, Gaitskell and Dalton. Indeed, the two most prominent MPs in CSM were convinced members of the Keep Left group, Driberg and Anthony Greenwood.

Greenwood was the son of another Labour MP, Arthur, who had been defeated for the party leadership by Attlee. Born in 1911 in Leeds, he went on to study at the Merchant Taylors School and Balliol, Oxford, where he became President of the Union. He served as an RAF intelligence officer in the war and was elected to Parliament at the 1946 Heywood and Radcliffe by-election. In 1950 his constituency was renamed Rossendale, and he remained its MP until 1970. Elected to the NEC in 1954, he soon had a shadow ministerial position at the Home Office, although after taking part in the first Aldermaston march in 1958 he resigned from the Government in October 1960 over Gaitskell's support for the H-bomb.

The following year, in an attempt to force Wilson into standing against Gaitskell, Greenwood announced his own candidature, whereupon Wilson decided to stand himself and then had to bully Greenwood into standing down. Wilson lost, by 166 votes to eighty-one, but when Gaitskell died in 1963 he had already laid down a marker and won easily. In his first Cabinet in 1964 Wilson appointed Greenwood Colonial Secretary, as one of his few left-wing allies, and a year later made him Minister of Overseas Development before in 1966 appointing him Minister of Housing and Local Government. Like Wheatley before him, he was a success at Housing and in 1967 managed to build a record 400,000 homes before the devaluation of the pound in 1968 led to Draconian cuts in the housing budget and a consequent fall in his own political stock. In 1969 he left the Cabinet, having unsuccessfully stood in 1968 for General Secretary of the party, and the following year he resigned his seat to become Chair of the Commonwealth Development Corporation.

Greenwood's fortunes were markedly different from Driberg's, not least because he was married to the extremely able artist Gillian Greenwood. Wilson clearly saw Driberg as useful but unreliable, and Greenwood was soon his sole ally in the Cabinet. Yet at the formation of CSM their perspectives on the Labour Party were remarkably similar. Opposed to Gaitskell's political agenda, they, together with the other Bevanite, Soper, led CSM with a left-ward gait. Indeed, in the first year of *CSM News* the sole dissenting voice to stand up for the party leadership was Tom Sargent's, and even he could only bring himself to say, 'Although I have always been an advocate of unilateral renunciation, I am convinced that the campaign in its present form is diverting a tremendous amount of moral effort and enthusiasm from what should be the main duty of the Labour Party today.'[14]

Despite the attempt to create a broad movement and the emphasis on unity in *Papers from the Lamb*, there was a clear majority on the new executive, which was dominated by Soper, in favour of unilateralism and a strict interpretation of common ownership as State ownership. Charles Record wrote in the February 1963 edition of *CSM News*, 'It is inevitable and has been invariable that Christian Socialists tend to the left of their more politically involved contemporaries.' Not everyone agreed, for key members of the executive failed to support the 1961 annual meeting's unilateralist resolution, and in 1965 Christopher Powell attacked CSM for being too concerned with the mechanics rather than the morality of politics and for supporting a form of Utopianism, effectively believing that the Kingdom of God could be realised by political action.

In the meantime Wilson had been elected both Leader of the Labour Party and Prime Minister, with Driberg's and Greenwood's support. Wilson himself had been brought up a Congregationalist and was married in Mansfield College Chapel, so he was a welcome guest at the 1964 annual meeting. Indeed, the *Christian Socialist* maintained that he was a member of the movement, although Eric Wright, at various times General Secretary and Treasurer of the movement, denies he ever paid a membership fee. None the less he stated, 'I can say that for me – because *I* am a Christian I must be a Socialist. I will also say that if any man is in a political party which is not the expression of his Christian ideals, he ought to get out of it.'[15] When Wilson became Prime Minister and had appointed his Cabinet one of his first ideas was to hold a service for the new Government in the Crypt Chapel of the House of Commons, at which he asked Stockwood to preach and Soper, whom he knew as a neighbour in Hampstead Garden Suburb, to lead the prayers. Soper's alignment with the left had led him to claim at a Tribune meeting in 1960 that he could vouch that CSM's 600 members would not support Gaitskell's leadership, but with Wilson at the helm he seemed much more comfortable; his prayers were later used by Wilson in his peroration during a party conference speech, and the service was repeated after the successful 1966 general election.

CSM's biggest beef with Gaitskell had been the attempt to rewrite the Labour Party's 1918 commitment to

> secure for the workers by hand or by brain the full fruits of their industry and the most equitable distribution thereof that may be possible upon the basis of the common ownership of the means of production, distribution and exchange, and the best obtainable system of popular administration and control of each industry or service.

Soper believed that 'Clause Four expresses, within the framework of a contemporary economic situation, what I believe to be the ultimate principle that emerges from our Lord's teaching,'[16] a view which he reiterated to *Tribune* in the 1995 debate on Tony Blair's rewriting of Labour's aims and values.

For CSM in the 1960s and 1970s, common ownership was the essence of Christian Socialism. When Evans wrote a study outline of Christian Socialism in 1962 he maintained, 'socialism is the common ownership of the means of production, distribution and exchange,'[17] and Soper was keen to point out that the early Church, on the descent of the Holy Spirit at Pentecost, had immediately formed a community where everything was held in common. So common ownership was not an issue. The question was: what kind of common ownership? So a working party, set up in 1964, reported back in 1966 that common ownership should be made the basis of all industry, but in different forms based on trusteeship. While in theory the report called for variety, in practice it urged homogeneity, with a demand for the national-isation of nearly every industry except retail. Another attempt at an industrial policy based on common ownership was made in 1971 as a result of a resolution at the annual meeting calling for the extension of 'social ownership' rather than 'common owner-ship'. A subcommittee consisting of Philip Bagwell, Edward Charles and Arthur Downes then produced a seventeen-page pamphlet, much of which was written by the one serious econ-omist in the group, a Roman Catholic called Paul Derrick, whose personal campaign for an extension to common ownership was to dominate CSM's industrial policy well into the 1980s. Here there was a serious discussion of municipal ownership, of State share-holdings, of 'people's capitalism' and of the socialisation of the company, but the main thrust of *Common Ownership and the Common People* is clear: socialism ineluctably 'will involve sub-stantial increases in nationalisation'[18] and socialists 'should pay much more attention to forms of common ownership other than state ownership: in particular to co-operative ownership and to municipal ownership'.[19]

Broadly speaking, every return to this subject in the history of CSM has brought the same response. So in the 1970s it was with great delight that the Common Ownership Act was passed, as the result of a Private Member's Bill in the House of Commons. And when Tony Blair in 1995 sought to amend the Labour Party's constitution a meeting of the CSM executive, at which neither the Chair nor the General Secretary was present, voted overwhelm-ingly to delay the Special Conference at which the new constitution was to be debated and to support the retention of the existing Clause Four. When the NEC's new wording was made public in March, CSM's Annual General Meeting spent a fraught couple of hours trying to decide whether to hold a postal ballot of all members or to vote there and then on the suggested amendment, many of those who were opposed to the new wording opposing the ballot. A ballot was agreed, and the result was 77.4 per cent in favour of change, effectively voting to ditch Labour's commitment to common ownership.

It is difficult to guess at the exact reason for CSM's voting pattern, unless it is simply that the CSM membership was far less doctrinaire than its executive. Some will argue that the reason was that Tony Blair had put his leadership on the line, and members were voting for or against him rather than on the issue. But my own suspicion is that while the extension of common ownership is a hope for nearly all Christian Socialists, very few are prepared to see a return to the centralised State that large-scale nationalisation implies. Co-operation, communal responsibility, sustainable communities – these seem more important than taking the 'commanding heights of the economy' in creating a just society. It is not ownership that matters so much as the exercise of power that goes with ownership. Nationalised industries, especially when they form monopolies, can act as little in the interests of the poor as can multinational corporations, and municipal services can seem more alienating and inaccessible to change than a responsible private company.

Christian Socialism in the 1960s and 1970s was not the exclusive prerogative of CSM. Indeed, the combination of its identification with the Labour Party and its left-wing bias conspired to keep the Movement small, never getting above 450 until a major push for members in the 1980s. Many radical Christians preferred to work through non-aligned denominational groups or single-issue campaigns. New theological insights from Europe and Latin America meant that CSM seemed out of date and parochial, its concerns dominated by the battles of the 1930s, when many of its leading lights had cut their political teeth. For CSM the question was whether taxes should pay for nuclear weapons. For others it was whether Christians could support armed insurrection. Street politics, student politics, struggles abroad, the women's movement – all these were far more exciting, especially for a generation of people who were so young in the Second World War that it had barely affected them.

A typical example of the 1960s search for new forms of Christian Socialism was the set of twenty-something Roman Catholics, most of them Cambridge students, who formed the informal Slant Group which in 1964 published, in association with the Dominicans and the publishing house Sheed and Ward, the magazine after which they were named.

*Slant*'s history went back to the December Group who in 1958 inaugurated an annual meeting at Spode House at which they debated the conclusions of Vatican II and tried to frame a Catholic response to Marxist materialism. The key figures, Terry Eagleton, Francis MacDonagh, Herbert McCabe, Brian Wicker and Adrian and Angela Cunningham, all went on to widely divergent careers: Eagleton and the Cunninghams in academia; McDonagh in the shanty towns of Brazil; Wicker as a unilateralist; and McCabe as one of the leading British Dominicans. From 1964 to 1970, when *Slant* ceased publication, they devoted much of their energies to developing a theology for 'New Left Church'. Drawing partly on Vatican II but more heavily on the Marxist literary critical analysis of the role of language, and therefore of theology, in society, they defined a critique of Catholic systematic theology with its reliance on natural law that was the most philosophically astute Christian–Marxist dialogue since MacMurray.

Eagleton in particular showed a remarkable level of political confidence at a time when Roman Catholics were still rarely admitted to the political caste in Britain. In his book *The New Left Church* he puts a remarkably triumphalist case for Christian communitarianism as the hub of all history, for 'since the resurrection, the meaning of human community has been Christ. Whenever two or three are gathered together, in a pub or discussion

group or works committee, Christ is the ground of their communication, the living principle of their community.'[20] He goes on
to argue that 'the idea that the experience of the worker under
capitalism is one of alienation is one of Marx's most basic insights,
and forms the centre of Marxist humanism,'[21] from which point
he states that 'the radical response to an alienated society is the
response of community – community as the way of life in which
all men can be simultaneously free subjects, present to each other
without mutual exploitation. For the Christian there is a proto-
typal society in which this can happen, and this is the liturgy.'[22]

In John Kent's words Slant ended up as a 'strange concoction
of an existentialist ecclesiology and a Marxist political analysis',[23]
but for many English Roman Catholics at this time the search for
a political theology which could replace the easy pietism and
superstition of much parish life was an essential part of reading
the signs of the times. Vatican II had taken off some of the stops
and Roman Catholic theologians across the world were determined to experiment – and nowhere more so than in Latin
America.

Rimac is the oldest slum in Lima. Its old colonial houses, which
once resplendently housed one family, now house a family per
room. Unemployment, underemployment, overcrowding, malnu-
trition, illiteracy, disease are all rife in a city and a continent
where to be poor is not to be part of a minority, as in Britain, but
to be part of the overwhelming, teeming majority. Many of those
who live in the ever-expanding Peruvian capital, with its extensive
shanties, have left their homes in the jungle or the mountains to
seek wealth and fortune but have to struggle in a harsh world
with little sanitation or political hope.

One of the priests in Rimac, who runs the Bartolomé de Las
Casas centre, was born in Lima in 1928, the son of a *mestizo*
family who wanted him to be a doctor. Gustavo Gutierrez,
however, decided to train for the priesthood. He was soon
identified as one of the clerical high-fliers and was sent to finish
his training at Louvain and Lyons, where he met the revolutionary

priest Camilo Torres, who was killed with a machine-gun in his hand in 1966.

In 1959 Gutierrez returned to Lima to teach at the Catholic University and to work in Rimac, where he remains. His theological training was designed to make him an eminent systematic theologian in the European mould, but Gutierrez's life in the midst of the suffocating poverty of Rimac made him want to reinterpret the Christian faith in the light of that experience. Throughout the 1960s, at a series of theological consultations in Latin America and Europe, he tried to formulate an expression of the Gospel that was actually 'good news to the poor'.

In 1968 he drafted the key chapter on peace which was included in the Medellín conference of Latin American bishops and which condemned institutionalised violence against the poor as a sin, and in 1971 he published *Theology of Liberation*, finally naming what was already a major body of theology across the continent.

Liberation theology is far from monolithic, but its basic premises are straightforward. For it asserts that theology itself comes second – it is the afterthought that prompts new action, a process of reflection upon our current situation in the light of God's word. Consequently the context in which we do our theology is an essential part of its meaning. True Christian theology must speak either from among the poor or from an attempt to make their liberation a reality because God himself chose poverty for his son so as to show that 'blessed are you poor'. The theologian must then embrace solidarity with the poor to be able to articulate a Christian Gospel that will involve either a radical political commitment or a personal decision to live and work with the poor. For the Church this must mean choosing the same 'option for the poor' as Christ did, assaulting political orthodoxies such as the concept of 'national security' which sustained many Latin American dictatorships from the 1960s to the 1980s and speaking up for those who have no voice.

Because the first premise of Liberation theology has always been its method, it has not been limited to any one denomination and has travelled well, leading to an enormously creative and

275

imaginative re-reading of Christian doctrines and biblical stories, most notably the liberation of the Israelites from slavery in Egypt. It has also involved a direct challenge to most European understandings of the concept of the Church. For whereas Rome might see the Church in terms of its own hierarchy, Liberationists like Leonardo Boff would argue that the Church is where the preferential option for the poor to which the Latin American Bishops committed themselves in successive conferences in Medellín and Puebla comes to life in a community inspired by the spirit. Or, in the words of Shakespeare's *Coriolanus*, 'The People are the City.'

Where the work of Gutierrez and Boff, Juan Luís Segundo, Jon Sobrino, Ernesto Cardenal, José Miranda and their Protestant counterpart José Miguez Bonino had a real effect and, they would argue, found their inspiration was in the numerous Basic Ecclesial Communities that started to spring up across Latin America throughout the 1960s. These were groups in the shanties and slums, sometimes associated with the official Church, sometimes not, who would meet together to read the Bible, to reflect upon their situation and to renew their commitment to corporate action and to change. Of course, the old divide between spiritual and material was condemned because spirituality itself was no more than reflection upon action that led to further action. And, of course, the refusal of European theology to acknowledge the causes of poverty was seen as one of its most basic flaws. As Gutierrez says, 'When I discovered that poverty was something to be fought against, that poverty was structural, that poor people were a class and could organise, it became crystal-clear that in order to save the poor, one had to move into political action.'[24] Gutierrez's own work has brought him into sharp conflict with many of Peru's leaders, and to a general support for the United Left of Manuel Barrantes, but much of his theology is the result of listening to the poor articulate their own experiences and commitments and has been reflected in the pioneering work of bishops like Helder Camera of Recife and the murdered Archbishop of El Salvador, Oscar Romero.

Not all Liberation theology, of course, has been Latin American. African and South-East Asian Christians have also been at the forefront of a contextualised theology with a commitment to the poor, and the Black theology of James Cone, some of the radical feminist theologies of the 1980s, and the lesbian and gay Christian theologies have used a Liberationist method as well.

Yet for the British Christian left the most significant influx of Liberationist thought came from South Africa, where Trevor Huddleston, Desmond Tutu and Alan Boesak came to represent the principle of Christian resistance to the oppressive and unjust apartheid regime. Here again was a theology that took the political situation and the oppression of the people seriously, that criticised the historical buttressing of apartheid by the Dutch Confessing Church and involved a radical commitment to creating a new society. Huddleston, who joined the Community of the Resurrection in 1939, maintains that he was politicised by working in the Community's Mission in the Sophiatown township in the 1940s, and when he was dramatically recalled to Britain in 1956 he became one of Britain's most respected and prophetic leaders, serving as Bishop of Masasi, Stepney and the Indian Ocean. His theology, like that of Tutu, is a close cousin of Liberation theology, giving little harbour to pious declarations but urging in words that could be those of his hero Gore, 'The Christian is bound to act politically, wherever he may be . . . [for] if the Church refuses to accept responsibility in the political sphere as well as in the strictly theological sphere, then she is guilty of betraying the very foundation of her faith: the Incarnation.'[25]

Back in Britain Liberation theology has inevitably had a more troubled history. For Britain's poor do not form a majority, and even the poor in Britain are rich compared to the poor of Rimac. So the context for all British theology is, by definition, not poverty but wealth.

None the less attempts at a Liberation theology for Britain have been made, most notably in the work of the Methodist John Vincent, whose Urban Theology Unit at Sheffield has used an analysis/reflection/action approach for several years. It has also had a consistent adherent in the shape of the Bishop of Liverpool,

David Sheppard, whose book *Bias to the Poor* was published in 1982. As much renowned for playing cricket for England as for his much trumpeted collaborative ministry with the Roman Catholic Archbishop of Liverpool, the late Derek Worlock, Sheppard's ministry began in the East End of London, where his evangelical emphasis on the Church's task of saving souls was challenged by the searing pain of poverty. Citing the Liberation theologians, he now argues:

> the Church is meant to be a transforming ferment in humanity[26] [because] God is to be found among the poor and powerless, those at the margins of society; a Church which seeks to be faithful must learn to listen to such, admit them to its decision-making, and then face the implications for its life as an established institution in society.[27]

God, for Sheppard, 'has a persistent tendency to favour those at a disadvantage',[28] not out of random prejudice but so as to include all.

So some of the insights of Liberation theology have fed into British Christian Socialism, and many of the older missionary societies now see themselves bringing the Gospel of the Poor to the West rather than the other way round.

One of the most potent concepts for Liberation theologians in the Old Testament, which Jesus referred to in his first sermon, is the year of Jubilee: by statute every seventh year shall be a year of remission (Leviticus 25), when debts shall be forgiven and slaves released.

In 1974, by accident, a new group of Socialist Anglo-Catholics was born and named itself, after some deliberation during which the title Catholic Crusade was rejected, the Jubilee Group. It is inevitably tempting to see Jubilee as the resurgence of a Noelite left wing, but in fact the band that gathered in the rectory kitchen at St Matthew's, Bethnal Green, almost a hundred years after Stewart Headlam had founded the Guild of St Matthew, had remarkably few direct links with Noel. Indeed, of the two who met with Noel to found the Crusade on 10 April 1918, sixty years after Maurice's, Ludlow's and Kingsley's *Politics for the People*, only Jack Putterill, his successor at Thaxted, was still alive. John Groser had died in 1966, Jack Boggis in 1969 and Jack Bucknall much earlier, so one of the few left who had played any real role in the Crusade was Gresham Kirkby, who had gone on to be Chairman of the SCL, had joined CSM and was then vicar of St Paul's, Bow Common. The Jubilee Group was a new generation, although it clearly saw itself as life-affirming and celebratory rather than puritanical and declared its allegiance to Headlam, Widdrington and Noel rather than Keeble, Clifford and Hughes.

The key figure in the formation of the Jubilee Group was Ken Leech, and it was thanks to a letter he wrote to some clergy friends, mostly in the East End of London, on 25 September 1974 that what was originally intended as no more than a support group for one another was started. Over the following months there were informal meetings at the rectory of St Matthew's, where Leech was then rector, and on 23 November the group was christened.

Jubilee's strength has always lain in its network of local groups and its publications rather than in a clear structure or efficient organisation – although there is an executive and an annual meeting. None the less there was an attempt at a manifesto, which Rowan Williams, now Bishop of Monmouth, and John Saward thrashed out in an Oxford pub. Written in short, staccato phrases more akin to a catechism than to a statement of aims, it started with the doctrine of the Trinity and man's creation in his image and proceeded to condemn 'the institutionalised egotism of all forms of capitalism, including the Soviet collectivised form'.[29] Proclaiming themselves 'subversive contemplatives' rather than 'shallow activists', they ended, 'Now that we are in the death-throes of late capitalism, which threatens to inflict even greater violence on mankind than it has done before, we must make our stand with the oppressed, with the movement for liberation throughout the world.'[30]

According to Ken Leech, this manifesto was described by Gresham Kirkby, the least triumphalist of all those involved in the early days of Jubilee, as a 'rant', and it was not adopted, but by December Leech himself was calling for the formation of 'a new militant movement with its own organ of opinion' organised on the basis of 'cells of holy discontent', and in 1976 he wrote another manifesto which declared: 'we have no real sympathy with the movements of bourgeois radicalism in the Church of England which seem to sit very lightly to doctrinal truths. We hold that these trends are misconceived and revisionist.'[31]

Jubilee has no formal membership and devotes its annual meeting to generalised debate, so its significance is difficult to gauge. It also has no formal policies, yet its political stance is firmly to the left of Labour, with a variety of Marxists rubbing shoulders with the occasional Labour Party member. Some of the group, though, have been and are still among the most consistently exciting writers and speakers on the Christian left, and Leech's work in founding the young homeless charity Centrepoint Soho when he was vicar of St Anne's, Soho, and as Director of the Runnymede Trust in tackling racism and the resurgence of Fascist groups in Britain, has made his place in history assured. Leech has also been the most accurate and insightful of all the historians of Christian Socialist thought. His own political position, however, is chimerical. He is often deeply critical of the Labour Party, although in the Wilson era of the late 1960s he perceived 'a sense of hope, of optimism, even of triumph', and in a 1994 pamphlet, 'Affirming Catholicism', he argued that 'in Britain the negative experience of the centralised state and of local state bureaucracies ... has made the whole identification of socialism with central planning and State ownership questionable.'[32] This would seem to suggest a call for a redefinition of socialism, and yet he criticises the Labour Party document *Looking to the Future* for mentioning socialism only once.

If much of Leech's work is political and theological, his clearest contribution to the Christian Socialist tradition, I believe, has been to inject a vital sense of the role of prayer and contemplation into social action. Drawing heavily on the work of many of the Christian mystics, including Julian of Norwich from the four-teenth century, St John of the Cross and Teresa of Avila from the sixteenth century and Thomas Merton from the twentieth, he argues that 'Christian contemplation ... is not a smug search for interior peace, for the resolution or reduction of conflicts and tensions.'[33] Instead it is 'a state of seeing, a deepening of vision, so that the will of God is more clearly seen, and the signs of the times more accurately discerned. It is this clarity of vision which makes Christian contemplation a truly subversive activity.'[34] This, of course, strikes very close to the work of the Liberation theologians, repeating the pattern of analysis, reflection, action, seeking a reinterpretation of the Western spiritual tradition.

The Jubilee Group has not only been about Ken Leech. Rowan Williams, Terry Drummond, Judith Pinnington, David Nicholls and the American John Orens have all played an equal role in attempting to resuscitate what they see as true Anglo-Catholicism. Jubilee publications have tried to reinterpret that peculiarly British tradition and to show that socialism is not an optional add-on to Anglo-Catholicism but is an inherent part of it. Thus there have been interesting pieces on Mary's 'song of high revolt', the Magnificat, relating it to Marx's *Communist Manifesto*; on the social theology of the Sacrament of Penance; on a Liberation theology of the Wapping disputes; and on the early Church fathers' social teaching. But the main body of Jubilee's work has been historical, retelling the stories of Noel, of Headlam and of slum priests like Joe Williamson of Stepney and Fr Dolling of Portsmouth. Leech's move to St Botolph's, Aldgate, as the Maur-ice Reckitt Community theologian has also enabled him to continue his work on racism in the predominantly Bengali area of Tower Hamlets, where in 1993 the British National Party won a notorious council by-election victory.

Jubilee and CSM, though independent, were not mutually exclu-sive. While Jubilee's remit was specifically Anglo-Catholic, and many of its members shunned Labour Party affiliation, others played a role in both organisations, most notably Gresham Kirkby, who sat on CSM's executive for several years as well as writing for Jubilee. Moreover, the 1960s and 1970s were years of a Christian Socialist diaspora, with countless different groups, many of them as small as, or smaller than, Jubilee ploughing solitary furrows.

On Friday, 4 May 1979, Mrs Margaret Thatcher, the conviction politician *par excellence*, became Prime Minister, having won the general election with a majority of forty-four, and signalled the end of the post-war consensus. Later that month a ONE for Christian Renewal conference on 'Power' came to the conclusion that small organisations working on their own would never be enough to defeat Thatcherism. Within a year nineteen Christian groups and movements, 'committed to co-operating in the struggle for a just, participatory and sustainable society',[35] had come together in a federation labouring under the ponderous title Christian Organisations for Social, Political and Economic Change (COSPEC). An inaugural meeting in Birmingham on 18 and 19 January 1980 agreed 'to encourage critical Christian support of, and participation in, the Labour Movement,'[36] but it soon became clear that the impetus for COSPEC was less support for Labour than opposition to Thatcherism. A council was started with representatives from all of the affiliated groups, including Brian Jenner from the Alliance of Radical Methodists; Canon Eric James from Christian Action; Ken Leech from Jubilee; Peter Gee from the Student Christian Movement; John Vincent from the Urban Theology Unit; Grace Crookall-Greening from the resurrected Quaker Socialist Society; the recently retired ex-Chair of CSM, Edward Charles, representing the Christian Peace Conference; and a new member of CSM's executive, a Hackney Council officer, John Collins. So on Easter Day 1980 COSPEC was launched.

There was a rash of publications. First off was David Haslam's and Rex Ambler's *Agenda for Prophets*, in which a serious attempt was made at articulating a 'political theology' which might harness some of the insights from Liberation theology in a

British context. Then Tony Holden, a Methodist working at the Bow Mission, Chair of Christians Against Racism and Fascism and editor of ONE for Christian Renewal, put together a special edition of the *Christian Action Journal* with contributions from Edward Charles, David Haslam and John Atherton, the Director of the William Temple Foundation in Manchester. Two further magazines were produced, and during the 1983 general election there was even a *Christian Manifesto*.

Meanwhile a pattern had already started to develop within COSPEC which was to prove its downfall. For though there was no formal leader of COSPEC, and Council members took it in turns to chair its meetings, it did start to take on a life of its own, especially when in 1983 it had the offer of its own offices in Goodge Street in London on the death of one of the council members, Bob Kemble. COSPEC's then convenor, Vaughan Jones, had a difficult task co-ordinating the work of some extremely forceful characters, and so much energy was dissipated in personal antagonism that work on one of the main aims of COSPEC, to develop a 'Christian Institute' for Britain, kept on being postponed from meeting to meeting. Furthermore, the formation from within COSPEC of 'Christians for a Change', which campaigned around the 1987 general election, led to a feeling that some members were working to their own agenda without reference to the member organisations. Eventually the simmering personal issues boiled over in a dispute between Vaughan Jones and Ian Rathbone, who represented Christians Against Racism and Fascism on COSPEC but was by this time also the editor of the *Christian Socialist*. After some vituperative correspondence, a 'reconciliation subcommittee' was set up to bring the warring parties together, though even its constitution was disputed.

None the less COSPEC did achieve some tangible results. For a start it maintained a radical witness at a time when the Labour Party's parliamentary opposition was next to useless and the left was divided by the creation of the Social Democratic Party. In 1984 it also organised Christian support for mining communities during the strike, and backed the blessing of the miners' strike by the Bishop of Durham, David Jenkins. Jenkins had himself been involved obliquely in COSPEC as a leading light in the Christians for Socialism group and, through his work at the World Council of Churches, had played a vital role in developing the theology of a 'just, participatory and sustainable society'.

In 1987, though, two of COSPEC's prime movers were promoted, which meant they had to resign most of their direct political involvement. David Haslam became an Executive Secretary at the then British Council of Churches, and Tony Holden became the Methodist Home Mission Divisional Secretary. At the meeting that these appointments were announced COSPEC started to review its situation. Vaughan Jones had resigned over the débâcle with Ian Rathbone, and Simon Barrow of Christian CND became the new convenor, reporting after a meeting with the CSM executive in October 1987 'a good deal of enthusiasm about the ideal of a network like COSPEC accompanied by an ever greater cynicism about whether anything can or will happen'.[37] The cynicism extended well beyond CSM, and the structural problems of an unaccountable convenor with no clear brief or resources were clear to all. Consequently a special meeting of all member organisations was convened in July 1988, although even the arrangements for this proved contentious, with the Council overturning Barrow's original agenda while he was abroad. Barrow fired off a five-page letter to Brian Jenner who had chaired the Council meeting, saying that the whole thing was 'a bloody mess'. The July meeting narrowly avoided disbanding COSPEC while also rejecting John Vincent's suggestions for a new structure. By April 1990 Jenner and Barrow were writing to member organisations asking for permission to close COSPEC down – permission for which was granted with a sigh of relief.

# 11

# *Reclaiming the Ground*

I hold it for indisputable, that the first duty of a State is to see that every child born therein shall be well housed, clothed, fed and educated, till it attains years of discretion. But in order to the effecting this the Government must have an authority over the people of which we do not now so much as dream.

John Ruskin, *Time and Tide*, Letter XIII

The rich have become richer and the poor have become poorer; and the vessel of the state is driven between the Scylla and Charybdis of anarchy and despotism.

Percy Bysshe Shelley, 'A Defence of Poetry'

In 1975 Donald Soper stood down as Chair of CSM and became its first President, almost ten years after becoming the first Methodist minister to be elevated to the House of Lords. His successor, Edward Charles, an Anglo-Catholic parish priest who had been a stalwart of the Council of Clergy and Ministers for Common Ownership, took over an organisation that, in the words of Peter Dawe, 'seemed to be under-performing and was still very dependent on Donald'.[1] Certainly it was still small, with no more than 500 members, and the executive continued to meet, once a month on a Tuesday evening, in Soper's Kingsway Hall in London, thus excluding those from outside the capital.

In 1976, as much by accident as by design, a small group of new members joined the Movement – one joined as the result of getting caught in a library by a torrential downpour and passing the time by reading a stray copy of *Christian Socialist*. At the annual general meeting, after some very critical remarks from one of these new members, John Collins, both he and Peter Dawe, a Methodist lay preacher from Walthamstow, were elected to the executive and to a small working party which was to consider CSM's long-term prospects. Out of this group, which also included the General Secretary, Leigh Hatts, and Stuart Masters, came a programme which was launched in October 1977; it set the targets of recruiting 2,500 members, inaugurating more local branches and reducing the number of executive meetings.

By 1983 these aims had been achieved in part. Membership had doubled; there was a very successful branch in Norwich, organised by a Salvation Army member, Harry Watson; and the executive had begun to grow away from its dependence on Soper. That same year Charles stepped down as Chairman and devoted his efforts to the Christian Peace Conference, which he represented on COSPEC. His successor was Peter Dawe, almost thirty years younger than he and one of the figures on the executive closely associated with the development plans. CSM was still a small organisation, with little clout and an extremely old-fashioned image, which fell between two stools, having neither the gravitas and resources to produce serious policy proposals nor the independence to be fully prophetic.

One of the idiosyncrasies of CSM's position in the 1980s was that neither of the two parliamentarians who most symbolised Christian Socialism in the public eye was a member of the Movement, although they both spoke on CSM platforms and wrote for the Movement. Their political positions, moreover, are radically different, for Tony Benn has, at least since 1979, been the frontman for the left, and Frank Field has maintained a resolutely right-wing socialist critique.

Just as CSM had tied its wagon to the Bevanite star in the early 1960s, so in the early 1980s it often succumbed to the allure of the Bennite agenda. Indeed, although Tony Benn considers himself a 'Christian without God' – he once replied to a fervent evangelical questioner at a Party Conference fringe meeting, when asked whether he acknowledged Jesus as his Lord, 'Since I don't believe in lords in any shape, it is a bit difficult to acknowledge Jesus as one' – his political message owes as much to the Levellers and Diggers as to Marx. With the earnestness of a prophet new-inspired he has consistently argued that 'the moral roots of socialism lie in religion' and that 'political agitation is groundless unless based on an independent moral and religious critique of society,'[2] seeing the Bible as 'a revolutionary document which, if it got into the hands of the common people, would stir up righteous fury at the injustices and tyrannies of the time'.[3] Yet he also insists on a Marxist class analysis because 'it is so self-evidently true. Without the bag of tools that Marx bequeathed to us, we cannot understand the world in which we live.'[4] In apocalyptic vein in an essay for CSM's twenty-fifth anniversary publication, *Facing the Future as Christians and Socialists*,[5] he also upheld the right to revolt as 'an ancient one that must always be held in reserve as a protection against the possibility that one day democracy and self-government might be removed, leaving us no alternative but to defend these rights by force'.

Elsewhere Benn has confessed that his 'political commitment owes much more to the teachings of Jesus – without the mysteries within which they are presented – than to the writings of Marx whose analysis seems to lack an understanding of the deeper needs of humanity',[6] and he always manages to catch the cadences of religious thinking: 'we may win elections from time to time. But all that is worthless unless our thoughts and actions are firmly grounded on moral truth.'[7]

Benn's influence within CSM was, for an agnostic, surprisingly significant, reinforcing an almost millenarian belief, in the words of John Ball, often cited by Benn: 'things cannot go well in England, nor ever shall, until all things are in common and there is neither villein nor noble but all of us are of one condition,'[8] a view with which many of the others who wrote in *Facing the Future*, including the communist Irene Brennan and fellow MP Eric Heffer, would have agreed.

Yet by no means all Christian Socialists agreed with Benn's agenda; indeed, the other MP who dominated much CSM thinking in the 1980s came, as we have noted, from the right wing of the party. Frank Field, since 1979 the MP for Birkenhead, has often been seen as something of a maverick within the Labour Party – a term he rejects. Yet he has the kind of mind that prefers to roam outside the allotted territory of a party MP as well as a fierce aversion to half-truths, which he sees as the basis of every heresy. Though he was Director of Child Poverty Action for ten years, 1969–79, and he founded the Low Pay Unit in 1974, he has always refused to accept the easy panaceas for poverty that many on the left have opted for. At times this has made him an infuriating colleague, and there were Militant Tendency attempts to deselect him as Labour candidate in the 1980s, yet his work, especially as Chair of the Parliamentary Social Security Select Committee, has earned him a moral authority that is respected across the party divide.

Field is a socialist and a Christian, but he would fight shy of the term 'Christian Socialist', not least because he believes that 'the Kingdom cannot be encompassed within the programme of any political party'[9] and reckons that the Christian left's greatest weakness has been its judgment that, in Lewis Donaldson's words, 'Christianity is the religion of which Socialism is the practice.' Instead he sees not one but two central strands to Christian political understanding, both founded on the primary concept of the Kingdom of God, the collective approach and the emphasis on individual piety, and he is opposed to 'the way exponents of one tradition deny the legitimacy of the other'.[10]

Furthermore, while he accepts as fundamental Christian concern for the poor and the weak, he is keen to urge Labour to adopt an enlightened attitude towards the market. Instead of seeking to replace the market with a command economy, 'Labour should embrace the market and spend the whole of its effort expressing its disapproval of the market's unacceptable faces – particularly its inability to tackle unemployment and its power to punish the poor and the least strong.'[11]

This, he believes, would allow Labour to play its strongest card, its ethical tradition, which emphasises both 'the opening up of opportunities so that individuals (rather than classes) can develop and use their talents to the full' and 'the protection and enhancement of the poor, the weak and the disadvantaged'.[12] Taking humanity seriously, both its capacity for altruism and its tendency to self-interest, would mean that Labour policies should be built on the 'fundamental fact' that 'self-interest is one of the most powerful of human characteristics.'[13]

Needless to say, Field's work has often been condemned by other Labour politicians as heretical revisionism. After all, a political system that deliberately appeals to self-interest seems inimical to any normally conceived moral society. Yet his arguments are persuasive, and he provides an enormously important corrective to the dewy-eyed romanticism of some forms of Christian Socialism, which have implied either that the Labour Party has a monopoly on truth or that unilateralism and common ownership or, more specifically, nationalisation would of themselves usher in the Kingdom of Heaven. Field's insistence that 'political activity for the Christian is inextricably interwoven with seeking the Kingdom'[14] places all that overbearing certainty in doubt and allies him with the earlier work of the Christendom Group.

In 1986 the Labour Party decided, after thirteen years, to reopen its lists for 'Socialist Societies', and the CSM executive resolved to seek affiliation. The then General Secretary, John Collins, argued that 'affiliation will give us a much higher profile within the Labour Party. We'd actually be in the conference hall – not just in a fringe meeting outside,'[15] and suggested that 'a higher profile *inside* the Labour Party would also make us more visible to Christians *outside*.'[16] Few seemed to disagree, though one member felt that 'affiliation may actually make it harder for us to carry our message into the churches if we are seen to be too tied up with the Labour Party,' and Harry Watson, later a Vice-Chair, stated, 'we won't always agree with everything that the Labour

Party says or does. But let's not be afraid to put our hands where our mouths are and be proud to be part of a socialist political party.'[17]

In fact CSM's links with Labour were already substantial. Seventeen MPs were listed as CSM members, including Labour's Chief Whip, the Salvationist Derek Foster, and the Shadow Chancellor, John Smith. So it was hardly a surprise when a postal ballot of members voted 86 per cent in favour of affiliation.

The immediate effects of affiliation could easily have been missed. Although CSM voted in the 1988 Labour leadership election, only a fifth of its members bothered to take part in the postal ballot, and the results were remarkable in that Tony Benn, who had recently given the Tawney Lecture, gained ninety-three votes to Kinnock's ninety-two, but Eric Heffer, a vociferous Anglo-Catholic Christian Socialist, lost out badly to Kinnock's running mate Roy Hattersley. The first CSM delegate to Conference, the executive member Will Sheaf, was more impressed by the folly of its labyrinthine processes than by the spiritual significance of CSM's presence, although he did find time to call the trade-union block vote a 'mockery of democracy' which 'must be decreased'.[18] None the less it did not take CSM members long to find their way in the party, and in 1992 and 1994 the membership voted overwhelmingly for John Smith and Tony Blair for leader and backed the 1995 constitutional change to Clause Four.

What is more, CSM's affiliation had a steady effect on its image within the Labour Party. No longer a spectator carping on the sidelines but a player in the field, CSM began to be taken more seriously, not least because it had a vote to cast. Steadily, more MPs joined, and several of its long-standing members came into prominence in the party. Chris Smith, the MP for Islington South, wrote frequently for the magazine and became a Vice-President; Keith Vaz from Leicester spoke at a Conference fringe meeting; Paul Boateng delivered a Tawney Lecture; John Battle, the Roman Catholic former Director of Church Action on Poverty and triumphant victor over the Liberals in Leeds West, became a regular speaker, as did Len Murray, the former General Secretary of the TUC, and Brenda Dean, the General Secretary of SOGAT during the Wapping disputes. And in 1991 the Shadow Employment Secretary, Tony Blair, joined the Movement and spoke at a fringe meeting at the Blackpool Conference.

So by the time of the 1992 general election CSM was a fairly effective Christian Union for the Labour Party. Yet it was still small, restricted largely to Methodists and Anglicans and, despite the publication of a collection of Tawney Lectures, *Fellowship, Freedom and Equality*, very limited in both its theological and its political contribution. A long-term working party had been set up and had consulted members as to what role the Movement should fulfil in society. Draft plans for an office and a full-time worker, a new magazine, major research projects and a membership campaign had been drawn up in *Plan for Action*, which saw a vital need for CSM to broaden its appeal. 'At present,' it stated, 'CSM is an association of people who accept the fairly precise description of Christian Socialism set out in its statement of aims, but we believe that CSM could and should be much more than this.'[19] Instead it should be a 'forum for the Christian left', not framing policies but influencing debates, 'helping Labour to regain the ethical ground' and adopting an exploratory rather than denunciatory style of political theology.

All these plans, meticulously researched by John Collins, came to most dramatic and providential fruition when John Smith, immediately after becoming Leader of the party, agreed, partly as a favour to his close friends Norman and Elizabeth Hogg, to give the 1993 Tawney Lecture. Many of his private office were against the move because such an overt Christian contribution from a party leader might easily be interpreted as self-righteous or fanatical. But Smith's own background was resolutely Christian. He had been the Church of Scotland representative on Churches Together in Britain and Ireland; he was a regular worshipper at his Edinburgh home church and a close friend of Norman Shanks, the present Leader of the Iona Community; and both he and his Parliamentary Private Secretary, Hilary Armstrong, like her father before her, were members of CSM. So on 20 March 1993 John Smith gave the Tawney Lecture at the Bloomsbury Baptist church.

Smith felt very happy with the Tawney legacy, with its equal emphasis on responsibility and equality. As he saw it, Tawney's democratic socialism 'sought to enhance individual freedom in a framework of collective common purpose and opportunity, in which fellowship was the bond of a community of equality'.[20] Citing Temple's dictum that 'the art of government in fact is the art of so ordering life that self-interest prompts what justice demands,'[21] Smith articulated a caution about saying that Christianity inevitably leads to socialism, which would have pleased Frank Field, further recognising that there are many other religious and non-religious paths to socialism. His lecture exuded an air of moral and intellectual confidence, for he clearly believed that democratic socialism, 'when tested in the experience of humanity . . . can be found to be a better explanation of the lives and purposes of men and women than its rivals on the *laissez-faire* right or Marxist left'.[22]

At a time when most Labour activists would still have condemned a concern with 'the aspirational classes' as revisionist, Smith was determined that Labour needed to build a society that was 'responsive to the aspirations of all our people', and he reiterated the claim that politics had to be based not only on practicable but also on moral foundations. 'Let us never be fearful of saying that we espouse a policy because it is, quite simply, the right thing to do. And let us not underestimate the desire, which I believe is growing in our society, for a politics based on principle.'[23]

Smith's speech, and the book *Reclaiming the Ground* that accompanied it, gave Christian Socialism a public prominence that it had not enjoyed for more than a hundred years. For he was speaking only a year after the general election. The Tory Government had promised tax cuts and implemented tax hikes; a series of scandals had seriously undermined John Major's 'Back to Basics' campaign; there was growing disquiet in the country about

Tory placemen on unelected quangos; the Scott Inquiry was beginning to suggest that ministers had been less than truthful, and there was a general sense that the moral high ground was up for grabs.

Naturally enough, not everyone welcomed Smith's Tawney Lecture. *Tribune* complained that 'Labour must not abandon secularism'[24] despite having had Soper as a lead columnist for more than a decade, and the *Daily Telegraph*, under the headline 'Sanctimonious Smith', accused him of claiming to be the leader of 'God's own Church'[25] when, in fact, Smith had explicitly argued that Christian faith might legitimately lead people to political conclusions different from his own. Several commentators recognised Smith's lecture for what it was, however. The Tory MP Michael Alison saw it as 'a definite, and confident, re-affirmation of the British Labour Movement's historical roots in Christian values and ideals',[26] and Sarah Baxter, writing in the *New Statesman and Society*, recognised in both Smith's lecture and Tony Blair's introduction to the book a 'reformist project' drawing a line under an era of ideological socialism and regrouping around an ethical socialism that might give 'moral underpinning to what might otherwise look like a purely opportunistic drift to the right'.[27]

John Smith was Leader of the party for less than two years, yet his determination to emphasise the moral and ethical foundation of Labour's approach made the style of Tony Blair's leadership both possible and inevitable.

Here is not the place to provide a full biography of Tony Blair. There are already plenty of journalists scanning the archives of Fettes College and St John's College, Oxford, listening to recordings of his student pop group and trying to find details of his period as a Ward Secretary in Hackney Labour Party. What we can do is try to assess exactly what Tony Blair and New Labour owe politically and philosophically to Christian Socialism.

Blair has often acknowledged his own indebtedness to the Christian faith, into which he was confirmed while at university through the influence of an Australian priest called Peter Thompson, who introduced him to the work of John MacMurray. His most unambiguous statement of the link between his faith and politics, however, is his foreword to *Reclaiming the Ground*, where he gives a fairly harsh and unremitting picture of what faith requires:

> Christianity is a very tough religion. It may not always be practised as such. But it is. It places a duty, an imperative, on us to reach our better self and to care about creating a better community to live in . . . It is judgmental. There is right and wrong. There is good and bad.[28]

From this judgmental faith he draws a set of principles:

> We are not uniform in character or position . . . but . . . we are entitled to be treated equally, without regard to our wealth, race, gender or standing in society[29] . . . Everybody should get the opportunity to make the best of themselves . . . We are not stranded in helpless isolation but owe a duty both to others and to ourselves.[30]

More significant than this recitation of principles, however, is the insertion of a new imperative, the need to 'rethink and re-examine our values', for

> by placing them alongside those of the Christian faith, we are able, politically, to rediscover the essence of our beliefs which lies not in policies or prescriptions made for one period of time, but in principles of living that are timeless. By doing so, we can better distinguish between values themselves and their application, the one constant and unchanged, the other changing constantly.[31]

Though written when Blair was Shadow Home Secretary, these are the words of a modernising politician whose first major speech as Leader would outline what he saw as the confusion of 'means such as wholesale nationalisation with ends: a fairer society and more productive economy'[32] and commit Labour to ethical rather than scientific socialism. Marxism as a deterministic economic theory, as he admitted in an interview in 1993, had come to represent the belief that 'personal responsibility was swallowed up in social responsibility,' and many Christians had deserted socialism because it seemed to assert that 'somehow a person was less important than the state.'[33] Blair's reinterpretation of the socialist message, then, is that 'social responsibility is important to reinforce personal responsibility, not as a substitute for it',[34] which in the end is what he believes the Christian religion is about.

Blair's campaign to rebuild the Labour Party is essentially moral, not only because it signals a return to an ethical rather than a 'scientific' socialism but also because to create a totem out of Clause Four, or to grant State ownership an absolute and eternal value, is heretically to confuse ends with means and unnecessarily to ignore the freedom of the individual in the laudable pursuit of a more just social order. Blair has written his own job description as leader in prophetic terms that sound like Solomon's building of the Temple, and there is a constant sense of his determination to say and do what he believes to be right rather than to curry favour with the Parliamentary Labour Party or the party activists. 'I am not interested in governing for a term, coming to power on a wave of euphoria, a magnificent edifice of expectations, which dazzles for a while before collapse. I want to rebuild this party from its foundations, making sure every stone is put in its rightful place, every design crafted not just for effect but to a useful purpose.'[35]

Blair's task does not end there, though. As he argued in his speech to the Labour Party Conference in October 1995, which was hailed by the *New Statesman* as Christian Socialism's coming of age, 'I didn't come into politics to change the Labour Party. I came into politics to change the country.' And his vision is couched in deliberately biblical terms: 'One Britain . . . where your child in distress is my child, your parent ill and in pain is my parent, your friend unemployed or helpless, my friend, your neighbour, my neighbour'.[36]

Blair is not alone in his belief that 'since the collapse of Communism, the ethical basis of socialism is the only one that has stood the test of time.'[37] Michael Meacher, a long-standing Anglican member on the left of the Labour Party, has asserted: 'what is vital is linking the State to the cause of socialist individualism,' for despite those for whom 'socialism is defined exclusively as state control over the commanding heights of the economy' what Labour must embrace is both a 'much more flexible state regulation' and 'a much more restrained market system.'[38]

Jack Straw, another member of Labour's front bench, who was confirmed as an Anglican in 1989, has also nailed his colours to the ethical mast, arguing that 'the message of the Christian gospels has been a powerful force over the centuries in moulding what we now understand as democratic socialism.'[39] Straw's assault on Clause Four in 1993 predated Blair's attempt to get Labour to reform its constitution, and it is interesting that in his *Policy and Ideology* he dismisses those who refuse to countenance any change in the constitution in theological terms. 'Some' he says, 'say [Clause Four] is an icon. But if so, there is no developed liturgy for its worship. Rather it is like some relic displayed in a church.'[40] Instead of giving the impression that 'under-achievement, crime or antisocial behaviour may be excused because it will have arisen as a result of the environment in which people may live', Labour should now emphasise the 'free will, the choice and responsibility' which were implicit in early 'Christian-based' socialism.[41] Straw's position, then, is very similar to Blair's, and a common strand is discernible in New Labour, a desire to return to a 'Christian-based socialism'.

Since becoming Labour leader, although he has spoken of 'spiritual doubt' and used biblical cadences, Blair has been keen not to be too explicit about his religious commitment, which he is reluctant to see institutionalised by the media, which have picked over every minuscule reference to God in his speeches and even speculated about whether he is an Anglican who goes to a Roman Catholic church because that is where his wife and family worship or is a Roman Catholic. Quite rightly, both he and Straw are hesitant to proclaim their Christian faith for fear of appearing self-righteous or exclusive and fanatical. For both of them faith has its inevitable political outcomes, but its real force is personal and private.

Indeed, of all Labour's front bench the most direct about his religion is Chris Smith, a Presbyterian with a strong sympathy for the Romanticism of Coleridge. Ironically, Smith's position as the first Member of Parliament openly to confess his homosexuality (and subsequently to increase his majority) allows him greater leeway than have either Blair or Straw, as no one would argue that his Christian Socialism is in any sense moralist or overly judgmental. His concerns, above all for the environment, stem from a keen estimation of God's immanence, and he has often expressed his political indebtedness to his religious understanding and the spiritual inspiration of God's beautiful Earth.

In Blair's case, despite his caution about self-proclamation, what is certain is that his brand of socialism is 'based on a moral assertion' – in his own words:

> that individuals are interdependent, that they owe duties to one another as well as themselves, that the good society backs up the efforts of the individuals within it, and that common humanity demands that everyone be given a platform on which to stand. It has objective basis too, rooted in the belief that only by recognising their interdependence will individuals flourish, because the good of each does depend on the good of all.[42]

Today's Christian Socialism is far from monolithic, and the New Labour version we have just looked at, espoused by many in CSM, has critics on both theological and political fronts. To gain a real impression of where modern Christian Socialism is placed, we shall look at three main critics: Ronald Preston as a representative of the cynics; Timothy Gorringe as a representative of the idealists; and Alan Duncan as part of the Conservative reaction.

For some twenty years the most acute criticism of Christian Socialism has come from one of Tawney's own disciples, Ronald Preston. Born in 1913, he met Tawney as an LSE student before he went to work for the Student Christian Movement and before ordination as an Anglican. From 1949 he taught Christian Ethics at Manchester University, becoming Professor of Social and Pastoral Theology in 1970, while also acting as Canon Theologian at Manchester Cathedral.

Broadly speaking, Preston allies himself with the socialist critique of capitalism, arguing that its overall philosophy should be condemned but also that 'some of its key institutions are of permanent usefulness to any economy.'[43] He abhors, however, the tendency of Christianity 'to take a static view of established institutions and to sanctify them',[44] a course which, he argues, was more plausible when the speed of social change was slow but which, with the advent of dynamic capitalist economies and the rapid social changes that accompany them, has been such a shock that a moral response like the socialist one was inevitable.

Part of Preston's aim is to get socialism to look again at its analysis of capitalism. Like Frank Field, he sees a valuable role for the market itself but is thoroughly aware that 'there is much scope for twisting it while paying lip service to it, especially by the free rider who makes a buck by flouting what he hopes his rivals will stick to'.[45] He questions Maurice's contention that competition is ethically dubious and expresses rather condescending surprise, when reviewing *Reclaiming the Ground*, that none of the contributors mentions 'the traditional nationalisation programme of the Labour Party'. In the light of subsequent events it is ironic that he even comments, 'Clause Four of the Constitution might not exist.'[46]

Preston's main contention, though, is not about policies but about how one does politics as a Christian. For, he avers, 'it is impossible ... to move directly from the Bible to the modern world.'[47] Instead Christians have to derive basic principles from the Bible, which he variously calls 'criteria' or 'middle axioms'. These are then brought to bear on the world after careful empirical research. It is irrelevant that the Bible remains silent about the operation of the market because theology's first task is to root out the ethical implications of the Kingdom of God, not uproot superficially supportive texts from their context. Part of these implications, he argues, 'are in line with the common moral insight of humankind, such as the Golden Rule, "Do to others what you would have them do to you" (Matthew 7:12). However, part go far beyond it, radicalising love for one's neighbour and requiring unlimited forgiveness for wrongdoers.'[48]

Preston goes on to suggest five key criteria for a Kingdom-based political theology, four of which – concern for the poor, concern for community and the diminution of social and cultural barriers, concern for abuses of power but not hostility to power as such, awareness of the power of sin – are common to most Christian Socialists. His final criterion, a reserve about human policies and causes, 'because the Kingdom of God ... is never exhausted in any political or social set-up',[49] allies him with Frank Field, but his argument goes further and risks alienating him from the actual practice of power. For if we can claim nothing for our policies, not even that we believe that they are morally or pragmatically true, we may avoid political hubris but we will also open the door to cynicism and apathy. If party politics is to be condemned as either sullying or morally irrelevant, then the whole of modern democratic politics is left to the moral nihilists or, by default, the Conservatives.

Preston's argument with Christian Socialism hinges, then, not on politics but on theology. In 1979 he wrote:

the recovery of a greater eschatological note in theology ... has destroyed the utopian element in the socialist case. This was a powerful note of the Christian Socialist movement.

Awareness of this in theological circles is undoubtedly the main reason why the Christian Socialist movement has run into the sand. It remains fixed in a theological and political attitude of the past; in neither is it flexible or pragmatic enough. Common ownership remains a panacea, and Christian principles are thought to be all too simply expressed by it.[50]

Yet for many Christian Socialists this is simply untrue. Few would claim that their political programme, whether it embraced common ownership or not, was in any sense God-given. Furthermore, as Charles Davis has argued, 'Because the Kingdom of God can never be identified with any political order actually achieved on earth does not mean that the Kingdom of God is not the ideal and standard for Christians in their political activity.'[51] It is right that the Labour Party should never become a Christian party. Not only does it seek to rule for many who are not Christian, but the very concept of such a close identification of one temporal programme with God's will is folly of the highest order, effectively doling out party-membership cards to the Persons of the Trinity. But if democracy is to be taken seriously by Christians, then a key element in Christian witness must be both the evaluation of each and every party programme against the objective standards of the Gospel and the attempt to assert those standards at the very heart of the political process.

Preston has not been the only critic of Christian Socialism, especially as it has been expressed in the present-day CSM. Many in the Jubilee Group would be equally suspicious of a Christian Socialist movement affiliated to a political party, for party politics is about compromise and consensus, about forming alliances, whereas the Christian injunction is absolute, to seek that Kingdom which must always transcend any political programme. Yet such caution about too close an identification of party with Kingdom does not always lead to the accommodating approach of Field and Preston, and many, instead of ditching the 'Utopian element' of Christian Socialism are keen to enhance it.

The most recent example of this is the work of Timothy Gorringe, an Anglican priest who spent several years working in India before returning to Oxford as chaplain at Tony Blair's old college, St John's, and, more recently, moving to St Andrew's University as Professor of Political Theology. Closely associated with other radical writers such as Rowan Williams and Chris Rowland, his most recent work, *Capital and the Kingdom: Theological Ethics and Economic Order*,[52] forms a fascinating counterpoint to both the work of Preston and New Labour.

Recalling the verse from Deuteronomy (30:19), 'This day I call heaven and earth as witnesses against you that I have set before you life and death, blessings and curses. Now choose life, so that you and your children may live . . .,' Gorringe hinges his argument on a deliberately simplistic two-way split – the way of death and the way of life. Demolishing the concept of natural law as central to ethics and attempting instead to build a 'messianic ethic' based on the Christ who became a slave, he argues that 'what is ethical is what enhances life, and what is unethical is what denies it.'[53] Capitalist economies are, then, to be evaluated according to whether, by producing wealth, they enhance life or whether they necessarily produce wealth at the expense of members of their own society. The Christian call is to rediscover a notion of redistributive justice and 'beyond that . . . the justice which is grace, which opposes every form of meritocracy'.[54]

Criticising the Conservative ideologue Brian Griffiths's belief that an egalitarianism implying equality of material reward is anti-Christian, he goes on to argue that if Christianity is to be more than an 'opiate for the people', it must advocate not only equality of opportunity, as Griffiths admits, but equality of outcome. He questions the survival, as Gore did at the turn of the century, of the wage system and urges the critical importance of a sustainable economy that ceases to plunder the Third World of its natural riches. After a discussion of the nature of work, leisure, human solidarity and resistance, he returns to the pith of his argument: 'The concern of Christian ethics is fulness of life, and this means that economics is at the heart of the ethical concern for, as Hilaire Belloc remarked, the control of the production of wealth is the control of human life itself.'[55] The answer is an egalitarian socialism, for the 'two ways' are seen in economic terms, 'a way of equality and a way of domination, a way of corporate justice and a way of concealed tyranny, a way of global nurture and a way of global suicide. The way of death is the prevailing economic system, based on cynicism and whistling for destruction, content to enjoy power and affluence at the expense of the Third World and future generations.'[56]

Gorringe is at pains to state that 'none of the proposals outlined . . . is Utopian'[57] but he imagines a world where work is purged of its element of toil, managers are interchangeable with other workers, the central concern of economics enable people to meet their needs and develop themselves, its operating system is decentralised, private ownership of the means of production is abolished, local public companies are wholly accountable and unbureaucratic, taxes are levied on land, not personal income (he cites Henry George), there is a maximum and a minimum wage, a basic income for all and a classless society. Certainly this sounds Utopian, for its posits a brave new world that might exist if only society were different, if only economics operated differently and if only human nature were altogether different.

Or at least so would run a Conservative critique of Gorringe's work. Interestingly enough, Gorringe's main attack on capitalism is based on its 'atavistic' regard for the individual, and Alan Duncan and Dominic Hobson in *Saturn's Children* argue that Christian Socialism is itself an atavistic cult of the State, dressing collectivism in its Sunday-best.

Claiming Christian Socialism as the child of High Toryism and of John Wesley, they maintain 'its inspiration was the paternalistic landed aristocrat of the Middle Ages employing, housing and feeding his tenants'[58] but see its most damaging residue as 'a continuing antipathy to market economics which is quite out of joint with reality'.[59] They go on, 'Christian Socialism desperately needs new doctrines of creation, sin, forgiveness and hope which can take account of its long-standing shortcomings and its denial by experience.'[60] Furthermore the simple fact of the Welfare State does not make people, communities or the nation any more caring. In truth the concept of community is 'the mask of despotism', depriving individuals of the right to dispose of their goods and themselves as they wish. The moral argument is, then, that since 'only the un-coerced individual is capable of a moral action' Christian Socialism is immoral because it denies individuals the right to 'act morally'.

It is almost churlish to take the Duncan–Hobson assault on Christian Socialism as a serious challenge. There are wild swipes at its being 'rooted in German metaphysics'; a bizarre statement that Jesus's 'whatever you did for one of the least of these brothers of mine, you did for me' (Matthew 25:40) was meant as a celebration of 'the uniqueness of every individual soul'; and an attack on clergy for criticising Government policy out of a desire to appear 'relevant' in this world instead of 'directing the attention of their congregations to the next world'. Indeed, the whole analysis smacks of the same naïveté about the nature of the Gospel as the rabid Conservative attacks on Tony Blair's Easter 1996 interview in the *Sunday Telegraph*, when Michael Fabricant MP condemned him for not only seeing himself as Prime Minister, 'but as Archbishop of Canterbury as well'. None the less it is right to take the Conservative challenge to Christian Socialism seriously, not least because the primary prosecution witness called by Duncan–Hobson is a reformed Christian Socialist, the Anglican priest and former Labour Deputy Leader of Sheffield, Alan Billings.

Billings's own case is clear, that the Church, and by this he means the Church of England, lost its theological bottle in the nineteenth century and has sought refuge in a semi-political role rather than in the true faith. The task of the Church must be that of 'evangelist and teacher', not politician, as Mrs Thatcher knew. Indeed, the 'failure of the church to hear what she was saying was a lost opportunity'.[61] Here it becomes difficult to tell whether it was the Church or Billings who lost their bottle, but the charge that Christian Socialism has at times been more interested in the collective than in the individual has been true, and the refusal by some Christian Socialists to take our individual responsibility seriously as part of the political agenda has weakened our case.

But the Duncan–Hobson argument is even more fundamentally flawed. For it relies on the same assumptions that Gore and Scott Holland attacked so fervently and effectively almost a hundred years ago. The assertion that the free market is a fact, a law of nature that nobody can deny, is at the heart of the Conservative critique of Christian Socialism, just as the belief that economics were made for man, not man for economics, and that no economic system can be a value-free zone, is at the heart of Christian Socialism's critique of capitalism. Nigel Lawson has stated that 'All that is left to socialism is the moral high ground,' thereby conceding much. What he and Duncan–Hobson fail to acknowledge is that no market operates without some limiting ethic, whether it be the primacy of short-term gain or the principle of a reserve price below which one will not sell, and every market, if it is not to consume its own children, needs rules to prevent abuse by those who have fewer moral scruples than the rest. Furthermore, while the market may be an effective means of ensuring good quality, well-priced television sets, it may be next to useless at delivering high-quality television programming.

So far this chapter has seemed to suggest that there is a fundamental split in Christian Socialism between those who believe an accommodation needs now to be made with capitalism and the idealists. I have also, I suspect, given the impression that most Christian Socialists are theologically liberal. Neither is true.

For many of today's advocates of Christian Socialism have a deeply conservative estimation of the Bible, of the magisterium of the Roman Catholic Church, of the sanctity of life and of the institution of marriage. Indeed, both the Anglo-Catholic Archdeacon of York, George Austin, and the evangelical Archdeacon of Northolt, Peter Broadbent, both of whom are associated within the Church of England with trying to return it to what they see as traditional teaching on sex, are Christian Socialists; the Roman

Catholic Von Hugel Institute has done much valuable work on Catholic social teaching; the Baptist minister Steve Chalke has spoken of the need for evangelicals to rediscover a biblical concept of justice; John Stott has argued for the spiritual significance of the social Gospel; Bob Holman, an ardent evangelical who has taken a radical option for the poor, has done some of the best socialist work on the Welfare State; and it is alleged that Cardinal Hume is a member of the Labour Party. There is also a sense in which Christian Socialism, in its determination to root out a doctrine older than capitalism, is essentially conservative.

As for the split between accommodators and Utopians, a thesis which has been propounded in nearly every history of Christian Socialism, splitting off the Christian Social Union from the Guild of St Matthew, the Church Socialist League from the Catholic Crusade, I believe this is profoundly misconceived. Oddly enough, Duncan and Hobson almost got it right when they said, 'The Christian Socialist critique of capitalism is not a technical one at all. It is a form of moral repugnance.'[62] Charles Davis has put the point more exactly: 'In a sense it is impossible to compare socialism and capitalism because they belong to different categories of reality and are thus essentially incomparable. Socialism is a political vision of a moral and religious character. Capitalism ... is a self-regulatory system.'[63] While we might want to add that capitalism is a self-regulatory system that needs external regulations, Davis is broadly right. The identification of Christian Socialism with any alternative to capitalism is flawed because that is not its nature or its task. Yet the sum total of all our theological strivings cannot simply be to say, 'This upsets my moral sense,' which is why what Preston calls 'the Utopian element of Christian Socialism' is so important.

For the question remains: is Christian Socialism just the random thoughts of a bunch of Christians who have adopted socialism for their politics, or socialists who go to church, who may see their political and spiritual values as consistent but vary in their conclusions? Or is there something that is identifiable as Christian Socialism?

When once we realise the essentially moral character of Christian Socialism it becomes clear that, if it gets its theology right, it can never be the straightforward theological and ideological back-up for any particular economic regime, however consonant it might seem with our dreams of a fairer society. Despite St Paul's injunction in Romans 14:1–7 that every State is ordered by God, and that Christians should therefore be subject to the State, the main body of New Testament teaching makes it clear that the ideal social order would be predicated on the Kingdom of Heaven. Jesus's own teaching elucidates elements of that Kingdom, but only obliquely, through a series of stories that emphasise radical neighbourliness, good husbandry, readiness, support for the weak. And his life – visiting the poor and outcast like lepers and tax collectors, taking water from a lone Samaritan woman in the sultry midday heat, touching the unclean, casting out the money-changers in the Temple – gives a glimpse of what human relations might be like in that Kingdom, but again the reference is oblique.

So, as Percy Widdrington argued, the Kingdom is undoubtedly the ideal against which all our political dreams must be measured. It cannot itself be identified with any political order achieved or achievable on earth, but it must remain for Christians the ideal in their political activity, not a stencil from which we may draw the contours of the Christian State, but a measure against which we may judge our world of economic, financial, judicial, social relations.

This is, of course, as liberating for the idealist as for the accommodator. For the Kingdom will serve as a Utopia, a place that does not exist but is a projection of all our best imaginings, a vision of society that will retain the outline of a world that we already recognise but will be radically different from anything we have ever known. State socialism, municipal socialism, international socialism – all will have to be held up to the light of the Kingdom just as critically as the 'national security' State or liberal democracy.

Preston's belief that because political solutions cannot be drawn off directly from the Bible, what theology has to do is define

306

'middle axioms' which can then be applied to political problems, is false. For axioms are by nature too unbending, too static for the Christian Gospel, and it is no accident that Jesus preferred to tell stories, or even to act them out, rather than to lay down rules for the good society. Narratives are both more easily and more subtly understood, and less prone to being fixed, than axioms. The strength of Utopian views of society is that they are nearly always predicated on stories rather than fixed so-called rules. So Thomas More's *Utopia* is a narrative written with irony and humour; the historical accounts of the Levellers, the Diggers and the Tolpuddle Martyrs, of Gore, Noel, Hardie and Acland, have become stories that point the heart towards a more co-operative society; and some of the most popular Christian Socialist writing has taken the form of novels and plays, like Kingsley's *Alton Locke*, Adderley's *Stephen Remarx* and Priestley's *An Inspector Calls*.

So far I have stressed the Utopian aspect of the concept of the Kingdom of God, but if Christian Socialism is to be more than a fanciful theological exercise for academics, it must be just as topical as it is Utopian. Every Christian Socialist we have looked at has held a profound belief that change is not only necessary but also possible, and that has taken them all into the realm of the practical and the practicable. So part of the Christian Socialist argument has been that others have simply misunderstood the essential nature of mankind or taken account of only one aspect of it. We are not just spiritual but also material beings, deliberately created as such by a God who became flesh. Ethics must then go with the grain of humanity, working away at the knots in the wood but taking mankind's material, historical, cultural nature seriously.

Furthermore, man is by his very nature individual, conscious of his own difference, his independence from others, but also ineluctably social, dependent on others, bound with others in a common humanity. Even more tellingly, man is capable of extraordinary self-sacrifice, able to delay pleasure, able to delight in the joy of others, *and* is motivated by a powerful and essential need to protect himself, to seek his own interest and that of those closest to him. This is not of itself sinful. After all, we are called to love our neighbour as ourselves, not more than ourselves, and the self-immolating martyr is as susceptible to pride as the wealthy tycoon. This conflict of the altruistic and the selfish is part of the essence of humanity, and any political system must work with it. Indeed, it is Conservatism's refusal to recognise the human capacity for co-operation that is one of its greatest weaknesses.

The best of the Christian Socialists have acknowledged this. Kingsley knew that sweated labour was a moral outrage, an offence against the Kingdom, but he also knew that human hearts would never be changed by legislation. Headlam understood that the grinding poverty of Bethnal Green was an iniquity, but he also realised that humanity has a deep-seated need to enjoy itself. Both Temple and Tawney acknowledged explicitly the importance of appealing to man's self-interest in any political agenda. Today Field and Gorringe equally know that the unbridled market economy is far from Utopian but accept as well that human ingenuity, innovation, enterprise can be thwarted by welfare regulations that encourage dependency and entrap people in poverty.

Christian Socialists have not always got it right about human nature. Maurice believed that universal suffrage was ill-conceived precisely because he did not think all men were equal. Johnson fell too readily for the blandishments of Stalin. Cripps, Henderson and Acland were all too keen to frame society in terms that left too little for personal freedom. Occasionally Christian Socialists have too readily identified the Kingdom with a particular political programme or policy. Johnson and Evans effectively believed that Soviet Russia was in the process of ushering in the Kingdom. Headlam fell for the Single Tax, and Reckitt for Guild Socialism. Soper believed that when the Labour Party adopted a unilateralist approach, the Kingdom had come. Thomas Hughes believed that the Co-operative associations would rapidly gestate the new world.

So why does the modern Christian Socialist Movement affiliate

308

to Labour? Certainly not because of a confusion of the Labour Party with the Kingdom of God. Few of us suffer under any such illusions. Nor, indeed, do many of us believe that if only Labour would adopt a particular set of policies, it would be building the New Jerusalem. What we seek to assert is that party politics is not a vile world wherein Christians have to sell or at least sully their souls, nor is it a separate world where ethics can have no sway. Ethics cannot be relegated to the privatised issues of personal moral choice: abortion, homosexuality, contraception, euthanasia. The moral dimension covers every aspect of the social order.

What affiliation did to CSM, in Leslie Griffiths's words, was to impose 'a discipline and a realism on Christians who wanted their thinking to shape the society we all live in'.[64] In effect affiliation has forced us to accept the realities of political life, to set our theology in a specific context. It has also forced us to think not about each topic in isolation but about how the whole of the nation's political life hangs together or falls apart. It has forced us to work with the grain of human nature, not condemning power but seeking ways of making power more accountable, not denouncing competition but seeking avenues for harnessing innovation and enterprise to a co-operative world economy.

But why should this be called socialism? The dictionary is unambiguous – socialism predicates the public ownership of the means of production, exchange and distribution – and what I have called socialism seems barely interested in such schemes. Yet Christian Socialism, as I hope I have shown, came before dictionary socialism, and Tony Blair's definition of socialism as 'a moral purpose to life' based on the simple truths 'I am worth no more than anyone else. I am my brother's keeper. I will not walk by on the other side' is right.[65]

The Kingdom of God is a permanent challenge to create a humane society of people equally able to live life in all its fullness. It is Utopian because it can never be fully realised, and society will always need to be re-formed. As Rowan Williams has said, 'Scripture and tradition don't give us a blueprint for society, but they give us a point of reference and a source of judgment, something to which we must come – a touchstone, a stone on which we test and are tested and may be broken in our assumptions.'[66] Just because Christian Socialism is Utopian does not mean that it is false. It is elusive but not illusionary. For in the end it is prepared to take human nature more seriously than most other political philosophies. We *are* members one of another. We *are* our brothers' and our sisters' keepers. We *are* material but spiritual; capable of free choice but often circumscribed by our history, our culture or our upbringing; capable of great acts of devotion and self-sacrifice both as individuals and as a group; co-operative and competitive. Above all, we live a part of our lives in dreams and visions of how the world might be, and these have the power to enslave or free us. After so many years of a Conservative ideology that has refused to acknowledge that morality has a role in economics and has maintained that ethics is the prerogative of the freestanding individual, it is time we rediscovered an older tradition, one that places the same value on equality as on freedom, on social responsibility as on personal accountability, on justice and peace as on enterprise and invention.

Some theorists have pointed to trust as the underlying principle of a successful good society. For others it is respect, or community. My suspicion is that for the next decade it will be unity informed by diversity. A sense of social cohesion, incorporating the myriad of different families modern life has created, giving every individual a role to play in shaping their own and their town's, their city's, their company's or their country's future – this is what people are already seeking, a genuine stake in our shared destiny. For that to happen, Parliament will have to change its constitution and its ways of working; openness and devolution will have to become a reality in the board room and the committee corridor; public service will have to return as the dominant social ethic of those in power; the Welfare State will have to be reinvented; and above all else education for jobs will have to become a national passion.

Vision is a much derided concept. Marx was almost as critical of Christian Socialism as of capitalism, and many have argued that the days of vision and of big ideas have gone. Certainly the centralist state has died, and many of the tidy options of the planned economy are no longer alive. But the Christian Socialist vision remains of a world where people would be valued not for what they owned or what they earned but for the strength of their character, where young people would be able to realise both their dreams and their potential, where the elderly could live without fear of penury or violence, where leisure was not the privilege of a few but accessible to all, where the market did not master us but we mastered it, where more could be accomplished in partnership than in fruitless competition, where all could enjoy clean air, clear water, a healthy diet and environment regardless of their race, their gender or their physical or intellectual ability, where all had a stake in society, in the economy, in democracy. Utopian this vision may be, and not such stuff as party manifestos are made of, but so many of the 'impossible' dreams of our forebears have now come to pass that it must be incumbent upon succeeding generations both to dream and to make their dreams, and those of others, possible.

# Postscript

You see things, and you say 'Why?' But I dream things that never were; and say 'Why not?'

George Bernard Shaw, *Back to Methuselah*

Because of the very nature of Christian Socialism this has not been a tidy history. Before they proceeded to recount its history others might have preferred to define Christian Socialism, as indeed Conrad Noel, Samuel Keeble, Maurice Reckitt and Stanley Evans did. Inevitably those figures who did not fit their rigid definitions were omitted. I have taken a different route and have told the stories of people who either defined themselves or were counted by others as Christian Socialists and, from their lives and ideas, have tried to distil the essence of Christian Socialism. I too have omitted much – there is little here of the influence of the Welsh valleys or the Celtic spirituality of the Highlands and islands of Scotland or of north-east England. I have said next to nothing about European or North American developments or even about the ecumenical movement in which many Christian Socialists have played such a vital role. My brief comments on Liberation theology are the barest minimum.

I have also left out the most recent developments in the Christian Socialist Movement. In 1993 I became the Movement's Chair. Eighteen months later we opened our new Westminster office, and a young Scottish Roman Catholic priest, David Cairns, became CSM's first full-time Co-ordinator in October 1994. Under his imaginative and energetic tutelage CSM has grown rapidly in activity and membership – now more than four thousand with forty-two MPs and half the Shadow Cabinet – with an expanded magazine, publications on the Welfare State (*What Justice Demands*) and the inner cities (*Keeping Faith with the Cities*) and evidence to the Nolan Committee. There have been consultations on the Borrie Report and the launching of new local branches. All this I have omitted.

Yet what I have tried to portray is a lively and diverse movement, less an economic ideology, more a body of Christians relaying a tradition of moral and social teaching. There are some core beliefs: that I am my brother's and my sister's keeper; that by its very nature humanity is both individual and social, material and spiritual, selfish and altruistic; that gross inequality is not how God would have us live; that rapacious greed and political indifference are not Christian options; that the market was made for humanity, not humanity for the market; that faith and politics are not worlds between which an unbridgeable chasm is stretched; and that Jesus's injunction to 'seek first the kingdom of God and His righteousness' entails a radical challenge to build a more just, more peaceful, more humane society. That God created us, became flesh and dwelt among us, broke bread and shared wine with us, went out of his way to reach out to the poor and required of his followers that they share their goods: this is the basis of our social-ism, though for others these natural common social values may find their source in the rivers of different faiths or understandings of life.

I said earlier that parables express truth more readily than philosophical treatises (or party manifestos). So I end with two images.

The first is a royal one. Several years ago the Queen's Christmas Day message came from Windsor, where she stood in the most spick-and-span of stables. Not a horse-hair out of place, not a tassle ungilt, not a cobble unpolished – for that matter, not a horse in sight. 'It was in a stable such as this,' Her Majesty began, 'that our Lord Jesus Christ was born.'

The second image is of a bishop in his resplendent palace advising me on why I was wrong to leave the full-time employ

313

of the Church of England. 'You see, my boy,' he expatiated, 'if only you could learn to keep your mouth shut, you have all the qualifications to be able to achieve what I have achieved. As a bishop I dine with Cabinet ministers. I count the Prime Minister as a close friend. I enjoy all the influence the Church can afford.'

There is bad religion. There is bad Christianity, and there are wilfully perverse readings of the Gospel. The soft theological inaccuracies of the conservative religious establishment are remarkably vulnerable to the hysteria of the religious right: almost as vulnerable as the American ecclesiastical establishment was fifteen years ago to the onslaught of the Christian Coalition. In the fight against the blandishments of 'prosperity teaching' and Christian apathy, Christian Socialism is essential. For bad faith can be defeated only by good faith.

Yet politics is not an easy realm for moralists. Consensus and compromise, upon which democracy rely, seem opposed to moral absolutes. Few Christian leaders understand economics. Many rely on understandings framed when they were at theological college and are hopelessly out of date. An over-hasty outburst from a prelate, however well-intentioned, is always harmful.

Yet the Churches, if only they could harness it, have an enormous resource of people who know the world as it is in every aspect. They enjoy weekly attendances way in excess of any political party's, and many Christians are the leading figures in the field. Intelligent, hard-headed, inspired thinking needs to be done about the moral life of the nation, and the truth about God's call to the nation cannot continue to be sacrificed at the altar of supposed impartiality and unity or for fear of the press. Gesture politics cannot be enough, for the exigencies of modern life and new technology, if left to an unbridled market economy, will inexorably drag society, and all her constituent parts, asunder.

A systematic response is vital if only because our social life is a seamless garment. The dreams of a new generation, harnessed to the wisdom of those who have seen more, might realise a new politics, more honest, less certain, more receptive, more imaginative, more responsible, less self-seeking, more possible. Above all, Christians need to be more prepared to think the unthinkable and be more radically inspired. New patches will not suffice. Old wineskins will not hold.

# Notes

## 1 Posthumous Comrades

1. J. Ball, cited in J. Froissart, *The Chronicles*, (Routledge, 1891), p. 180.
2. Cited in C. Oman, *The Great Revolt of 1381* (Clarendon, 1906), pp. 51–2.
3. G. Winstanley, *Gerrard Winstanley: Selected Writings* (Aporia Press, 1989), p. 10.
4. *A Light shining in Buckinghamshire* (no publisher, 1648).
5. Winstanley, *Selected Writings*, p. 13.
6. G. Winstanley, *The Law of Freedom and other writings*, ed. C. Hill (CUP, 1973), p. 389.
7. G. H. Sabine (ed.), *The Works of Gerrard Winstanley* (Ithaca, 1941), p. 292.
8. ibid., p. 331.
9. Winstanley, 'New Year's Gift' in *Selected Writings*, p. 81.
10. Sabine, *The Works of Gerrard Winstanley*, p. 210.
11. Winstanley, 'New Year's Gift' p. 95.
12. C. Rowland, *Radical Christianity* (Blackwell, 1988), p. 113.
13. E. Bernstein, *Cromwell and Communism* trans. H. J. Stenning (George Allen and Unwin, 1930), pp. 227–8.
14. K. Marx, *Capital* (Everyman, 1967), p. 257.
15. Cited in R. Porter, *English Society in the Eighteenth Century* (Penguin, rev. edn 1990), p. 177.
16. R. F. Wearmouth, *The Social and Political Influence of Methodism in the Twentieth Century* (Epworth, 1957), p. 253.
17. Cited in J. Marlow, *The Tolpuddle Martyrs* (Panther, 1974), p. 96.
18. Cited in M. Edwards, *Purge This Realm* (Epworth, 1994), p. 47.
19. ibid., p. 41.
20. ibid., p. 51.

21. ibid., p. 57.
22. *Ashton Standard*, 18 December 1858, cited in ibid., p. 115.
23. Rowland, *Radical Christianity*, pp. 112–13.
24. A. Kenny, in *Renaissance Thinkers* (OUP, 1993), p. 210.
25. Cited in ibid., p. 217.
26. N. Harpsfield, 'Life of Thomas More' in ed. E. Reynolds, *Lives of Thomas More* (Everyman, 1963) p. 105.
27. T. More, *Utopia*, ed. R. Adams (Norton, 1992), p. 84.
28. ibid, p. 108.
29. C. S. Lewis in ibid., p. 217.
30. Bunyan, 'I will pray with the spirit' in J. Bunyan, *Miscellaneous Works*, Vol. II (OUP, 1976), p. 253, cited in C. Hill, *The English Bible and the Seventeenth Century Revolution* (Penguin, 1994), p. 371.
31. P. Ackroyd, *Blake* (Sinclair Stevenson, 1995), p. 73.
32. Cited in ibid., p. 160.
33. W. Blake, 'London' in *Complete Poems and Prose*, ed. G. Keynes (Nonesuch, 1927), p. 75.
34. J. S. Mill, *Dissertations and Discussions* (Parker, 1867), Vol. 1, p. 403.
35. S. T. Coleridge, *Aids to Reflection* (Bohn's Library edn, 1860), p. 272.
36. S. T. Coleridge, *Confessions of an Enquiring Mind* (William Pickering, 1840), p. 52.
37. ibid., p. 75.
38. S. T. Coleridge, *The Constitution of the Church and State*, ed. J. Barrell (Everyman, 1972), p. 98.
39. Cited in S. E. Keeble, *Christian Responsibility for the Social Order* (Epworth, 1922), p. 138.
40. W. Wordsworth, *The Prelude* (Norton, 1979), Book IX.
41. Coleridge, *The Constitution of the Church and State*, p. 102.
42. S. T. Coleridge, *The Friend* (Bell and Daldy, 1866), Section I, Essay 16, p. 230.
43. J. Donne, 'Devotions', *Poems and Devotions*, ed. R. Van de Meyer (Fount, 1995), p. 162.

## 2 The Band of Brothers

1. J. F. Maurice *The Life of Frederick Denison Maurice, Chiefly Told in His Own Letters* (Macmillan, 1884), Vol. I, p. 13.
2. ibid., p. 56.
3. ibid., p. 229.

4. ibid.
5. J. Ruskin, *Praeterita: The Autobiography of John Ruskin* (OUP, 1978), p. 451.
6. J. M. Ludlow, *The Autobiography of a Christian Socialist*, ed. A. D. Murray (Frank Cass, 1981), p. 65.
7. ibid., p. 121.
8. F. E. Kingsley (ed.), *Charles Kingsley: His Letters and Memoirs of His Life* (Macmillan, 1891), Vol. 1 p. 12.
9. ibid., p. 335.
10. Cited in S. Chitty, *Charles Kingsley, Monk and Beast* (Hodder and Stoughton, 1974), p. 53.
11. Ludlow, *Autobiography*, p. 55.
12. Cited in N. S. Masterman, *John Malcolm Ludlow: The Builder of Christian Socialism* (CUP, 1963), p. 28.
13. Letter to Professor Lujo Brentano, 2–3 August 1882, cited in Masterman, *Ludlow*, p. 33.
14. Cited in ibid., p. 32.
15. Ludlow, *Autobiography*, p. 60.
16. J. F. Maurice, *The Life of Frederick Denison Maurice*, Vol. I, p. 458.
17. Cited in B. Colloms, *Victorian Visionaries* (Constable, 1982), p. 23.
18. C. Kingsley, *Politics for the People*, 6 May 1848.
19. J. F. Maurice, *The Life of Frederick Denison Maurice*, Vol. I, p. 463.
20. F. D. Maurice, 'Prospectus', *Politics for the People*, 6 May 1848.
21. J. M. Ludlow, *Politics for the People*, 3 June 1848.
22. C. Kingsley, *Politics for the People*, 17 June 1848.
23. Cited in Masterman, *John Malcolm Ludlow*, p. 75.
24. J. F. Maurice, *The Life of Frederick Denison Maurice*, Vol. II, p. 537.
25. ibid., p. 538.
26. F. E. Kingsley (ed.), *Charles Kingsley: His Letters and Memories of His Life* (H. S. King, 1877 edn.), Vol. I, p. 206.
27. C. Kingsley, *Alton Locke, Tailor and Poet: An Autobiography* (Macmillan, 1862), p. 383.
28. Cited by W. D. Morris, *The Christian Origins of Social Revolt* (Allen & Unwin, 1949), p. 179.
29. Cited in S. Chitty, *Charles Kingsley, Monk and Beast* (Hodder & Stoughton, 1974), p. 133.
30. J. M. Ludlow, *Fraser's Magazine*, XLI, January 1850, pp. 17–18.
31. G. J. Holyoake, *Sixty Years of an Agitator's Life* (T. F. Unwin, 1892), Vol. I, p. 39.
32. J. M. Ludlow, *Atlantic Monthly*, LXXVII, January 1896, pp. 109–18.
33. J. F. Maurice, *The Life of Frederick Denison Maurice*, Vol. II, p. 31.

34. ibid., p. 32.
35. ibid., pp. 33–5.
36. J. M. Ludlow, 'Labour and the Poor', *Fraser's Magazine*, XLI, January 1850, p. 18.
37. T. Hughes cited in B. Colloms, *Victorian Visionaries* (Constable, 1982), p. 72.
38. F. D. Maurice, *Sermons* (Macmillan, 1857–9), Vol. V, p. 24.
39. *Christian Socialist* Vol. I, pp. 49–50.
40. Cited in Masterman, *John Malcolm Ludlow*, p. 139.
41. J. M. Ludlow to E. Seligman, 24 July 1886, cited in P. Blackstrom, *Christian Socialism and Co-operation in Victorian England* (Croom Helm, 1974), p. 40.
42. Cited in Masterman, *John Malcolm Ludlow*, pp. 147–8.
43. J. F. Maurice, *The Life of Frederick Denison Maurice*, vol. II, p. 221.
44. Ludlow, *Autobiography*, p. 260.
45. ibid., pp. 261–2.
46. C. Mansfield, 27 April 1854, cited in Masterman, *John Malcolm Ludlow*, p. 152.
47. J. M. Ludlow, 28 April 1855, cited in Masterman, *John Malcolm Ludlow*, p. 153.
48. C. Kingsley, review in *Macmillan's*, January, 1864.
49. T. Hughes, *The Old Church: What shall We Do with It?* (Macmillan, 1878), p. 46.
50. J. M. Ludlow and L. Jones, *Progress of the Working Class, 1832–67* (Macmillan, 1867), p. 18.
51. T. Hughes, *Rugby, Tennessee, being Some Account of the Settlement Found on the Cumberland Plateau by the Board of Aid to Land Ownership Limited* (Macmillan, 1881), citing a speech at Rugby School, 7 April 1881, p. 123.
52. F. G. Bettany, *Stewart Duckworth Headlam: A Biography* (John Murray, 1926), p. 20.
53. J. F. Maurice, *The Life of Frederick Denison Maurice*, Vol. II p. 132.

## 3 The First Socialist Organisation in England

1. 'Why Dives lost his soul', cited in M. B. Reckitt, *Maurice to Temple: A Century of The Social Movement in the Church of England*, Scott Holland Memorial Lectures, 1946 (Faber & Faber, 1947), p. 111.
2. S. Headlam, *Maurice and Kingsley*, Fabian Paper, 1909.

3. F. G. Bettany, *Stewart Duckworth Headlam: A Biography* (John Murray, 1926) p. 33.
4. T. Hancock, *Church Reformer*, Vol. IV, no. 6, 15 June 1885.
5. C. Noel, *Commonwealth*, August 1904.
6. T. Hancock, *The Pulpit and the Press* (Brown, Langham, 1904), pp. 248–9.
7. T. Hancock, cited in M. B. Reckitt (ed.), *For Christ and the People* (SPCK, 1968), p. 37.
8. Hancock, *The Pulpit and the Press*, p. 45.
9. *Church Reformer*, Vol. III, no. 10, October 1884.
10. Bettany, *Stewart Duckworth Headlam*, p. 85.
11. *Commonwealth*, Vol. VIII, no. 6, June 1903.
12. *Church Reformer*, Vol. III, no. 8, August 1884.
13. W. E. Moll, *Church Reformer*, Vol. IV, no. 6, June 1885.
14. Cited in M. B. Reckitt, 'Charles Marson, 1859–1914, and the Real Disorders of the Church' in Reckitt (ed.), *For Christ and the People*, p. 90.
15. C. Marson in *Christian Socialist*, Vol. III, no. 34, March 1886.
16. P. Peach in *Christian Socialist*, Vol. III, no. 36, May 1886, pp. 179–80.
17. C. Marson, *God's Cooperative Society: Suggestions on the Strategy of the Church* (Longman, 1914), p. 37.
18. ibid.
19. G. Binyon, *The Christian Socialist Movement in England* (SPCK, 1931), p. 171.
20. Cited in P. D'A. Jones, *The Christian Socialist Revival, 1877–1914* (Princeton University Press, 1968), p. 146.
21. J. K. Hardie, *After Twenty Years: All About the ILP* (ILP, 1913), p. 12.
22. *Church Reformer*, Vol. XIV, no. 5, May 1895.
23. S. D. Headlam, *Church Reformer*, Vol XIV, no. 6, June 1895.
24. G. B. Shaw, cited in Jones, *The Christian Socialist Revival, 1877–1914*, p. 147.
25. Official Report of the Church Congress, Leicester, 1880.
26. S. D. Headlam, 'The Cultus of Our Lady' in *The Service of Humanity* (John Hodges, 1882), p. 18.
27. S. D. Headlam, *The Sure Foundation, an Address given before the Guild of St Matthew*, (F. Verinder, 1883), p. 6.
28. S. D. Headlam, *The Meaning of the Mass* (Brown, Langham, 1905), p. 134.
29. Bettany, *Stewart Duckworth Headlam*, pp. 210ff.
30. *Church Reformer*, Vol. XIV, no. 10, October 1895.

## 4 *The Army of Occupation*

1. S. D. Headlam, *Church Reformer*, Vol. VIII, no. 10, October 1889.
2. P. d'Arcy Jones, *The Christian Socialist Revival, 1877–1914* (Princeton University Press, 1968), p. 165.
3. C. Noel, *Socialism in Church History* (Frank Palmer, 1910), p. 257.
4. ibid.
5. H. S. Holland, 'The King of Terrors' in *Facts of the Faith*, ed. C. Cheshire (Longman, 1919) p. 41.
6. C. Gore, in S. Paget (ed.), *Henry Scott Holland: Memoirs and Letters* (John Murray, 1921), p. 243.
7. ibid., p. 248.
8. ibid., p. 12.
9. J. Heidt, 'The Social Theology of Henry Scott Holland' (unpublished Ph.D thesis University of Oxford, 1975), p. 24.
10. Paget (ed.), *Henry Scott Holland*, p. 81.
11. ibid., p. 69.
12. Letter to E. K. Talbot, cited in ibid., pp. 69–70.
13. ibid., p. 86.
14. Cited in G. L. Prestige, *Life of Charles Gore* (Heinemann, 1935), p. 43.
15. *Church Reformer*, Vol. VIII, no. 8, August 1888.
16. Paget, (ed.), *Henry Scott Holland*, p. 169.
17. K. Leech, 'Stewart Healdam' in M. B. Reckitt (ed.), *For Christ and the People* (SPCK, 1968), p. 86.
18. Letter, 17 May 1913, cited in Paget (ed.), *Henry Scott Holland*, pp. 285–6.
19. From *The Ground of Our Appeal* (CSU, 1890), cited in Paget (ed.), *Henry Scott Holland*, p. 171.
20. ibid., pp. 172–3.
21. J. Adderley, *The Parson in Socialism* (Richard Jackson, 1910), cited in N. Dearmer, *The Life of Percy Dearmer* (The Book Club, 1941), p 39.
22. C. Gore, in Paget (ed.), *Henry Scott Holland*, p. 242.
23. Letter to Dr Coppleston, August 1889, cited in Paget (ed.), *Henry Scott Holland*, p. 170.
24. Adderley, *The Parson in Socialism*, cited in Dearmer, *The Life of Percy Dearmer*, p. 38.
25. B. Tillett, *Dock, Wharf, Riverside and General Workers Union, A Brief History of the Dockers' Union* (Twentieth Century Press, 1910), p. 29.

26. B. F. Westcott, 'Socialism as Christian Social Reform' in J. Atherton (ed.), *Social Christianity* (SPCK, 1994), p. 81.
27. B. F. Westcott at Church Congress, 1890, cited in M. B. Reckitt, *Maurice to Temple: A Century of the Social Movement in the Church of England*, Scott Holland Memorial Lectures, 1946 (Faber & Faber, 1947), p. 144.
28. Westcott, 'Socialism as Christian Social Reform' in Atherton (ed.), *Social Christianity*, p. 87.
29. Cited in Prestige, *Life of Charles Gore*, p. 10.
30. ibid., p. 18.
31. Cited in A. Wilkinson, *The Community of the Resurrection* (SCM, 1992), p. 47.
32. ibid., p. 51.
33. Prestige, *Life of Charles Gore*, p. 218.
34. Cited in d'Arcy Jones, *The Christian Socialist Revival*, pp. 202–3; W. Stewart, *James Keir Hardie* (Independent Labour Party, 1925), p. 156.
35. Cited in Paget (ed.), *Henry Scott Holland*, p. 219.
36. ibid., p. 227.
37. Cited in d'Arcy Jones, *The Christian Socialist Revival*, p. 188.
38. L. Donaldson in *Commonwealth*, Vol. X, no. 7, July 1905, pp. 218–20.
39. ibid.
40. C. Gore, *Christianity and Socialism* (CSU pamphlet No. 24, 1908).
41. ibid.
42. ibid.
43. Prestige, *Life of Charles Gore*, p. 353.
44. Cited in Wilkinson, *The Community of the Resurrection*, p. 149.
45. H. S. Holland in C. Gore (ed.), *Property, its Duties and Rights* (Macmillan, 1922) p. 186.
46. Letter to E. Talbot, September 1893, cited in Paget (ed.), *Henry Scott Holland*, p. 202.
47. Holland in Gore (ed.), *Property, its Duties and Rights*, p. 306.
48. Gore, *Christianity and Socialism*, p. xxi.
49. ibid., p. xv.
50. C. Gore in Paget (ed.), *Henry Scott Holland*, p. 242.
51. Holland in Gore (ed.), *Property, its Duties and Rights*, p. 197.

## 5 A New Jerusalem

1. Cited in Alan Wilkinson, *The Community of the Resurrection* (SCM, 1992), p. 120.
2. Cited in H. Moncrieff, *Roots of Labour* (Linden Hall and Industrial Pioneer, 1990), p. 145.
3. J. K. Hardie, *From Serfdom to Socialism* (George Allen, 1907), p. 35.
4. Cited in G. C. Binyon, *The Christian Socialist Movement in England* (SPCK, 1931), p. 193.
5. ibid., p. 189.
6. C. Noel, *Autobiography* (Dent, 1945), p. 60.
7. *Church Socialist*, Vol. 1, no. 1, January 1912.
8. R. J. Campbell, *Christianity and Social Order* (Chapman and Hall, 1907), p. 36.
9. P. Bull, *Socialism and the Church* (Community of the Resurrection, Manual No. 4, no date), pp. 12–31.
10. Cited in Noel, *Autobiography*, p. 57.
11. Cited in R. Groves, *Conrad Noel and the Thaxted Movement* (Merlin Press, 1967), p. 12.
12. P. Snowden in *The Labour Prophet*, April 1898, pp. 169–70.
13. P. Snowden, *The Christ that is to be* (ILP, 1903), p. 7.
14. ibid., p. 13.
15. J. Adderley, *A Little Primer of Christian Socialism* (CSL, no date), p. 27.
16. B. Pinchard in *Church Socialist Quarterly*, Vol. IV, no. 3, July 1909, pp. 236–7.
17. G. Lansbury, *My Life* (Constable, 1928), p. 75.
18. R. Postgate, *The Life of George Lansbury* (Longmans, Green, 1951), p. 56.
19. G. Lansbury, *These Things Shall Be* (Swarthmore Press, 1920), p. 15.
20. Lansbury, *My Life*, p. 41.
21. Noel, *Autobiography*, p. 107.
22. J. N. Figgis, 'The Sword and the Cross' in *Challenge*, 18 September 1914.
23. H. S. Holland, cited in M. B. Reckitt, *Maurice to Temple: A Century of the Social Movement in the Church of England*, Scott Holland Memorial Lectures, 1946 (Faber & Faber, 1947), p. 155.
24. Cited in Wilkinson, *The Community of the Resurrection*, p. 142.
25. Noel, *Autobiography*, p. 60.

26. C. Noel, *The Battle of the Flags: A Study in Christian Politics* (Labour Publishing, 1922), p. 7.
27. C. Noel, *Jesus the Heretic* (Dent, 1939), p. 31.
28. P. E. T. Widdrington in *Christendom*, March 1947, p. 23.
29. P. E. T. Widdrington in *Church Socialist*, November 1912.
30. M. B. Reckitt, *Faith and Society* (Longman, 1932), p. 108.
31. Cited in Wilkinson, *The Community of the Resurrection*, p. 118.
32. J. N. Figgis, *The Fellowship of the Mystery* (Longman, 1914), p. 101.
33. J. N. Figgis, *Churches in the Modern State* (Longman, 1913), p. 36.
34. J. N. Figgis, *Political Thought from Gerson to Grotius, 1415–1625* (Longman, 1916, 1960 edn), p. 236.
35. Figgis, *Churches in the Modern State*, p. 36.
36. M.B. Reckitt, *P. E. T. Widdrington* (SPCK, 1961), p. 75.
37. L. Thornton in *Church Socialist*, September 1919.
38. M. B. Reckitt (ed.), *The Return of Christendom* (George Allen & Unwin, 1922), p. 9.
39. ibid., p. 10.
40. ibid., p. 90.
41. P. E. T. Widdrington in Reckitt (ed.), *The Return of Christendom*, p. 113.
42. P. E. T. Widdrington in M. B. Reckitt (ed.), *Prospects for Christendom* (Faber & Faber, 1945), p. 253.
43. Cited in Reckitt, *P. E. T. Widdrington*, p. 97.
44. J. Oliver, *The Church and Social Order* (Mowbray, 1968), p. 81.
45. W. Temple in *The Pilgrim*, January 1922.
46. G. D. H. Cole, *Self Government in Industry* (Bell, 1917), p. 117.

## 6 *Faith of Our Fathers*

1. J. Wheatley, *Forward*, 6 July 1912.
2. C. MacKenzie, *Catholicism and Scotland* (Routledge, 1936), p. 185.
3. J. Wheatley, Glasgow Observer, 24 February 1906.
4. *Forward*, 10 November 1906.
5. Cited in F. Davis, 'The Lost Radical of English Catholicism', *Allen Review*, no. 6, Hilary 1992, p. 14.
6. Cited in D. Simpson, *Manning: the People's Cardinal* (Industrial Pioneer Publications, 1992), p. 8.
7. Cited in Davis, 'The Lost Radical of English Catholicism', p. 14.
8. Cited in M. B. Reckitt, *Faith and Society* (Longman, 1932), p. 101.
9. ibid., p. 17.

10. Cited in Simpson, *Manning*, p. 31.
11. *Rerum Novarum*, para. 5.
12. ibid., para 1.
13. ibid., para 6.
14. ibid., para. 31.
15. ibid., para. 49.
16. ibid., para. 9.
17. ibid., para. 26.
18. ibid., para. 48.
19. Cited in F. Davis, 'Whose God?', *Radical Quarterly*, Autumn 1991.
20. *Rerum Novarum*, para. 37.
21. J. Wheatley, *Mines, Miners and Misery* (Catholic Socialist Society, 1909), p. 22.
22. C. D. Plater, *The Priest and Social Action* (Longman, 1914), p. vii.
23. *Graves de Communi.*
24. Plater, *The Priest and Social Action*, p. 240.
25. Hansard, 25 July 1924, Vol. 176, paras. 1703–4.
26. *Glasgow Eastern Standard*, 8 November 1924.
27. *Quadrogesimo Anno* (St Paul's Editions, 1931), p. 58.
28. ibid., p. 57.
29. ibid.
30. ibid., p. 14.
31. ibid., p. 41.
32. ibid., p. 40.
33. ibid., p. 51.
34. D. Dorr, *Option for the Poor: Catholic Social Teaching* (Gill & MacMillan, 1992 edn), p. 86.
35. K. Leech, *Social God* (Sheldon Press, 1981), p. 18.
36. Dorr, *Option for the Poor*, p. 147.
37. *Mater et Magistra*, para. 71.
38. *Gaudium et Spes*, para. 69.1.
39. *Populum Progressio*, para. 26.
40. *Octagesima Adveniens*, para. 31.

## 7 Two Boys from Rugby

1. G. S. Kennedy, *The Hardest Part*, cited in W. Purcell, *Woodbine Willie: A Study of Geoffrey Studdert Kennedy* (Mowbray, 1962), p. 115.
2. *National Mission of Repentance and Hope* Paper 3 (National Mission, 1916).

3. Bishop Woods in *The Chronicle of Canterbury Convocation* (Church of England, 1918), p. 216.

4. ibid., p. 344.

5. *The Church and Industrial Problems* (SPCK, 1918), p. 80.

6. G. S. Kennedy, *Democracy and the Dog Collar* (Hodder & Stoughton, 1921), p. 221.

7. W. Temple, 'The Church and the Labour Party', *Economic Review*, April 1908.

8. W. Temple, *The Kingdom of God* (Macmillan, 1914), pp. 96–8.

9. Cited in F. A. Iremonger, *William Temple, Archbishop of Canterbury: His Life and Letters* (Clarendon Press, 1948), p. 123.

10. R. Kenyon in 'Politics and Citizenship', *The Proceedings of COPEC*, Vol. X (Longmans Green, 1924), p. 107.

11. 'Industry and Property', *The Proceedings of COPEC*, Vol. IX (Longmans Green, 1924), p. 190.

12. ibid., p. 195.

13. J. Kent, *William Temple* (CUP, 1994), p. 122.

14. Iremonger, *William Temple*, p. 342.

15. E. Norman, *Church and Society in England 1770–1970* (Clarendon Press, 1976), p. 340.

16. R. H. Tawney, Presidential Address to LSE Student Union, *Speeches on Various Occasions* (LSE Archive), p. 22.

17. J. E. Heringham to Mansbridge, 21 February 1908, Workers' Educational Association Archive.

18. Tawney, Presidential Address to LSE Student Union, *Speeches on Various Occasions*, pp. 11–12.

19. R. H. Tawney, 'Labour Honours', *New Statesman*, 22 June 1935.

20. Cited in A. Wright, *R. H. Tawney* (Manchester University Press, 1990), p. 11.

21. R. Terrill, *R. H. Tawney and His Times* (André Deutsch, 1973), p. 49.

22. 22 December 1915, Beveridge Collection L.1.211 Additional A.

23. Terrill, *R. H. Tawney and His Times*, p. 21.

24. Wright, *R. H. Tawney*, p. 19.

25. R. H. Tawney, *The Acquisitive Society* (Bell, 1921, Fontana edn, 1961), p. 183.

26. R. H. Tawney, *Religion and the Rise of Capitalism* (John Murray, 1926), preface to the 1937 edn, p. vii.

27. ibid., p. 73.

28. Tawney, *The Acquisitive Society*, p. 31.

29. ibid., p. 82.

30. ibid., p. 97.

31. R. H. Tawney, *Equality* (Allen & Unwin, 1931), p. 110.
32. ibid., p. 113.
33. ibid. (1938 edn).
34. ibid.
35. R. H. Tawney, 'British Socialism Today' in R, Hinden (ed.), *The Radical Tradition: Twelve Essays on Politics, Education and Literature* (Allen & Unwin, 1964), p. 176.
36. Tawney, *The Acquisitive Society*, p. 30.
37. ibid., p. 291.
38. Iremonger, *William Temple*, p. 428.
40. W. Temple in *Malvern 1941* (Longman, 1941), p. ix.
41. Editorial, *Christendom*, March 1941.
42. Temple in *Malvern 1941*, p. ix.
43. D. L. Sayers in ibid., p. 77.
44. V. A. Demant in ibid., p. 149.
45. Temple in ibid., p. 58.
46. ibid., p. 65.
47. ibid., p. 69.
48. W. Temple, *Christianity and the Social Order* (Penguin, 1942; Shepherd-Walwyn 1976), p. 97.
49. R. H. Tawney in T. Wilson (ed.), *Discourses upon Usury* (Bell, 1925), p. 15.

## 8 Parliamentary Lives

1. Cited in K. Harris, *Attlee* (Weidenfeld & Nicolson, 1982), p. 97.
2. Arthur Henderson to J. Ramsay Macdonald, 2 January 1911, MacDonald's papers, cited in F. M. Leventhal, *Arthur Henderson* (Manchester University Press, 1989), p. 20.
3. *Labour and the Nation* (Labour Party, 1928).
4. 15 November 1935.
5. G. Lansbury, *My Life* (Constable, 1928), p. 37.
6. J. MacMurray, *Search for the Reality of Religion*, (Allen & Unwin, 1965, p. 19.
7. J. MacMurray, *The Philosophy of Communism* (Faber & Faber, 1933), pp. 79–80.
8. J. MacMurray, *Persons in Relation* (Faber & Faber, 1961), p. 60.
9. ibid., pp. 157–8.
10. The Cripps Memorandum.
11. M. Stockwood, *The Chanctonbury Ring* (Hodder & Stoughton, 1982), p. 62.

12. K. Ingram, *Taken at the Flood* (Allen & Unwin, 1943), p. 42.
13. Cited in M. Waterson, *The National Trust: The First Hundred Years* (BBC Books, 1994), p. 120.
14. R. Acland in *Malvern 1941* (Longman, 1941), p. 155.
15. Stockwood, *The Chanctonbury Ring*, p. 65.
16. Cited in C. Cooke, *The Life of Stafford Cripps* (Hodder & Stoughton, 1957), p. 361.
17. Harris, *Attlee*, p. 354.
18. Cited in D. Collins, *Partners in Protest: Life with Canon Collins* (Gollancz, 1992), p. 143.
19. Stockwood, *The Chanctonbury Ring*, p. 73.

## 9  United in Diversity

1. F. Hughes, *Socialist Christian*, Vol. XIII, no. 3, May–June 1942.
2. J. T. Harris, *Three Papers on the Responsibility of the Society of Friends to the Social Problem*, Tract No 4 (Socialist Quaker Society, 1907).
3. *Ploughshare*, November 1919.
4. Cited in G. Carnall, *Socialist Christian*, Spring 1953.
5. H. P. Hughes, *Social Christianity* (Hodder and Stoughton, 1890), p. 14.
6. ibid., p. 49.
7. S. E. Keeble, *Industrial Daydreams* (Elliot Stock, 1896, 2nd edn 1907), p. 152.
8. S. E. Keeble, *Methodist Recorder*, 2 May 1907, p. 16.
9. J. Trevor, *Theology and the Slums* (Labour Prophet Tract No. 1, no date), p. 2.
10. R. J. Campbell, *Primitive Christianity and Modern Socialism* (Progressive League Series No. 1, no date). p. 2.
11. *The Catholic Crusade, 1918–1936*, ed. R. Groves (Archive One, 1970).
12. Cited in K. Brill (ed.), *John Groser: East London Priest* (Mowbray, 1971), p. 169.
13. Fabian Lecture, 1950, cited in ibid., p. 18.
14. Cited in ibid., p. 164.
15. *Socialist Christian*, Vol. 1, no. 4, January 1929.
16. ibid.
17. D. O. Soper, *Calling for Action* (Robson Books, 1984), p. 31.
18. V. Brittain, *Testament of Experience* (Fontana, 1980), p. 164.
19. R. Sorensen, *Socialist Christian*, November 1935.

20. Soper, *Calling for Action*, pp. 37–8.
21. C. Record, *Socialist Christian*, Vol. XII, no. 2, April–May 1941.
22. Private interview, 19 June 1995.
23. *Socialist Christian*, Summer 1953.
24. G. MacLeod, cited in R. Ferguson, *George MacLeod: Founder of the Iona Community* (Collins, 1990), p. 115.
25. ibid., p. 114.
26. ibid., p. 155.
27. *Christian Socialist Movement News*, No. 1, July 1960.
28. C. Record, *Socialist Christian*, Spring 1953.
29. S. Purkis, *Socialist Christian*, June 1956.
30. M. Stockwood, *The Chanctonbury Ring* (Hodder and Stoughton, 1982), p. 106.
31. *Dictionary of National Biography 1961–70* (OUP, 1981), p. 592.
32. Hugh Gaitskell, *1960 Labour Party Conference Report* (Labour Party, 1960).
33. Cited in W. Purcell, *Odd Man Out: A Biography of Lord Soper of Kingsway* (Mowbray, 1983), p. 144.
34. R. Woodifield, *Socialist Christian*, Spring 1954.

## 10 A Moral Crusade

1. *Papers from the Lamb* (Christian Socialist Movement, 1960), p. 1.
2. ibid.
3. ibid., p. 2.
4. *CSM News*, No. 2, September 1960.
5. A. Duncan and D. Hobson, *Saturn's Children* (Sinclair Stevenson, 1995) p. 281.
6. *The Times*, 13 August 1976.
7. John 10:10.
8. *Papers from the Lamb*, p. 8.
9. ibid., p. 26.
10. Private Interview, August 1995.
11. S. Evans in D. Ormrod, *Fellowship, Freedom and Equality* (Christian Socialist Movement, 1991), p. 22.
12. Duncan and Hobson, *Saturn's Children*, p. 279.
13. Evans in Ormrod, *Fellowship, Freedom and Equality*, p. 23.
14. T. Sargent, *CSM News*, No. 3, December 1960.
15. *Christian Socialist*, No. 20, April 1964.
16. D. O. Soper in W. Purcell, *Odd Man Out: A Biography of Lord Soper of Kingsway* (Mowbray, 1983), p. 111.

17. S. Evans, *Christian Socialism: A Study Outline and Bibliography* (CSM Pamphlet No. 2, 1962), p. 4.
18. *Common Ownership and the Common People* (CSM, 1971), p. 20.
19. ibid.
20. T. Eagleton, *The New Left Church* (Sheed and Ward, 1970), p. 142.
21. ibid., p. 158.
22. ibid., p. 166.
23. J. Kent in R. Ambler and D. Haslam (eds.), *Agenda for Prophets* (Bowerdean Press. 1980), p. 80.
24. G. Gutierrez, cited in J. Atherton, *Social Christianity: A Reader* (SPCK, 1994), p. 35.
25. T. Huddleston, *Naught for Your Comfort* (Fount, 1985), p. 171.
26. D. Sheppard, *Bias to the Poor* (Hodder & Stoughton, 1983), p. 145.
27. ibid., p. 158.
28. ibid., p. 225.
29. K. Leech (ed.), *Who shall Sound the Trumpet?* (Jubilee Group, 1994), p. v.
30. ibid., p. vi.
31. ibid., p. 4.
32. K. Leech, *Politics and Faith Today* (Darton, Longman & Todd, 1994), p. 10.
33. K. Leech, *The Social God* (Sheldon Press, 1981), p. 54.
34. ibid., p. 56.
35. Aims of COSPEC, outlined in *Christian Action Journal*, Winter 1980.
36. *Christian Action Journal*, Autumn 1980.
37. COSPEC papers, 31 October 1987.

## 11 Reclaiming the Ground

1. Private interview, August 1995.
2. T. Benn, *A Future for Socialism* (Fount, 1991), pp. 7–8.
3. ibid., p. 8.
4. T. Benn in D. Ormrod, *Fellowship, Freedom and Equality* (CSM, 1991), p. 107.
5. D. Ormrod (ed.), *Facing the Future as Christians and Socialists* (CSM, 1986), p. 41.
6. T. Benn, *Arguments for Democracy*, ed. C. Mullin (Cape, 1981), chapter 7.
7. Benn, *A Future for Socialism*, p. 64.

8. J. Ball, cited in J. Froissart, *The Chronicles*, (Routledge 1891), p. 180.
9. F. Field, *The Politics of Paradise* (Fount, 1987), p. 137.
10. ibid., p. 93.
11. F. Field, *An Agenda for Britain* (Fount, 1993), p. 20.
12. ibid.
13. ibid.
14. Field, *The Politics of Paradise*, p. 135.
15. Cited in *Christian Socialist*, no. 124, Spring 1987.
16. J. Collins, 'Give Labour a Christian Voice', *Christian Socialist*, no. 125, Summer 1987.
17. 'AGM backs affiliation', ibid.
18. W. Sheaff, *Christian Socialist*, Winter 1988.
19. *Plan for Action*, report to the Movement by CSM Working Party, December 1992.
20. J. Smith in C. Bryant (ed.), *Reclaiming the Ground* (Spire, 1993), p. 127.
21. W. Temple, *Christianity and the Social Order* (Penguin, 1942), p. 65.
22. Smith in Bryant (ed.), *Reclaiming the Ground*, p. 137.
23. ibid., p. 128.
24. 26 March 1993.
25. 22 March 1993.
26. M. Alison, 'Reaffirming Labour's Christian Roots', *House Magazine*, 10 May 1993, p. 13.
27. 19 March 1993.
28. T. Blair in Bryant (ed.), *Reclaiming the Ground*, p. 12.
29. ibid., p. 10.
30. ibid.
31. ibid., p. 11.
32. T. Blair, *Socialism* (Fabian Pamphlet No. 571, 1995), p. 5.
33. T. Blair in 'Practising for Power', *Third Way*, October 1993, p. 16.
34. ibid., p. 17.
35. T. Blair, *Let Us Face the Future* (Fabian Pamphlet No. 571, 1995), p. 5.
36. T. Blair, speech to Labour Party Conference, 3 October 1995.
37. Blair, *Let Us Face the Future*, p. 12.
38. M. Meacher in C. Bryant (ed.), *John Smith: An Appreciation* (Hodder & Stoughton, 1994), pp. 72–3.
39. J. Straw, *Policy and Ideology* (Blackburn Labour Party, 1993), p. 5.
40. ibid., p. 12.
41. ibid., p. 29.

42. ibid., p. 12.
43. R. Preston in M. Taylor (ed.), *Christians and the Future of Social Democracy* (Hesketh, 1982) p. 9.
44. R. Preston, *Christian Conservatism or Christian Socialism* (IEA Health & Welfare Unit, 1994), p. 24.
45. ibid., p. 32.
46. ibid., p. 30.
47. Preston in Taylor (ed.), *Christians and the Future of Social Democracy*, p. 9.
48. Preston, *Christian Conservatism or Christian Socialism*, p. 24.
49. Preston in Taylor (ed.), *Christians and the Future of Social Democracy*, p. 9.
50. R. Preston, *Religion and the Persistence of Capitalism* (SCM, 1979), p. 109.
51. C. Davis, *Religion and the Making of Society* (CUP, 1994), p. 176.
52. T. J. Gorringe, *Capital and the Kingdom: Theological Ethics and Economic Order* (Orbis, 1994).
53. ibid., p. 41.
54. ibid., p. 42.
55. ibid., p. 159.
56. ibid.
57. ibid.
58. A. Duncan and D. Hobson, *Saturn's Children* (Sinclair Stevenson, 1995), p. 297.
59. ibid., p. 283.
60. ibid.
61. A Billings, cited in Duncan and Hobson, *Saturn's Children*, p. 289.
62. Duncan and Hobson, *Saturn's Children*, p. 291.
63. Davis, *Religion and the Making of Society*, p. 173.
64. L. Griffiths in C. Bryant (ed.), *John Smith*, p. 58.
65. T. Blair, speech to Party Conference, 3 October 1995.
66. R. Williams, *Justice and the Demands of the Gospel* (Diocese of Llamdaff Board of Responsibility, 1994), p. 21.

# Bibliography

## Periodicals

*Politics for the People*, 6 May to 29 July 1848
*Christian Socialist, A Journal of Association*, 2 November 1850 to 27 December 1851 and 3 January to 28 June 1852
*Church Reformer*, 1882 to 1895
*Christian Socialist, A Journal for Thoughtful Men*, 1883 to 1891
*Commonwealth*, 1896 to 1921
*Church Socialist Quarterly*, formerly *The Optimist*, January 1909 to April 1911
*Church Socialist*, February 1912 to December 1921
*Ploughshare*, November 1912 to November 1915
*Socialist Christian*, formerly *New Crusader*, October 1928 to November 1959
*Christian Socialist*, formerly *Christian Socialist Movement News* February 1960 to today
*Slant*, 1964 to 1970

Ackroyd, P., *Blake* (Sinclair-Stevenson, 1995)
Acland, R. D. T., *The Forward March* (George Allen and Unwin, 1941)
  *Unser Kampf* (Penguin, 1940)
Adderley, J., *The Parson in Socialism* (Richard Jackson, 1910)
  *In Slums and Society: Reminiscences of Old Friends* (T. Fisher Unwin, 1916)
  *Stephen Remarx* (E. Arnold, 1893)
Atherton, J. (ed.), *Social Christianity: A Reader* (SPCK, 1994)
  *Christianity and the Market* (SPCK, 1992)
Bettany, F. G., *Stewart Duckworth Headlam: A Biography* (John Murray, 1926)

Binyon, G. C., *The Christian Socialist Movement in England* (SPCK, 1931)

Blair, T., *Socialism* (Fabian Pamphlet No. 565, 1994)

Blake, W., *Complete Poetry and Prose*, ed. G. Keynes (Nonesuch, 1927)

Bryant, C. (ed.), *Reclaiming the Ground* (Spire, 1993)

Bull, Paul B., *Socialism and the Church* (Mirfield Manuals for the Million No. 4, no date)

Campbell, R. J., *Christianity and the Social Order* (Chapman and Hall, 1907)

Chitty, S., *Charles Kingsley, Monk and Beast* (Hodder & Stoughton, 1974)

Christensen, T., *Origins and History of Christian Socialism 1848–54* (Aorhus, 1962)

Coleridge, S. T. C., *Selected Poetry, Prose, Letters*, ed. S. Potter (Nonesuch, 1933)

Colloms, B., *Victorian Visionaries* (Constable, 1982)

Cooke, C., *The Life of Stafford Cripps* (Hodder & Stoughton, 1957)

Cripps, S., *Towards Christian Democracy* (George Allen and Unwin, 1945)

Davis, C., *Religion and the Making of Society* (Manchester University Press, 1994)

Dearmer, N., *Life of Percy Dearmer* (The Book Club, 1940)

Dearmer, P., *The Parson's Handbook* (Grant Richards, 1899; OUP, 1932)
  *Socialism and Christianity* (Fabian Tract No. 133, 1907)
  *The Beginnings of the CSU* (CSU, 1912)

Demant, V. A., *Religion and the Decline of Capitalism* (Faber & Faber, 1952)

Dolling R., *Ten Years in a Portsmouth Slum* (Brown, Langham, 1896)

Dorr, D., *Option for the Poor* (Gill and MacMillan, rev. edn, 1992)

Eagleton, T., *The New Left Church* (Sheed and Ward, 1970)

Edwards, M. S., *Purge This Realm: A Life of Josph Rayner Stephens* (Epworth, 1994)

Estorick, E., *Stafford Cripps* (Heinemann, 1949)

Evans, S., *The Church in the Back Streets* (Mowbray, 1962)
  *The Social Hope of the Christian Church* (Hodder and Stoughton, 1965)

Ferguson, R., *George MacLeod: Founder of the Iona Community* (Collins, 1990)

Field, F., *The Politics of Paradise* (Fount, 1987)
  *An Agenda for Britain* (Fount, 1993)

Figgis, J. N., *The Fellowship of the Mystery* (Longman, 1912)
  *Churches in the Modern State* (Longman, 1914)

Frere, W. H., *God and Caesar: or the Laws of Church and State* (Mirfield Manuals for the Millions, no date)

Frost, B., *Goodwill on Fire* (Hodder & Stoughton, 1996)

Gore, C. (ed.), *Lux Mundi* (John Murray, 1889)

*The Social Doctrine of the Sermon on the Mount* (CSU, 1893)

*Christianity and Socialism* (CSU Tract No. 24, 1908)

(ed.), *Property, Its Duties and Rights* (Macmillan, 1922)

*Christ and Society* (Allen & Unwin, 1928)

Gorringe, T. J., *Capital and the Kingdom* (SPCK/Orbis, 1994)

Gray, D., *Earth and Altar* (Alcuin Club, 1986)

Groves, R., *Conrad Noel and the Thaxted Movement* (Merlin Press, 1967)

Gunnin, G., *John Wheatley: Catholic Socialism and Irish Labour in the West of Scotland 1906–24* (Garland Publishing, 1987)

Gutierrez, G. A., *Theology of Liberation* (Orbis, 1973)

*The Power of the Poor in History* (SCM, 1983)

Hamilton, M. A., *Arthur Henderson* (Heinemann, 1938)

Hancock, T., *Christ and the People* (Brown, Langham, 1875)

*The Pulpit and the Press* (Brown, Langham, 1904)

Hardie, J. K., *Can a Man be a Christian on a Pound a Week?* (ILP, 1905)

*From Serfdom to Socialism* (George Allen, 1907)

Headlam, S. D., *Christian Socialism* (Fabian Tract No. 42, 1891)

'The Socialist Church', in *The Labour Ideal* (George Allen, 1907)

*The Meaning of the Mass* (Brown, Langham, 1905)

*Maurice and Kingsley* (Fabian Tract, 1909)

Hobson, J. A., *The Problems of Poverty* (no publisher given, 1891)

*John Ruskin: Social Reformer* (J. Nisbet, 1898)

Hobson, S. G., *Pilgrim to the Left* (E. Arnold, 1938)

Holland, H. Scott, *The Labour Movement* (CSU, 1897)

*Our Neighbours a handbook for the C.S.U.* (CSU, 1911)

*A Bundle of Memories* (Wells, Gardner, Darton, 1915)

Holman, B., *Good Old George* (Lion, 1990)

Hughes, H. P., *Social Christianity* (Hodder and Stoughton, 1890)

Hughes, R., *The Red Dean: the Life and Riddle of Dr Hewlett Johnson* (Churchman, 1987)

Illingworth, Mrs J. R., *Life and Work of J. R. Illingworth* (John Murray, 1917)

Ingram, K., *Christianity – Right or Left?* (Allen & Unwin, 1937)

Iremonger, F. A., *William Temple* (Clarendon, 1948)

Johnson, H., *The Socialist Sixth of the World* (Victor Gollancz, 1939)

Jones, P. D'A, *The Christian Socialist Revival 1877–1914* (Princeton University Press, 1968)

Kee, A. (ed.), *A Reader in Political Theology*, (SCM, 1975)

Keeble, S. E., *Industrial Daydreams* (Elliot Stock, 1889)

'Christianity and Socialism' in *The Labour Ideal* (George Allen, 1907)

*Christian Responsibility for the Social Order* (Fernley Lecture Trust, 1922)

Kent, J., *William Temple* (CUP, 1994)

Kenyon, R. A., *History of Socialism* (Mirfield Manuals for the Millions, no date)

Kingsley, C., *Yeast: a Problem* (Macmillan, 1851)

*Alton Locke: Tailor and Poet* (Macmillan, 1862)

*Life and Letters*, 2 vols., edited by his wife (H. S. King, 1884)

Lansbury, G., *My Life* (Constable, 1928)

Leech, K., *The Social God* (Sheldon, 1981)

*Politics and Faith Today* (Darton, Longman, Todd, 1994)

(ed.), *Who Shall Sound the Trumpet?* (Jubilee, 1994)

Leventhal, F. M., *Arthur Henderson* (MUP, 1989)

Ludlow, J. M., 'Some words on the ethics of Cooperative Production', *Atlantic Monthly*, LXXV (March 1895)

'The Christian Socialist Movement of the Middle of the Century', *Atlantic Monthly*, LXXVII (January 1896)

*The Autobiography of a Christian Socialist*, ed. A. D. Murray (Frank Cass, 1981)

Lyttleton, E., *The Mind and Character of Henry Scott Holland* (Mowbray, 1926)

MacMurray, J., *The Philosophy of Communism* (Faber, 1933)

*Persons in Relation* (Faber, 1961; Humanities Press, 1979)

Manning, H., *The Rights and Dignity of Labour* (Burns and Oates, 1887)

Mansbridge, A., *Edward Stuart Talbot and Charles Gore* (Dent, 1935)

Marlow, J., *The Tolpuddle Martyrs* (Panther, 1974)

Marson, C. L., *God's Co-operative Society: Suggestions on the Strategy of the Church* (Longman, 1914)

Masterman, N. C., *J. M. Ludlow: Builder of Christian Socialism* (CUP, 1963)

Maurice, F. D., *The Kingdom of Christ* (Rivington, 1842)

*Social Morality* (Macmillan, 1872)

Maurice, F. (ed.), *Life of Frederick Denison Maurice, Chiefly Told in His Own Letters*, 2 vols. (Macmillan, 1884)

Mayor, S. H., *The Churches and the Labour Movement* (Independent Press, 1976)

More, T., *Utopia*, ed. R. Adams (Norton, 1992)

Noel, C., *The Labour Party: What it is and What it Wants* (Fisher Unwin, 1906)

# Bibliography

*Socialism in Church History* (Frank Palmer, 1910)

*Jesus the Heretic* (Dent, Religious Book Club, 1939)

*An Autobiography*, ed. Sidney Dark (Dent, 1945)

Norman, E., *The Victorian Christian Socialists* (CUP, 1987)

Oliver, J., *The Church and Social Order* (Mowbray, 1968)

Ormrod, D. (ed.), *Fellowship, Freedom and Equality* (CSM, 1990)

Paget, S., *Henry Scott Holland: Memoirs and Letters* (John Murray, 1921)

Plater, C. D., *The Priest and Social Action* (Longman, 1914)

Porter, R., *English Society in the Eighteenth Century* (Penguin, rev. edn 1990)

Postgate, R., *The Life of George Lansbury* (Longmans, Green, 1951)

Prestige, G. L., *Life of Charles Gore* (Heinemann, 1935)

Preston, R. H., *Religion and the Persistence of Capitalism* (SCM, 1979)
and Novak, M., *Christian Capitalism or Christian Socialism?* (IEA, Religion and Liberty Series No. 1, 1994)

Purcell, W., *Woodbine Willie: A Study of Geoffrey Studdert Kennedy* (Mowbray, 1962)

*Odd Man Out: A Biography of Lord Soper of Kingsway* (Mowbray, 1983)

Raven, C. E., *Christian Socialism 1848–54* (Macmillan, 1920)

Reckitt, M. B. (ed.), *The Return of Christendom* (Allen & Unwin, 1922)

*Faith and Society* (Longman, 1932)

*As It Happened: An Autobiography* (Dent, 1941)

(ed.), *Prospect for Christendom* (Faber & Faber, 1945)

*Maurice to Temple: A Century of Social Movement in the Church of England* (Faber & Faber, 1947)

*P.E.T. Widdrington* (SPCK, 1961)

(ed.), *For Christ and the People* (SPCK, 1968)

Reid. A. (ed.), *The New Party: Described by Some of Its Members* (Hodder, 1894)

(ed.), *Vox Clamantium* (A. D. Innes, 1894)

Rowland, C., *Radical Christianity* (Polity, 1988)

Royden, A. M., *Political Christianity* (G. P. Putnam, 1922)

Ruskin, J., *Selected Writings*, ed. K. Clark (Penguin, 1991)

Sheppard, D., *Bias to the Poor* (Hodder & Stoughton, 1983)

Simpson, D., *Manning: the People's Cardinal* (Industrial Pioneer Publications, 1992)

Smith, L., *Religion and the Rise of Labour* (Ryburn Publishing, 1993)

Snowden, P., *The Christ that is to be* (ILP, 1905)

*Autobiography*, 2 vols. (Nicholson Watson, 1934)

Stockwood, M., *The Chanctonbury Ring* (Hodder & Stoughton, 1982)

Stubbs, C. W., *Christ and Economics* (Isbister, 1893)

Studdert-Kennedy, G., *Democracy and the Dog-Collar* (Hodder & Stoughton, 1921)

Tawney, R. H., *The Acquisitive Society* (Bell, 1921)
  *Equality* (Allen & Unwin, 1931)
  *Religion and the Rise of Capitalism* (John Murray, 1926; Penguin 1990)
  *The Radical Tradition* (Allen & Unwin, 1964)

Taylor, M. H. (ed.), *Christians and the Future of Social Democracy* (Hesketh, Ormskirk & Northridge, 1981)

Temple, W., *The Kingdom of God* (Macmillan, 1914)
  *Readings in St John's Gospel*, 2 vols. (Macmillan, 1939)
  *Christianity and the Social Order* (Penguin, 1942)

Terrill, R., *R. H. Tawney and His Times: Socialism as Friendship* (André Deutsch, 1974)

Tillett, B., *Memories and Reflections* (Long, 1931)

Trevor, J. *Theology and the Slums* (Labour Prophet Tract No. 1, no date)

Wearmouth, R. F., *Methodism and the Working Class Movements of England 1800–1850* (Epworth, 1937)

Westcott, B. F., *Social Aspects of Christianity* (Macmillan, 1888)
  *Socialism* (Guild of St Matthew, 1890)
  *The Christian Social Union* (CSU, 1895)

Wheatley, J., *Mines, Miners and Misery* (Catholic Socialist Society, 1909)

Wheen, F., *Tom Driberg: His Life and Indiscretions* (Chatto & Windus, 1990)

Wilkinson, A., *The Community of the Resurrection* (SCM, 1992)

Winstanley, G., *Gerrard Winstanley: Selected Writings* (Aporia Press, 1989).

Wood, I., *John Wheatley* (Manchester University Press, 1990)

Wright, A., *R. H. Tawney* (Manchester University Press 1990)

# Index